Also by Wilmont R. Kreis

The Allards Historical Series:
The New World
The Hunter
Peace and War
The Voyageur
The City in the Wilderness
The Medallion
The Witch
The Chief

Fearful Passage North

1634—Return to the New World

Contemporary Medical Thrillers
The Labyrinth
The Pain Doc
The Corridor

Available in print and e-books from Amazon.com

Visit the author at
www.wilmontkreis.com
And on Facebook

THE
BEAVER
WARS

Wilmont R. Kreis

Port Huron, Michigan
2017

Spanish civilization crushed the Indian; English civilization scorned and neglected him; French civilization embraced and cherished him.

—Francis Parkman

Get your facts first, and then you can distort them as much as you please.

—Mark Twain

The man who does not read good books has no advantage over the man who cannot read them.

—Mark Twain

READER REVIEWS

"Another great read by one of my favorite authors! Excellent historical perspective via a captivating story! Amazing writing..." –S. Steve

"The author does what all family genealogists long to do—based on actual historic facts, he uses his gifted imagination, inspired insight and visionary intuition to breathe life into dreary statistics and a rough outline of events..." –L. Rockwell

"He's done it again! And he keeps getting better at it. Based on a true story, this historical novel takes us back in time..." –fellow writer

"As an avid follower of the Allard sagas, I was once again happily swept back to 17th century Québec by Wilmont Kreis. The writing is significantly faithful to history, yet easily engages the imagination as we're invited along with the early French settlers to experience the early French Canadian Wilderness..." –S. Williams

"Dr. Kreis has done it once again. With over 12 books under his belt, this fast moving novel cleverly combines historical fact with historical fiction. The book transports you mentally back to the 1600s involving England, France, the Dutch, Canadian Québec and the native Indians..."
–R. and S. Champine

For the French-Canadian Heritage Society of Michigan that stoked my interest in this wonderful history, and to the members of FCHSM for their support as well as their own excellent work and research of French-Canadian ancestors.

And for Susan, my wonderful wife of almost fifty-years. We first met at a junior high dance and she has thrilled and guided my life ever since.

. Acknowledgements

Since writing the first Allards book at the turn of the century, I have humbly realized more each year that writing is a team effort. With each book I have expressed my appreciation for the help of my editor, Susanna Defever, my map and cover creator, Carrie Mclean and especially my wife and most valuable critic, Susan—but there are many others:

Members of the French-Canadian Heritage Society of Michigan have provided not only support, but excellent ideas and advice from their never-ending work on French, French-Canadian, and Detroit history. Readers I meet at presentations, on the web and even in the grocery store, offer interesting insights and often good suggestions.

I must not forget my grandmother, Julia Allard, who held me on the swing as a tot, as she filled me with tales of growing up on her fourth-great-grandfather's ribbon farm where we both were born and where we were still swinging.

As with all my works, I am happy to discuss any questions on my blogs, both at www.wilmontkreis.com and on Facebook.

Thanks for stopping by.

Erratum: I was born in Detroit at the end of WWII. My family moved back to the farm when I was a young toddler. WK

The Percheron Express

For those of you who are not sailors:

Sailing upstream or upriver is traveling into the current (away from the ocean)

Sailing downstream or downriver is traveling with the current (toward the ocean)

Preface

History records the known past through a collection of facts generally taken from written records. In writing *historical-fiction*, the author is allowed to fill in the missing details—those interesting bits of life that may have escaped the historian's pen, or may have happened only in the author's imagination.

When I began The Allards Series many years ago, I began writing a family history but soon fell prey to the historical-fiction sirens, asking for a broader tale of all French Canadians, whispering to add details, bringing the stories of these courageous and enigmatic people to life. Since this change was well received, I continued it throughout my writing historical-fiction. The Allards stretched from the mid-seventeenth century to the mid-twentieth. Since its completion, readers have asked for earlier stories about *Québec* and its people *before* that time. The result was **1634—Return to the New World.**

The year 1634 was chosen as a starting point because it seemed to represent the beginning of French-Canada as a viable entity with the arrival of families aboard the so-called *Percheron Express,* the ship that sailed the Atlantic that year to bring these few families from the region of Perche, France, to their new home…

And now… the rest of the story!

From: <u>1634—Return to the New World</u>

The final chapter

<u>Beauport, *Québec:* September 15, 1642</u>

The morning was as bright and spectacular as it could be, even for early autumn in *Québec.* "When you go to the docks, you can take Robert, Marie-Nicole and Agnes-Anne to the convent school," Françoise instructed her husband as she served breakfast. "I promised Marguerite we would go collect the chestnuts today. Jean-Pierre will stay with Félicity-Angel."

As Noël sat down, he told her, "Just don't go beyond the pasture."

"We are only going to the big chestnut tree," she reassured him.

Once Noël and the older children had left for the city, she dressed the two youngsters and led them and Tutu over to Jacques-Henri's camp. Leaving young Jean-Pierre with Félicity-Angel, mother, daughter and dog headed to the giant chestnut tree at the back of their cleared lot, kicking the falling maple leaves as they went. "It is good we are going before the giant oak leaves fall," she told her three-year-old daughter, "They hide the nuts." Once they arrived, she set down her two large buckets and explained to Marguerite how to identify the best chestnuts.

Normally this chore took only a short while, but the day was fine and Françoise had no other jobs, so she delighted in her daughter's interest. Picking up each nut to examine it, she would ask, "Is this one good, Mama?" If Françoise said yes, she put it in her bucket; if no, she gave it to Tutu who would bite it before spitting it out while the little girl giggled.

As they began to sing nursery songs to the chirping of the birds, Françoise felt a searing pain in her right thigh. She looked down in disbelief to see an arrow penetrating the leg—an *Iroquois* arrow. Looking up in panic, she saw no one in the forest. She turned to pick up Marguerite but realized the leg would not hold her. As she fell to the ground, she screamed, "Marguerite! Run to Félicity-Angel's!" Her daughter only looked and sobbed. "Go now! Quickly! Take Tutu!" The youngster turned and calling the dog began to run for the camp.

From her viewpoint on the ground, Françoise searched the woods to her north but saw nothing. Looking at her bleeding leg, she thought of the Algonquin who nearly bled to death but for the aid of Sister Marie-Forestier at the Algonquin camp. She tried again to stand, but the leg would not hold her. Re-examining the woods in front of her, she decided to attempt crawling back. Her progress was tortuously slow and painful as she made her way slowly south.

⚜

THE BEAVER WARS

CHAPTER 1

Beauport, Québec: September 20, 1642

Where was she? Except for a ray of moonlight that broke the darkness through what appeared to be a window, she felt disoriented until she realized, it was her window, and she was in her room. She reached for Noël, but he was not there. She lay alone in their bed. Trying to sit up, she was stopped by a severe pain in her left thigh. As her eyes adjusted to the darkness, she saw the cabinet her husband had built. It certainly was her room—where was Noël? What was happening? Another attempt to sit up resulted in more severe pain. "Noël!" she cried out, "come help me!"

The bedroom curtain pulled back allowing in more moonlight from the front room window. A figure carrying a candle appeared, not her husband. "Félicity-Angel!"

Françoise groaned, recognizing her Indian neighbor. "Where is Noël? Something is wrong with my leg. What is happening?"

Her friend came to the bedside. "You bad hurt, Françoise. We thought you would die, but Sister-nurse came and cut your leg. Help heal, she say. She be back today. Will be happy you awake."

"But where is Noël? Where are the children?"

Félicity-Angel sat on the edge of the bed. "Your husband take his shallop to sail soldiers to post at *Trois-Rivières*. Robert is at our camp with Jacques-Henri and our sons. Girls and little Jean-Pierre next-door with Madame Boucher. Everyone okay."

"But, what…"

Her friend took her hand, "Sister Marie-Forestier come soon from hospital. She know. You must be calm, go sleep."

Feeling a wave of dizziness, she lay back and shut her eyes, trying to remember. She recalled going chestnut gathering with her three-year-old daughter, Marguerite. Their dog, Tutu, was with them, but something happened that she could not recall. The last she remembered was her leg hurting.

"Sister here!" The voice jarred Françoise awake. By now, the sun had replaced the moon, shining through the window. She felt much better and more alert. The young woman in her gray habit of the Augustinian nursing nun entered. Even in that shroud-like garment, she was attractive. "Well, you certainly look improved," Sister asserted as she set her bag on the table. Coming to the bedside, she added, "You gave us quite a fright."

"Sister, what happened to me?"

4

To remove Françoise's gown, the nun pulled back the sheets. "First let us take a look." Unwrapping the bandage from the left thigh, she saw it was soaked in pus. The *religieuse* smelled it and announced, "The infection is improving." Putting her finger in the wound made her patient wince, but Sister declared, "Much better," and proceeded to inspect the abdomen, "The baby seems all right. When is it due?"

Françoise groaned, "Félicity-Angel says three months— two months before she is due herself."

"We shall let the wound breathe," the nun explained, as she sat on a small stool by the bedside. Taking Françoise's hand to hold as well as take her pulse, she continued. "We are not certain what happened. As I understand it, you took your little girl to collect chestnuts in the clearing by Jacques-Henri's camp behind your house. When the sobbing child and dog returned to the camp, Jacques-Henri went to investigate, finding you unconscious by the tree with an arrow in your thigh—an Iroquois arrow. He removed the arrow and dressed the wound. He says you were stable but confused and the next day became disoriented. That is when he sent for me. I applied a poultice, but the next day you were much worse—delirious. I lanced and drained the wound and applied a wick, the one I just removed. Thank the Lord, the infection is now resolving."

"So what do they think happened to me?"

The nun paused for a moment. "We really don't know. From the arrow, we assume an Iroquois shot you, but no one has seen any in Beauport and you have no recollection. Little Marguerite was frightened but seems clear she saw no one as well." Pausing for a second, she decided to go on. "One other thing... Two men were killed near Sillery—two *engager* who were taking a day to go fishing. One shot by an arrow and one killed by a knife."

Jacques-Henri had tutored Françoise in the identity of native arrows. "Was it an Iroquois arrow?" she queried.

"Yes…" the nun replied, "and one man was scalped."

Obviously greatly upset by this information, Françoise became silent. Sister Marie-Forestier returned to the task at hand. Reapplying a wick to the wound, she wrapped it snugly before moving the leg. Françoise grimaced. "Does that hurt?" the nun asked.

Gritting her teeth, "Yes."

"I'm afraid the arrow may have cracked your femur bone."

"Oh? Is that bad?" (It sounded bad).

"It will take a few months to heal," Sister Marie-Forestier answered, "and you dare not bear weight on it for at least two months."

"But… how will I get around? I have the children, the farm…"

The nurse began to pack her bag. "I will have a brace made and bring crutches in a few days, but you must be *very* cautious."

"But…"

Sister Marie-Forestier closed her medical pack and looked at her patient with the classic stern nun-stare that held generations of Catholics in fear for centuries. "*Madame* Langlois," she began with a hint of sarcasm, "You have good friends, not to mention your Indian neighbors and the school to look after the children, and your *sous-sieur* husband has a team of tenant farmers and *engager* to look after his *concession*," referring to the farm. "You will survive. I shall see you in a few days." She turned and was gone.

Looking about her room, Françoise realized the nun was correct. She and her husband had gone from poor French immigrants, coming eight years before as early settlers of the colony, to being managers of a large tract of land worked by a bevy of farmers who had arrived after them. In addition, her husband, Noël, worked as a river pilot, sailing boats along the *Saint-Laurent* for *Québec*. She also knew she had avoided the obvious question; why had he taken a group of soldiers to the post at the town of *Trois-Rivières* located upstream between *Québec* and *Montréal*?

As the sun rose toward the center of the sky, Françoise was sitting up in bed. Following the lecture by the nun, she had retrieved a knitting project abandoned near the bed before the accident and was now hard at work on it. Félicity-Angel entered with a bowl of porridge. "You must eat—Sister's orders."

Putting down the knitting, Françoise said, "Why don't you bring the children over. Let them see I am improving." Her Indian companion headed toward the door when Françoise added, "Oh, Félicity-Angel, what day is it?" Her friend told her and she did the math, "Why school begins in two days! I had entirely forgotten."

It was not long before Félicity-Angel had the children lined up to enter the room in age rank, beginning with the youngest. First was Jean-Pierre, age a year and a half. He stared at her and she smiled. He smiled and she patted his head as three-year-old Marguerite, who had accompanied her mother that fateful day, stepped forward with Tutu, their large Indian-dog, also with them that day. He had not left the girl's side since. These two children would be the only ones staying home this school term. Her older son would attend the school at the Jesuit Monastery and the older girls the facility at the Ursuline Convent.

Next came Agnes-Anne, age six, who hugged her mother while sobbing. The oldest sister, Marie-Nicole, age seven, followed her. Her eyes were dry when she kissed her mother. Last was Robert, age eight, who looked through his tearless blue eyes and stated with adult-like maturity. "We all prayed for your recovery, Mother," adding a little lie, "I knew God would not allow you to die."

Trying not to wince, she sat up straight, and told them, "School begins in two days. I will not be able to accompany you on the first day. Madame Boucher will be in charge. I expect all of you to be on your best behavior. Are there any questions?"

Agnes-Anne stepped forward. "We will be all right, Mama, don't forget the older children went for orientation last week, the day you were hurt." Françoise nodded. Actually in the confusion, she had forgotten about the orientation. It had been the reason she had been free to collect chestnuts with Marguerite.

Félicity-Angel then marched the troops out, explaining to them their mother must rest. As she shut the curtain, Françoise began to sob—tears of joy and thanks.

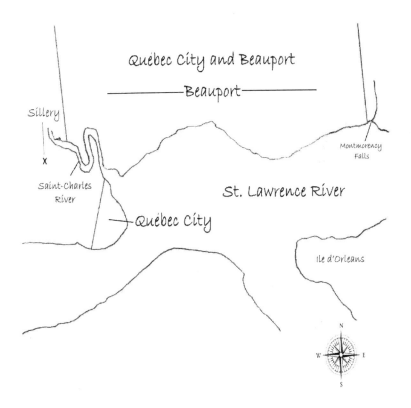

Québec City and Beauport

Beauport

Sillery

X

Saint-Charles
River

Québec City

St. Lawrence River

Montmorency
Falls

île d'Orleans

N

W   E

S

9

CHAPTER 2

Awake since well before daybreak, Françoise was filled with anticipation for the first day of school. Françoise's childhood had been anything but privileged. At the age of eight, her parents abandoned her at an orphanage near Paris where the nuns taught her basic skills of reading, writing and numbers. She now considered education of enormous value. Although confined to bed while Félicity-Angel did all the work, she still wanted to experience this day. "Remember," she told her children, "make me proud." Finally, each of them kissed her goodbye before they assembled by the canoe dock at the riverbank. Jacques-Henri would ferry them across the *Riviére Saint-Charles* for the hike to the upper town where both schools were located. Living a relatively short distance from the schools, they would be coming home each evening, unlike the native children and those from further away who boarded at the monastery or convent. Once winter descended and travel became difficult, however, some, if not all, of the children might spend the nights as well.

Françoise knitted and napped until midday when Félicity-Angel announced, "Madame Boucher here."

Nicole Boucher lived next-door. Shorter, fuller-figured and ten years Françoise's senior, she was the first friend Françoise had made when she arrived at *Mortagne* in the *Perche* region of France. Six years later, Françoise, along with her fiancée, Noël Langlois, joined four other families from *Perche* to come to *Québec*. The five families received large land *concessions* in Beauport, a village that stretched along the northern bank of the *Fleuve Saint-Laurent* from the mouth of the *Riviére Saint-Charles* to the thunderous Montmorency Falls.

Nicole entered her old friend's room. Félicity-Angel followed, bringing a pot of black-root tea and three cups. "All the children are now enrolled in school," Nicole announced, as she sank, exhausted into a chair, "including Félicity-Angel's two boys. It looks like a very good year. The new Ursuline Convent is just opening, and in a few weeks they are having a showing for the citizens." She poured tea before continuing. "Most of the mothers at the school expressed concern about recent random attacks by Iroquois—like yours." Françoise merely nodded, sipping her tea while Nicole continued. "I hope when your husband returns, he can give us some insight."

Félicity-Angel added, "My husband say small raids in our region unusual for Iroquois. He also look into it." The women turned to common gossip until Françoise began to fade, and they left her to sleep. She only awoke when the children returned, filling their mother's room with tales of the new school year and the new convent. Discussion was suddenly curtailed when the door opened loudly, and Robert exclaimed, "Papa is home!"

Racing to the front door, the children mobbed the returning Noël Langlois. Of average size, Noël was the sort of man who caught a woman's eye. His smile was accentuated by striking blue eyes, a trait from the Viking side of his Normand ancestry. Quickly patting the head of each younger child, he hastened to the bedroom. Sitting on her bed, he took his wife's hand, "I have been in a frenzy worrying about you. When we landed in town, I heard you were recovering. I rejoice it is true."

He came closer and took her in his arms. It was awhile before his wife replied, "I have been frantic. I could not imagine why you were so late." She told him what little she knew of her assault before she asked, "What have you heard about the Iroquois raids?"

"Immediately after your attack," he began, "Governor Montmagny called me to the main fort. Small bands of Iroquois have been menacing the fort upriver at *Trois-Rivières*. He sent a small contingency of troops with me to improve their defenses."

"Did you see any trouble there?" his worried spouse asked.

"Not there, but afterward we continued on across the twenty miles of *Lac Saint Pierre* where we found a regiment beginning to build a fort at the mouth of the Richelieu River. We left some reinforcements and did see a few random Iroquois snooping around but had no trouble."

"I know you have told me before," his wife stated, "but refresh my memory. If there is only one river at *Trois-Rivières,* why is it called three rivers?"

"You are correct to question it," he explained with his wonderful smile. "*Rivière-Saint-Maurice* flows to the

Saint-Laurent from the north and once was the primary route of the fur trade, but now the beaver there are mostly trapped out. As it enters the *Saint-Laurent*, the *Saint-Maurice* forms three mouths that appear to be separate rivers."

Nodding, she added, "And *Lac Saint Pierre* is not a lake at all."

Laughing, he told her, "That is also correct. The *Saint-Laurent* widens there and the early explorers thought it was the river ending in a lake rather than just a wide space in the river itself." Standing, he added, "I almost forgot the best news. Young Pierre Boucher returned with us. He is up at the fort."

She sat up suddenly at the news, wincing as she turned her leg, but managed to reply, "Oh! You must go next door and tell Nicole. When can we see him?"

Noël looked out the window before responding, "He is going to be very busy reporting to the governor, but there is to be an opening of the new convent to the public after mass in two or three weeks, I suspect he will be there."

The following day Sister Marie-Forestier arrived as promised with a brace and crutches. "I had these made by *Monsieur* Morin, the carriage-maker. He said he knew your size." Françoise smiled, "I knew him from my early days in *Québec*." The brace was a wooden splint. The nun showed her and Félicity-Angel how to secure it with binding. "It is bent at the knee," she demonstrated, "to prevent you from bearing weight."

"Rather awkward," Françoise complained with a grimace as she tried to move it.

The nun retorted, "You will get used to it. I became used to a heavy woolen habit in the heat of summer," adding with a smile, "We all have our crosses to bear." Producing the wooden crutches, she challenged Françoise. "Shall we give it a go?"

Françoise nodded and, with the nun on one side and Félicity-Angel on the other, came to standing. "Take your time," Sister Marie-Forestier counseled, "you may be dizzy at first." Françoise took three hopping steps, remaining upright only with the help of her two friends. "Takes some practice," the nun said with a smile.

They continued the drill, sitting to rest on occasion, but by the afternoon, Françoise could actually do it with minimal help. After one last turn, she returned to the bedside, pivoting to the bed. Doing so, she caught a glimpse of herself in a mirror Noël had given her. "Dear God!" she shrieked, "Is that me?" Although not known for beauty, Françoise was a handsome woman with a pleasant figure, long wavy brown hair and deep brown eyes. The creature in the mirror, however, was a haggard old woman with blotchy skin and uncontrollable hair.

Gently pulling her away from her reflection and seating her in bed, the nun said, "You have been severely injured and very ill—you almost died. It takes time to recover." As Françoise lay down, Félicity-Angel said, "I go to my camp, get potions—make you fine again."

The nun collected her things, "Good, Félicity-Angel, I leave her to you. This is not my specialty." The Indian returned with several jars. Rubbing a cool ointment into Françoise's skin made her relax as Félicity-Angel massaged her scalp with a different potion before bushing it out of her wavy hair. With mint oil, she massaged her teeth and gums. By dinnertime, Françoise looked almost herself again.

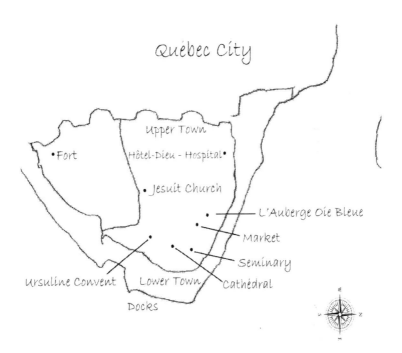

Québec City

Upper Town

•Fort

Hôtel-Dieu - Hospital•

• Jesuit Church

L'Auberge Oie Bleue

Market

Seminary

Ursuline Convent   Lower Town   Cathédral

Docks

CHAPTER 3

Québec: Sunday, three weeks later

As the bell tolled, the congregation spilled from the chapel into a spectacular *Québec* October day. Abundant maples had reached their peak of Canadian splendor as their red and golden leaves floated to the ground. Parishioners were anxious to exit the cramped quarters of the Jesuit chapel. Two years earlier, Champlain's church, *Notre-Dame de la Recouvrance,* had burned to the ground. Determined to avoid another disaster, the congregation was building a new facility entirely of stone, *Notre-Dame de la Paix* which required considerable time. In the interim, the colonists worshiped with the Jesuits. Today, however, the community was interested in another new stone structure, the recently completed Ursuline Convent and School for girls.

Françoise exited slowly behind the crowd. Although she had become independent on her crutches, she remained very slow. Noël walked, supporting her on the left side, while Nicole Boucher and her husband, Gaspard, strolled on the right. Gaspard's brother, Marin, and his wife, Perrine brought up the rear of the slow procession.

"Father said the showing would begin this afternoon," Nicole informed them, "We have time to stop for lunch." Reaching the square, they headed for *Québec's* famous eatery, *L'Auberge Oie Bleue*. Others were already gathering, most seated at outdoor tables under the canopy of Canadian maples.

The proprietor, Étienne Fortin, greeted them. "I have a special table—just for you," he announced, coming to Françoise's side, "very convenient for Madame Langlois. I see you are recovering from the wounds of those devil Iroquois, Madame. Those savages will not prevail!" There were few secrets in the small town of *Québec*, especially among saloonkeepers.

"I can scarcely wait to see Pierre!" exclaimed Nicole Boucher. "Even though he has been home three weeks, he has been too busy to take leave from the fort." Pierre Boucher had only been eight years old when Françoise first met him in the *Perche* region of France. Even then, he was a precocious child. Coming to Canada and educated by the Jesuits, he had become Governor Montmagny's chief Indian language interpreter as well as an officer in the army. In spite of his youth, his opinions on many topics were becoming well regarded.

After *Monsieur* Fortin brought pitchers of local beer, Marin Boucher raised his glass, "To Canada." As dinner arrived, talk turned to the Ursuline Convent. Marin was a master mason and knew all the nuances of the new facility.

"After the fire at the old church, we decided stone is the way to go," adding with a smile, "that should be more difficult to burn."

Following their meal, they made their way to the new convent. Set on a long front lawn, the muted-white stone structure was now a gem of the upper town, only surpassed by Fort St. Louis, which overlooked the entire landscape from high on *Cap Diamant*. At the front door, a nun wearing the habit of the Ursuline met them. She appeared formidable in this austere black shroud, but smiling widely, she greeted them warmly, "How nice of you to visit." This was the foundress and Mother Superior, *Marie de l'Incarnation*. She had traveled with Françoise to the Indian camps to see and learn the ways of the natives and study their language, and the two women had remained good friends. She ushered them into the vestibule where a young novice waited. "Sister Monique," she explained, introducing them to the young lady, "will guide you."

Following the novice into the great hall, they heard a booming voice from behind. "I will take these guests, Sister."

As the young guide stopped, Françoise turned slowly toward the familiar voice. "Sister Marie-Claude!" She tried to approach the enormous nun and almost fell in her excitement.

"My goodness, child!" the nun shouted, "Do not damage yourself any further." Fully one head taller with twice the girth of Françoise, the nun embraced her. They had first met in France where both worked at the church school in *Mortagne*. After Françoise had departed for *Québec*, Sister Marie-Claude went to the Ursuline Convent of Tours and arranged to go to the colony with the first group of nuns.

18

"Follow me!" this corpulent *religieuse* ordered, embarking on their tour of the impressive facility.

The great hall was the largest room the visitors had ever experienced, and its austere white stone made it seem all the greater. Sister Marie-Claude told them, "We fear this may be cold in winter." Then putting her hands on her large abdomen, she chuckled, "but I am built for it." The dining room contained rows of tables facing a small altar to facilitate meditation while dining, and the chapel, awash with wooden décor and statues, was certainly the most impressive.

Coming to the end of the tour, they encountered a young man in a sergeant's uniform following a much younger native girl. "Pierre!" shouted Nicole Boucher, recognizing her son. Mother and son embraced before Pierre greeted his neighbors. Although only 22 years old, he appeared older and acted much older.

Once free of his mother's embrace, he told them, "This is *Ouébadinoukoué*. She is a student here and giving me a tour."

The young native curtsied and said, "My Christian name is Marie-Madeline Chrétienne. I have already met Madame Langlois." Stepping back, she looked at Pierre, "Now that you have found your family, sir, I should leave you."

As she walked away, Nicole said, "My, what a mature child. How old is she?"

Pierre shrugged, but Françoise answered, "I believe she would be about ten. Two years ago, *Marie de l'Incarnation* asked me to see her. Iroquois had raided her village to the west, and missionaries brought her here. At first she would not even speak, but we managed to bring her out and now I hear she is one of the best students in the school."

Changing the subject, she asked, "Pierre, what can you tell us of the situation upriver?"

He looked to make certain no one else was listening before he reported, "I have the next two days on leave, so I was planning on coming home tonight—we can speak more freely there."

"Excellent," Françoise declared, "You can come home with us. Due to my condition," lifting the crutches, "we brought the cart over the bridge."

The three families bid farewell to the nuns and headed back to the Jesuit chapel where the cart awaited. Pierre had been gone for nearly two years and marveled at the changes and improvements that had occurred since his departure. When Governor Montmagny replaced the deceased Samuel Champlain in 1636, he began building roads. Now a small road ran in front of the farms of Beauport on the north bank of the *Saint-Laurent* to a small bridge crossing *Riviére Saint-Charles*. From there the road continued into the lower town and then up to the upper town and on to the gates of Fort Saint-Louis at the top of the foreboding *Cap Diamant*. Noël had managed to obtain an ox that pulled the cart much better than their old cow. At Beauport, they unloaded, agreeing to meet at the Langlois house before dinner.

All five men of the original Beauport settlers were artisans in the building trades and initially built simple log structures to house their families. Eventually fires, hard winters, and an abundant supply of *Québec* fieldstone caused them to use their talents to convert these simple dwellings to larger stone houses reminiscent of their native Normandie. The long porch on the Langlois dwelling now allowed space for all five Bouchers, Noël, and Françoise as well as Jacques-Henri and Félicity-Angel to gather.

Félicity-Angel brought ale brewed by one of the Normand tenant farmers. Pierre had shed his uniform for more traditional and comfortable *habitant* garb. Taking a sip of ale, he began, "Last year, the Iroquois proposed a peace with Governor Montmagny. In exchange, they wanted free access to the beaver on the Huron lands. Montmagny told them the Huron were long-term friends and allies, and we wanted no part of such a plan. In response, the Iroquois declared war on the French. There were a few skirmishes near the mouth of the Richelieu River, but we were able to chase them off.

"As you know, the Richelieu is the route north from Iroquois country to the *Saint-Laurent*. In fact, it was once known as the Iroquois River. We began to put small groups of men along it to impede the travel of the Iroquois. Before I departed, we began construction of a proper fort where the Richelieu enters the *Saint-Laurent*. Small battles occurred in many places, some in *Montréal* resulted in deaths, and there have been a few raids in Sillery just west of *Québec*."

"That's where Sister Marie-Forestier is at the *Hotel Dieu,*" Françoise reported with obvious concern, referring to the Augustinian Convent and hospital.

Marin's wife, Perrine Boucher, who had remained silent, asked her nephew, "Why don't the Iroquois stay where they live?"

"Well," said Pierre, "traditionally they live around the Dutch and English colonies to the south and west, but the beaver of the Hudson River Valley have been all but trapped out. Now they must come north, where beaver still flourish, to trap and continue their trade. To do this, they must encroach on Huron land. Their fight is really with the Huron—we are just in the way."

21

"Well," his aunt continued, "why don't the Huron fight them?"

Pierre paused for a while, sipping his ale. "Normally the Huron are a force to reckon with, but they have been plagued by disease the last few years, and their numbers are falling—rapidly. Even as we speak, the Jesuits led by Isaac Jogues are trying to help negotiate, but the Iroquois don't favor the missionaries." He put his cup down and stood, before adding, "And there is one other factor."

"What is that?" his aunt queried.

Pierre looked out at the river with intensity, "The Dutch have sold guns to the Iroquois!"

That evening when Françoise and Noël readied for bed, she asked, "Did you know about the Iroquois having guns?"

Her husband shrugged, the way he always did when he was trying unsuccessfully to seem unconcerned. "Yes— actually I just heard rumors."

"But what does it mean?" she persisted.

Lying down and pulling up the covers, he concluded, "I suppose it means we must be more careful." Neither of them slept well that night.

CHAPTER 4

Québec: December 25, 1642

"This must be the warmest Christmas ever!" Nicole exclaimed as they left the Jesuit chapel. The snow was only two inches deep, the river had yet to freeze, and the sun bounced gleefully off the few flakes remaining on trees.

"I agree," said Françoise, using her free hand to shield the sunlight as she stabilized herself with her solitary crutch, while the two women worked their way into the market square followed closely by their husbands. Her progress had been excellent, and now she bore full weight with a single crutch held in her right hand as dictated by Sister Marie-Forestier. In truth, she never used it in the house but kept this fact to herself.

Christmas weather was rarely so kind to the colonists, but today was the exception as they made their way to the Ursuline Convent, open for a celebration. Taking time to maintain Françoise's balance in the snow, they eventually reached the grand structure where Sister Marie-Claude greeted them at the door. The rotund *religieuse* gave Françoise a hug, stepping away laughing. "You are as prominent as I am." she chuckled, while holding her ample midsection, comparing it to Françoise's great with child. "When are you due?"

"Félicity-Angel says any day," she replied. They proceeded to the great hall where the nuns and the community were gathering. The refreshments differed from *L'Auberge Oie Bleue* consisting of tea and crackers, with a limited taste of low-end communion wine for the desperate.

"What do you hear from your boy?" the *religieuse* inquired of Nicole.

"He is up-river and reports the new fort on the Richelieu River is complete. They are calling it Fort Richelieu."

"I'm certain the Cardinal will be pleased," Sister Marie-Claude offered. "They say he had little use for the colony until the King put him in charge last year."

"We shall see," Nicole replied. "At any rate, Pierre says there has been little trouble with the Iroquois."

"Oh, look," said Françoise. "There is *Monsieur* Robert Caron and his wife." When the couple approached, she introduced him to her friends, explaining, "*Monsieur* Caron does business with Noël."

Bowing to the ladies, he replied, "This is my wife, Marie-Crevet."

After exchanging some small talk, the Carons went on their way, which allowed Françoise to continue. "Noël said Marie-Crevet came from Normandie—in the region of Calvados." Both women smiled at the name of France's famous beverage. "She was one of the first to come as a *fille à marier*."

Sister Marie-Claude chuckled, "I know what Calvados is, but what is a *fille à marier?*"

They gathered in close as Françoise reported, "Since the beginning, men have come to *Québec* in much greater numbers than women. As a result, many of the men leave at the end of their three-year *engagement.* Some marriages have occurred with native women, but not enough to solve the issue. A short while ago, the government began to recruit eligible French women without prospects who were willing to come alone to *Québec* with the hope of marrying a *habitant*—the *filles à marier.* This improved things somewhat but has not solved the problem—there are still not nearly enough women.

"Monsieur Caron came from around *La Rochelle,"* she continued. "He came the same time as we did, but on another ship. As an unmarried *engager,* he went to work for *Monsieur* Giffard. On completion of his three-year contract, he decided to stay and became a tenant farmer in *Beaupré.* A few years later, she came alone, met and married *Monsieur* Caron."

After exchanging holiday pleasantries, the *Québécois* departed the convent, some heading for stronger libation while others, like the Langlois, for home. Collecting the children from their own party at the convent school, Noël pointed his ox toward the *Riviére Saint-Charles* Bridge. Looking to the northwest sky, he predicted, "It seems as though our wonderful weather is coming to an end," and urged the beast on. By the time they reached the bridge, the violent northwest blizzard lowered visibility to twenty feet and more than a foot of new snow lay on the ground. Finally reaching their destination, they could scarcely see the house as the two older children helped their mother, impaired on two fronts, pregnancy and injury, to the door while Noël led the snow-covered ox to the barn.

Beauport: January 1, 1643

Winter raged for five days but the past two had been only cold and cloudy. The *Saint-Laurent* remained passable for the time being and Noël had been sent to deliver reinforcements to the fort at *Trois-Rivières.* "I wish they could have sent someone else," he told his spouse, "with the baby due and everything."

His wife had laughed. "Don't worry—you are useless around childbirth, it will be better to have you away. Maybe you can visit with Pierre Boucher while you are there. I believe it is his current post."

So on the first day of the year, Françoise rose to bright sunshine, the first in a week, and she walked out on the porch to greet the day. Suddenly she felt the flow of liquid down her leg. She waited for the amniotic fluid to slow to a trickle before she reentered her house with its clean floor, "Robert, take your brother and go to Jacques-Henri's camp. Tell Félicity-Angel it is time. You boys stay there until we call for you. The girls may stay here."

Her Indian friend arrived immediately, inspected the puddle on the porch and entered. No novice to childbirth, Françoise had already put a special sheet on the bed, water on to boil and assembled the other necessary items. Félicity-Angel, who was nearly as pregnant as her friend, instructed her to lie down. She inspected the patient and announced. "Not turned."

Françoise became worried, "You mean not head first?"

Félicity-Angel shrugged, "No, but we okay."

"Should we send one of the girls for Nicole?"

Her friend looked around. "No, we have Marie-Nicole," referring to the seven-year-old. "Time she learn." She asked the young girl to come over and began to manipulate the abdomen while she instructed her. Soon the girl was helping, and Françoise said, "I'm having strong contractions!" Félicity-Angel continued to speak softly to the child, while Françoise became frantic. "They are very strong, like I'm about to deliver!"

"That good," her friend replied.

"But it's breach!"

"It's all right, Mama," Marie-Nicole declared. "I turned it!"

Three contractions later, the baby began to cry as Félicity-Angel helped the infant's sister bring it completely into the world. Félicity-Angel held up the screaming, blood-soaked infant. "Nice big girl. Good lungs." She and her assistant returned it to the bed and dealt with the cord. They dried the baby, wrapped it in a towel and delivered it to its astounded mother. "Time to eat," Félicity-Angel said. The infant agreed.

Marie-Nicole came to watch her new sister nurse, "What will we call her, Mama?"

Françoise looked at her usually reserved daughter, "I don't know—how about Marie II?"

The youngster made a face and countered, "How about Jeanne?"

Her mother smiled, "That's it, Jeanne it is."

Once things were in order, Félicity-Angel sent Agnes-Anne for Nicole Boucher.

One week later Noël returned. While he held his new daughter, his eldest described her role in the event—in detail. "When I grow up, I'm going to be a *sage-femme!*"

Marie-Nicole informed him referring to the French term for mid-wife. "I'll deliver *all* the babies. I will be the best."

When Françoise finally had all the children in their bedroom lofts and was alone with her spouse, she brought two glasses of Calvados. Actually, it was a local attempt at apple brandy, which was well short of the mark of the real thing—but calling it *Calvados* seemed to make it taste better.

"I can scarcely believe Marie-Nicole," he told her. "I have never seen her so lively. She is usually so shy."

Sipping her drink, she replied, "I think she is over that stage. But tell me, how was your trip?"

He stood to stoke the fire while replying, "Brutal. Two days longer and we would not have been home this season. Fortunately, we had just enough room in the ice to maneuver. The narrows by *Riviére Saint-Charles* can now be crossed on foot. Soon even the carts will be safe on the ice." Returning to his rocker, he continued, "Things seem to be quiet in *Trois-Rivières.* They say it is calm at the new Fort Richelieu as well."

"Did you see Pierre Boucher?"

"Yes, I did. In fact, I had dinner with Commandant LaViolette. I have known him for a long time. He invited Pierre to join us. I think that reflects well on his opinion of the boy—actually, I think Pierre knows more about the Indian situation than anybody does. They think the Iroquois will lay low until the weather breaks, but don't think they are going away."

"What should *we* do?"

Her husband frowned, "I don't think there is much we can do. Just be careful and prepared."

Six weeks later, Félicity-Angel gave birth to her first daughter. Françoise went to help and brought Marie-Nicole who begged to come. Like most native women, Félicity-Angel was accustomed to giving birth with minimal assistance but told the youngster she could not have done without her. She named the child Marie-Angel.

Things remained quiet in *Québec*, the ice broke on schedule and spring arrived as always. The first ship of the season entered the port early on May 10, 1643, causing the citizens to flock to discover what it brought. As usual, there were soldiers, *engager*, animals and equipment. The ship also brought a few single women, but very few. Unexpected was the news that His Grand Eminence Armand-Jean du Plessis, Cardinal de Richelieu, had died December 4, 1642, at the age of 57. He would never know about the fort in the new world named for him.

In addition, the ship brought something no one knew about or had expected—something the colony did not need.

CHAPTER 5

Québec: May 20, 1643

Since April, it had been apparent this would be a wonderful spring, and for Noël Langlois, good weather produced plenty of work. As the colony grew each year, the need for shipping within the colony expanded, and although Governor Montmagny was building roads in the city and larger towns, the waterways continued to be his main highways. Piloting crafts larger than canoes, called small shallops, was the job of the river pilots, and initially that was Noël and Abraham Martin. Now they were training other men, but Noël and Abraham were in charge and did scheduling on days like today when they were both in town.

Noël was typically early and stopped by the lower town docks, taking a seat at Étienne Fortin's original establishment for a cup of *Québécois* coffee. Catering to a rougher trade than *L'Auberge Oie Bleue* in the upper town, the *Taverne Terre Sauvage* was busy with dockworkers, ship hands, and the occasional *voyageur* passing through on his way to the wilderness. Today, two men in *voyageur* dress soon joined Noël.

Some years ago, he had met Benoît and Bernier through Abraham Martin. Considered the most experienced and reputable *voyageurs* in the fur trade, they also provided a reliable source of information. "Good mornin' Captain," Benoît greeted, "May we join you?" Noël nodded and the two men sat as Benoît hailed the waiter, "Shots and beers, *garçon!*" Bernier remained silent. This enigmatic backwoodsman rarely uttered a word in public.

Noël nursed his coffee, while the pair swallowed their shots in one gulp and washed them down with mugs of beer. Benoît slapped his mug on the table and signaled, "*Garçon,* two more!" Turning his attention to Noël, he told him, "I hear you was up to *Trois-Rivières,* Captain." For someone who spent most of his time in the wilderness, Benoît seemed to know everything that occurred in the entire colony.

"Yes, I was."

"Seen any of them Iroquois rascals?"

"A few," Noël responded, "but mainly down by the new Fort Richelieu."

"Word is they's goin' back on the warpath," Benoît declared, "especially down by *Montréal.* Folks down there are takin' precautions, but they ain't got much to work with."

"Are you two hoodlums bothering the captain?"

The threesome looked up at the speaker. "Well, if it ain't Captain Abraham Martin, hisself." Benoît declared. "We was just discussing them Iroquois, yer honor."

Taller than Noël and much heavier, Abraham Martin cut a rugged figure with his long unruly hair and thick white beard. Sitting down while ordering coffee, he reported, "Well, I have just seen something equally as disturbing at the fort."

One of the very first colonists in Champlain's colony, Abraham had now lived here longer than almost anyone except a few voyageurs. When Champlain first set his new fort on *Cap Diamant*, Abraham Martin requested the land behind it. Now when he came to town, it was necessary to traverse the Cap. "When I leave home for the docks," Abraham continued, "I must walk through the fort, and that is the place to pick up gossip and other news. It seems," he continued, "that the first ship of the season arrived from France two weeks ago. A few crew and passengers were ill and placed in the small hospital of the fort. They all have fever and a rash, and yesterday, one of them died!"

The two *voyageurs* listened intently. Suddenly Bernier spoke the first word either of the two captains had heard him utter, "*Peste…*"

Noël's eyes widened, "Like the pox?"

"That's what I thought," Abraham answered, turning to the voyageurs, "You men have probably seen more than any other white men. What do you think?"

Benoît set his mug aside, "Sounds like it to me, yer honor…"

No one in *Québec* knew when or why these two odd men came to Canada. Rumor had it Benoît was a highly educated aristocrat who fled to the new world escaping something. In spite of his rugged demeanor, it was clear he was not the average backwoodsman. Looking out over the river, he continued, "We seen more than I can recall, yer honor. Almost all in the Huron tribes."

Noël asked, "Where does it come from?"

Benoît looked back from the river, "From the black robes."

"The Jesuits?" Noël queried, *"How do you know that?"*

"Can't *know* fer sure, Captain, but every time we see it, the black robes is in the camp."

Noël protested, "But, that doesn't mean…"

Benoît interrupted, "And each time it was a priest what got it first. Lots of names for it: pox, *peste*, plague. Dutch calls it *mazelen* or measles. Anyhow, I remember I had it as a boy. Sick for a while, then got better. I heard you never get it again. Seems like it wasn't so bad for Europeans, but the Indian… why it runs through the camp like a fire in a drought. Seen it kill whole tribes."

Wrinkling his brow in thought, Noël asked, "Why do we only see it *rarely* in the French?"

Ordering another round, the voyageur explained, "Got some thoughts on that, Captain. Most the French here was born in Europe. It seems the Indians born here gets it easy, because the *peste* is never been in their world. What worries me is now we're getting' all these new kids who been born here—ain't never been in Europe."

Abraham Martin stepped in, "That doesn't make any sense."

Benoît shrugged, "Probably, yer honor—just thinkin'."

The two captains excused themselves and Abraham picked up the tab. "Never hurts to have men like these on your side," he counselled Noël. They made their way to the shipping office at the dock and assigned two short runs to two of their new men and Noël took a longer run west.

Québec: Six days later:

"How is everything in *Trois-Rivières?*" Abraham asked, while securing Noël's shallop to the dock.

"Quiet," Noël replied, "There were a few Iroquois sightings upriver, but no trouble."

Abraham stood, stretching his back, "No Indian activities here either, but three more passengers from that ship took sick." He looked upriver for a minute before continuing, "Another of the first sick ones died."

Noël stopped, "What do they…"

"Sister Marie-Forestier came over from the *Hôtel-Dieu.* She says it's what the Dutch call measles."

"Anything else?"

"No, she just said, wait and see."

Noël arrived home to excitement as the children were coming home from their last day of school. When the children were in bed, he and his wife had time together on the porch enjoying the long day of sunlight, "A new Sister came on that last ship," she told him. "She began teaching at the school, but she took sick two days ago."

"Oh?"

"Yes, Sister Marie-Forestier says it is measles."

During the next two weeks, the nuns cautioned citizens to avoid close contact with new arrivals from the ship. There were no more cases among the passengers, no more deaths, and all the surviving affected passengers had recovered.

CHAPTER 6

<u>Beauport: June 1, 1643</u>

"Agnes-Anne, try to make your row straighter. Look how straight your sister's is."

"I think mine is straight enough, Mama," her daughter replied. "You always think Marie-Nicole's are better."

"That's because they are!" her older sister declared with a slight tinge of superiority. When her mother turned her head, Agnes-Anne stuck her tongue out at Marie-Nicole.

Even though Noël was able to hire out all the farm labor to his *engager* and tenant farmers, Françoise felt obligated to maintain a large kitchen garden and expected the girls to do their part. At seven and eight, Agnes-Anne and Marie-Nicole were to do their share while four-year-old Marguerite helped two-year-old Jean-Pierre pick up sticks. Françoise had recovered sufficiently from her leg wound to carry young Jeanne *en papoose*.

As the sun rose high in the sky, Françoise noticed Nicole Boucher approaching. "All right, girls," she announced, "time for lunch. Marie-Nicole, take them in, stir the porridge and set the table. I am going to visit with Madame Boucher."

As the girls headed for the porch, Marie-Nicole told her sister, "Maybe you can set the table straight." Her sister pushed her, eliciting a response from her mother. "Agnes-Anne, behave!" and a subtle stuck-out tongue from her older sister.

Françoise turned to her neighbor, "Why can't these girls get along?"

"Oh, it's the age," Nicole responded, "Didn't you…oh, I forgot, you had no sisters. Believe me, this is how it is at this age."

Françoise took the solitary cane she still used for walking any distance and led her friend to the porch. Taking seats on the porch rockers, Nicole told her, "I came to see if you had heard about Sillery."

"No, what?"

Nicole answered, "The men have had some concerns with Iroquois in the area and last night a few braves attacked the *Hôtel-Dieu* and Augustinian Convent."

"Oh, my God! What happened?"

Nicole leaned in to whisper, "The Iroquois burned a barn and killed one of the hired men."

"What will the Sisters do?"

"That's what I came to tell you. My Gaspard said Sister Marie-Forestier came by the church construction where he is working and told him this was not the first scare. Apparently, they are considering moving the convent and hospital back to the city for safety. Of course, they will need to build a new convent and hospital. They would have to use the old *Hôtel-Dieu* for now and live with the Ursuline."

Françoise stood, looking out across the river thinking of Sillery just behind the city of *Québec*. Looking back at her friend, she said, "Keep me informed, I had better see to the children."

By the time Françoise entered the house, the girls had lunch ready. Following the meal, Agnes-Anne said, "I don't feel good, Mama, may I go to bed?"

Still thinking about Sillery, she answered curtly, "No, get back to work. It is good for you."

Returning for dinner, Noël had more news. "The Iroquois came back and tried again to set fire to the Augustinian convent in Sillery. They were able to extinguish it, but two more outbuildings burned. Montmagny sent men to move the nuns to safety even as we speak."

Three days later, he reported, "I heard two children from the upper town have been stricken with the measles. Both attended the Ursuline school." Opening the door, he stepped out onto the porch, looking about as if he expected natives in the trees. Returning, he added, "We had word from *Montréal* today, a raiding party killed two women and hung and scalped a man." He shut and latched the door.

The next morning, Agnes-Anne would not get out of bed. She had a fever and a rash. During the ensuing two weeks, dozens of *Québécois* fell ill, mostly children, but also a few adults who had not had the disease in France. All of those involved had been at the school or closely related to someone who was. In Beauport, there was illness in several homes, and some had multiple cases. At the height of the epidemic, the Langlois family had four: Along with

37

Agnes-Anne, Marie-Nicole, Robert and young Jean-Pierre were also stricken. The first fatality was a native girl from the school, then two young French children. Eventually there were no more new cases, and the afflicted began to improve, including Robert, Jean-Pierre and Agnes-Anne, but Marie-Nicole lingered as her siblings healed— until she finally gasped her last.

In such an epidemic, the deceased is interred as soon as possible to avoid further spread. Therefore, in late June 1643, accompanied by neighbors and her grieving parents and siblings, Marie-Nicole Langlois, who had been destined to become the great *sage-femme*, was put to rest at the cemetery by the yet-to-be-completed church of *Notre-Dame de la Paix*, close to the Father of Canada, Samuel Champlain.

Cap Tourmente to Ile De Jesus (Montreal)

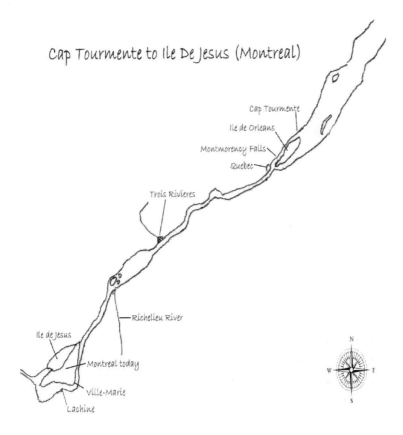

Cap Tourmente

Ile de Orleans

Montmorency Falls

Quebec

Trois Rivieres

Richelieu River

Ile de Jesus

Montreal today

Ville-Marie

Lachine

CHAPTER 7

Montréal: The same day

As one travels upstream from the City of _Québec_, the course of _Fleuve Saint-Laurent_, as the French called their great river, runs south and west for 130 miles before taking a short turn due west. Here one finds one of its largest islands, a triangle with a hill-covered interior. Legend has it when the great explorer, Jacques Cartier, first saw the peak on the interior of the island in 1535, he declared, "_Quel Mont Royal!_" The name endured, but since that time, the island remained a wild place with only occasional transient Indian camps and the rare camps of French voyageurs.

In early 1641, this had begun to change, when a group of French citizens formed _l'Association de Montréal_. Coming to _Québec_ the following year, they organized and sailed an unusual boat they had constructed to the island in May of

1642. They set their village of *Ville-Marie* just around the point of the triangle where waters of *Fleuve Saint-Laurent* were navigable. Farther round the bend, as the river turns westerly, one encounters a spectacular wonder of nature, a series of rapids not navigable by any craft—rapids passable only on foot or long arduous portage of canoes. The same Cartier had believed this was the route to China and named it, *Lachine.*

This was not far from Huron Country. Although the Huron spoke a form of Iroquois dialect, they shared a culture with the Algonquin. More importantly, they were friends of the French. The Huron had controlled the fur trade in this area since time immemorial, but recent episodes of war and disease had greatly diminished their numbers. The remaining Huron saw the future. Beaver to the south and to the east were virtually gone and the trade would depend on trapping to the north and west—in traditional Huron territory.

The French had started the small community based on religion named *Ville-Marie* on the large island of *Montréal.* The tribe, however, heard there was a French contingent that anticipated it would be simple and economical to trade for the Indian furs trapped to the north and west with French goods and money here, rather than transport the merchandise all the way to *Québec.* Familiar with the area, the tribe came to *Lachine* with plans to begin a village and a trading post with sixty braves from the traditional Huron lands. Arriving at a clearing in view of the rapids, they found something unexpected—an Iroquois camp.

The Huron stopped on the edge of the clearing to discuss their options, but the Iroquois were soon aware of their presence and three Iroquois approached them—unarmed and holding a standard of peace. The Huron chief decided

41

to take a chance and approach them with similar numbers also unarmed. In typical native fashion, they began by avoiding the obvious and made small talk of the recent winter and the current weather. There had been recent skirmishes between these two tribes but generally on a small scale.

Ultimately, the Iroquois chief broached the issue. "We have come from the south where the beaver is scarce. We know the beaver is now here and to north and west."

Pointing east toward the new settlement of *Ville-Marie,* he declared, "These people have no interest in trade. They are here to convert and enslave the Indian—they come with the black robes. As we speak, they have taken in some Algonquin who are working for them, like slaves, farming."

Pointing downstream toward *Québec,* he continued, "Our scouts tell us there are men in *Québec* who are coming here to establish a post for trade." Pointing next to the Huron leader, "We have not enough numbers alone, but if we join our forces, we will be able to control the trade without the Algonquin." The men conversed further without making any decisions but decided to part for the night.

The Huron set their camp on the opposite side of the clearing, and as the Iroquois went to sleep, the Huron chief and his advisors held a meeting. "Once the Huron nation was large enough to defeat the Iroquois," the chief began, "but after years of the *peste,* our numbers are too few. Perhaps we should consider joining these people to achieve an advantage in the new fur trade."

In the morning, the three Iroquois returned to the Huron, "We are going to find some of these Frenchmen and show them the power of the Indian. Send three of your men with our band and you will see what we can achieve together." The Huron chief agreed and sent three of his strongest braves.

The group of nearly forty men started toward *Ville-Marie*. Close to the village, they came upon six Frenchmen hewing timber. They descended on them suddenly, brutally killing three and taking the other three back to Lachine where they tied them and began to taunt and abuse them. Feeling they needed to make a stand of solidarity, some of the Huron joined in the abuse of the unfortunate three. That night they had a campfire and celebrated their victory.

The two tribes returned triumphant to their respective camps. Before sunrise, however, the Iroquois descended on the hapless Huron with a vengeance far greater than that taken with the French as they tortured and slaughtered at will. A few Huron managed to escape into the interior of the island, the rest were dead, tortured, or kept as prisoners. Of the three French captives, two were burned to death, but one escaped and made it back to his village where he reported the terrible event. The French in *Ville-Marie* understood, this was no skirmish—the real Beaver Wars had begun.

CHAPTER 8

Québec: April 1644

Noël brought the large shallop to the dock with his typical precision. The crowd of prominent citizens and gray-clad Ursuline nuns waited with excitement as he had the gangplank lowered for him to escort his passenger to land. Wearing a long gray gown similar to the Ursuline habit, Madame de la Peltrie stepped ashore ending her nearly two-year absence from *Québec* city. After greetings by public and church officials, Canada's richest woman was led to a carriage in which she would be taken to the new Ursuline Convent she had financed but not seen since its completion.

Madame de la Peltrie, born into the aristocracy in *Alençon*, France, in 1603, had married young and was a widow at 22. From an early age, she read the *Relations of the Jesuits*, and at the death of her husband decided to devote her life—and enormous fortune—to the Canadian missions. Coming with the first Ursuline nuns in 1639, she financed the voyage. So great was her fortune that when the ship could not transport all her belongings, she hired her own ship to carry her, the nuns, and her cornucopia of belongings to *Québec*. In 1642, she had accompanied the first French settlers to *Montréal* to found the settlement of *Ville-Marie*, but with the growing hostilities of the Iroquois, Madame decided to return to the capital.

Françoise was waiting for her husband as he disembarked. After a warm welcome, she informed him, "There is a banquet tonight at the convent, and *we* are invited. They have also asked that Jacques-Henri attend."

That evening, the Ursuline convent served a tasteful banquet to welcome their benefactress back to *Québec*, after which Madame de la Peltrie asked a few officials and citizens to remain for a discussion, Françoise, Noël and Jacques-Henri among them. Once assembled, she began, "The settlement at *Ville-Marie* shows great prospect for success. The return of the Iroquois to violence, however, threatens everything. This spring they attacked Commandant Maisonneuve and his party outside the village. But for the grace of God, he returned with only a few losses. In March, they made two raids on the village, both with loss of lives. Around the same time, the devout Italian Jesuit, Joseph Bressani was taken hostage after the murder of his Algonquin guide and tortured almost to death. The community has done all it could to ensure safety. A moat now surrounds the village and palisades are being erected.

"The problem remains—there is no means of knowing when and where these Iroquois savages are and how they can be thwarted. *Ville-Marie* needs your help and advice."

Looking over the audience, she saw Jacques-Henri, "*Monsieur,* I have been told you are a wise Algonquin. What do you say?"

Jacques-Henri looked shocked having been singled out by this formidable woman but simply stood and replied, "Dogs." No one spoke, so he continued, "Indian-dog is highly intelligent creature—easy to train. We have abundance of them here. Can tell man's tribe from his scent and sense if the man proposes mischief. A group of these could alert the citizens when and where trouble lurks."

Madame de la Peltrie appeared perplexed, "But, dogs? What manner of breed?"

Jacques-Henri replied, "Mostly Northern Wolf."

Aghast, she queried, "Wolf?"

"With some cross breeding," he answered, "with other wild dogs."

Françoise stood, "It is true, Madame, many of the farms have one or more. They pull sleds, hunt and are excellent guard dogs. I can think of more than a few times my dog has kept me from harm."

"Could you," Madame de la Peltrie questioned Jacques-Henri, "provide a number of these animals?"

"Oh, yes Madame," he told her. "Good breeders—have large litters; I could easily get 20 animals. I also have two men who could go with them to *Montréal*—to train citizens." The Indian's joke was lost on her.

"Well," Madame sighed, "I hope I have my answer. I wonder if you would all join me in the parlor. *Monsieur* Fortin, who supplies our communion wine, was kind enough to bring another libation for the evening." The small entourage retired to the parlor where Étienne Fortin himself stood behind a table pouring cups of Calvados. When each surprised guest had a cup of the famous

Normand libation, Madame de la Peltrie raised her cup, "To Canada." Shocked at this toast from this austere religious woman, they all raised their glasses, as she added with a muted smile, "You know I *am* a Normand." Then turning to Noël, "*Monsieur,* I understand you are also from near *Alençon.*"

"Yes, Madame, *St. Leonard du Parc*—as is my sister, Madame Martin."

"I must thank you," she continued, "for bringing Jacques-Henri. He adds a great deal to our knowledge of the area. I pray he can gather these canines and you can deliver them."

Fleuve Saint-Laurent: June 1644

During his ten years as river pilot, Noël had carried all manner of cargo and passengers, but this voyage was truly unique. Along with his venerable first mate, André Bergeron, he carried two soldiers for Fort Richelieu, two nuns, two Indians and twenty Indian-dogs with ten pups who lay quietly in a corner of the deck. "Gorgeous day to sail, Captain," Bergeron noted, as he climbed up from the hold. "Should be in *Trois-Rivières* in an hour or two." Surveying the deck, he added, "Still can't get over how these hounds behave. If only we could get sailors and women to do as well."

Laughing at his own joke, Bergeron went to the rail to speak with the two natives, Achak and Machk, friends of Jacques-Henri. Although they had accepted Christianity, they retained their native names and felt the rules of religion were mere—suggestions. They were, however, skilled dog handlers and planned to remain in *Montréal* until the dogs and colonists were comfortable with each other. They would return in the canoe now towed behind the shallop.

Approaching the *Trois-Rivières* harbor, Machk went to the rail. Looking at the patient group of canines, he called softly, "Pilot." A large female approached and sat before him. When they were close to where the dockhand stood at the ready, he said, "docking." The dog took the line in her teeth and jumped to the dock, delivering it to the shocked hand. She then returned to the shallop and ran to the rear, taking the aft line and delivering in it the same fashion.

The amazed dockhands secured the lines, and as Noël stepped ashore, he heard, "What's the problem, Captain, cannot find sailors?" Noël turned to see his old friend, Commandant LaViolette.

Shaking his hand, Noël replied, "No, just delivering some Indian-dogs to *Ville-Marie*." LaViolette looked over the rail at the patient brood. "Dear God! Come to my office, I believe I need a drink."

Walking up the hill to the fort, they entered LaViolette's office to find a friendly face hard at work. "Pierre!" Noël said, "Your mother will be pleased I saw you." Looking at his uniform, he added, "I see you've had another promotion."

"Young Boucher is now the official interpreter of *Trois-Rivières*," the commandant explained. "Couldn't live without him *these days*. You are staying the night, I hope?"

"Yes, it will be dark soon and I have two nuns aboard, as well as your supplies."

"We shall get them over to the convent for the night, and you and your men can stay at the fort. Pierre, you must come out and see what else the captain has on board."

When they reached the dock, Machk and Achak were unloading the hounds that disembarked single file and assembled peacefully on the lawn. "Indian-dogs are very trainable," Pierre told LaViolette. "I believe they will serve the purpose well."

Following dinner, the three men retired to the camp tavern. "How are *things* in *Québec?*" LaViolette began. *Things,* at this time referred to Iroquois attacks, and Noël told him about the problems at Sillery. "This spring," his host responded, "a Jesuit came through. When he left, the Iroquois captured him and tortured him to within an inch of his life. Eventually, for some reason unknown, they sold him to the Dutch. A voyageur passing through told us the Dutch put him on a ship to La *Rochelle*. I don't know if he lived."

After sharing tales of raids, LaViolette concluded, "The problem is this is not like a real war—the sort we had in Europe. There, you had two sides, organized battles and everyone knew what they stood for. These savages, however, with these small but vicious random attacks— they are not armies, and they are not soldiers. They are terrorists! That is what they are. You try to negotiate with one tribe but the next one disagrees. It's not civilized—like Europe."

Noël merely nodded, relieved Jacques-Henri was not here.

The next morning, they were on their way at sunrise—or what should have been sunrise, but the sky was black with threatening storm clouds. The soldiers were above deck and the nuns below while the dogs sat obediently in their allotted space. Soon the boat entered the area known as *Lac Saint Pierre*. As Noël had explained to his wife, it was a long wide segment of the river where one frequently lost sight of land.

As Noël had feared, as soon as land was out of sight, the storm hit—thunder, lightning, pelting rain and hail battered by violent winds. The seasoned seamen trimmed the sails and explained the situation to the passengers. The nuns below deck were petrified, Noël tried to coax them above deck. "You will feel better if you can see," he explained.

When the hysterical *religieuse* declined, Machk said, "I know." Going above deck, he returned with two dogs who sat below with the nuns. Ten minutes later, both women were asleep, lying against the patient hounds.

As the tempest built, Noël noted, "I think even the dogs are becoming nervous." The Indians laughed and an hour later, the storm departed as quickly as it had arrived, leaving smooth sailing to the mouth of the Richelieu River and the newly constructed Fort Richelieu. When they disembarked, the nuns each kissed the ground and headed to the small chapel, while Noël and the soldiers went to the office of the new fort, where Commandant Durocher showed the two soldiers to their new quarters before inviting Noël to dine.

The conversation was not much different than at *Trois-Rivières*, "Had a big battle here just last week," Durocher reported. "Tribe of Iroquois attacked a band of Huron and Algonquin traveling together. The good news is they blew those devil Iroquois away—big victory and big celebration. If all the tribes would join against the Iroquois, I think they could chase the vermin back home."

When they retired to the small tavern, the topic changed. Referring to the French organization that controlled the colony, Durocher asked, "What do you hear about the Company of 100 Associates, Captain?"

Noël sipped his drink, "I hear they are low on funds."

"Going out of business, I hear," The commandant reported, "I also heard they are going to form a committee of *Québec* citizens to take over management."

Noël was not certain he wanted to share everything he knew, "Oh?"

"Yes. Can you imagine it, a colony run by its citizens instead of aristocrats? I don't know what the world is coming to." Noël merely nodded.

Daybreak was as bright as yesterday had been gloomy, and the passengers boarded with renewed spirit. "Good luck in *Montréal*," Durocher said, while Pilot brought the docking lines aboard. "I pray those Iroquois rats are not still on the warpath."

Heading into the great river, the two nuns stood confidently along the rail, each guarded by their new best friend. The banks near *Québec* and *Trois-Rivières* had become more populated as time had progressed. When Noël first began in 1634, he would see nothing here but wilderness, but now it was spotted with the occasional camp or cabin, and random parties of fishermen and traders. Upstream of Richelieu, little had changed. The pristine water ran by miles of virgin forest with no sign of human life, only the occasional bear, moose, or other creature coming to drink, or eagle diving for fish. It seemed the world here was still free of man—at least European man. Only when they were a few hours from the island community did a canoe with two Indians come alongside. The two conversed with Machk while both crafts continued to move. When the natives departed, Machk came to Noël.

"Huron from north of here, I have met one of them. They say things are…" Machk was not as adept as Jacques-Henri in translating various native dialects to French.

"...*worrying* for white man in *Ville-Marie*. Iroquois bands becoming more common. There have been small attacks on village and some more worse on traders, missionaries and hunters outside village."

A stranger approaching the new settlement of *Ville-Marie* might miss it all together. The dock sat behind a small point. There were no structures directly on shore and most buildings inland were small. As Noël approached the small dock, three men came to meet them in a canoe. He did not come to *Ville-Marie* often and was not as familiar with it as he was with the first two ports of the voyage. Before they reached the dock, a tall man in uniform boarded. Noël had briefly met Commandant Paul de Chomedey, Sieur de Maisonneuve. He had heard he was rich, capable, and had handled himself well fighting the Iroquois, but little else.

"Well, Captain," the commandant began, "last week *Monsieur* Abraham Martin told me Madame de Peltrie was sending you with dogs to help run our city. Please tell me this is not true."

Noël looked at Achak as they approached the dock, and Pilot jumped with the forward line bringing it to a waiting officer. Returning quickly to the shallop, she took the aft line to the dockhand. Machk then began to order the dogs to disembark, causing them to leave the boat single file and with military precision. They marched down the dock and lined up on the shore. "I am afraid it is true, Commandant," Noël reported, fighting back his smile. "Here are the other passengers." The two nuns appeared with their two new canine friends. "The Sisters seem to like them," Noël added.

Monsieur Bergeron began to help the dockhands unload the cargo from *Québec* and the two Indians led the dogs inland, while Maisonneuve led Noël and the nuns to the small *Hôtel-Dieu* where they would double the size of the convent to four nuns. Smaller than the other two forts visited, *Ville-Marie* was a small village of wooden shacks, a small wood chapel, a small fort, an office, a few cabins and Indian huts. A moat, which appeared easily crossed, was the solitary barrier apart from the unfinished palisade. A small mud path crossed the tiny town.

Maisonneuve invited Noël to dinner in his rather cramped quarters. "As you can see," he began to tell Noël, "We are making little progress. Funds are low, but the biggest obstacle is the Iroquois. The village weathered two large attacks, but the small raids are our biggest problem, and I fear our palisade will not be finished soon."

"Hopefully the Indian-dogs will help." Noël answered cautiously. Maisonneuve frowned, but Noël continued. "I was skeptical at first, but I must say they are amazing."

Maisonneuve shrugged, changing the subject, "I hear the Company of 100 Associates is failing."

"Yes," Noël replied, "I believe we are going to have a committee of citizens."

"Sounds odd to me," the commandant replied, "but, I think there is a move afoot to make the whole island of *Montréal* over to the new Sulpician Order in Paris." Leaning over as if someone might be listening, he added, "It works for me—the Jesuits are too damned independent."

In the morning, Noël met again with Maisonneuve. "Machk and Achak will remain until the dogs are trained. Then they will return to *Québec*." The commandant frowned. "I cannot believe we are doing this."

Noël smiled, "Well, it was Madame de la Peltrie's idea."

Reminded they were a gift from Canada's richest woman, Maisonneuve said, "Yes, I hope it works."

As Noël approached the shallop, he saw Machk, "I'm leaving, my friend. I hope you do well training the dogs."

Machk smiled, "Dogs already trained, need train Frenchmen."

In late August, Noël found himself stranded in *Trois-Rivières* by a ferocious storm. While gale force winds and hail battered the roof, he found shelter in the tavern with Commandant Champfleur, who had only recently replaced LaViolette.

"May I join you, gentlemen?" Looking up at the tall stranger in voyageur garb, they nodded. "Not going anywhere tonight." The men just nodded when he added, "Are you the captain of the shallop at the dock?"

Noël nodded, and the voyageur continued, "Are you the man who brought the Indian-dogs to *Ville-Marie?*" Noël nodded again, he had not heard about the dogs since his return. "I was just up there a few weeks ago," the voyageur exclaimed. "I could hardly believe it,"

Noël sipped his poorly distilled *Trois-Rivières* Calvados, replying simply, "Oh?"

"Yes, each morning they go on patrol outside the perimeter. If they suspect an Iroquois, they bark and return to town so the citizens know what is up and are prepared. One bitch with a litter of pups is particularly talented."

"Is her name, Pilot?" Noël asked.

"Why, yes."

Noël smiled, "I guess she trained the Frenchmen well."

CHAPTER 9

<u>Beauport: February, 1645</u>

She could hardly hear Félicity-Angel for the gale outside the door, "One more push!"

Françoise pushed, felt the relief, and then heard the healthy scream.

Agnes-Anne strained her neck around the Indian to get a peek at the action. "Oh, look!" she shouted as her eyes opened wide, "It's a girl, Mama!" Félicity-Angel handed the infant to the girl who snuggled her new sister, carefully displaying her to Françoise. The infant hollered again while her sister looked at their mother and asked, "Why are you crying, Mama?"

Françoise reached out for the child, replying, "I was just thinking of your sister, Marie-Nicole."

"Father Lalemant told me she is in heaven and we should all rejoice."

"I know," her mother replied, "I just miss her."

"So do I, Mama… I wish we hadn't fought so." Agnes-Anne pondered for a moment, "Maybe we should call the baby Marie-Nicole."

"It might be a little soon to do that, dear."

As the gale continued, Françoise told her, "From the sound of this tempest, I think we have time to decide. It will be several days before we can get to the church."

Agnes-Anne climbed onto the bed and gently stroked the infant's abundant dark brown hair, "I can't wait that long! How about Elisabeth?"

Jesuit chapel, *Québec*: March 3, 1645

"I can barely believe how warm it is," Françoise exclaimed, exiting the chapel with the newly christened Elisabeth in her arms. Looking up at the sun, she added, "Why don't we go to the tavern? I'm well recovered and I can feed Elisabeth anywhere." Her neighbors on each side of their home, Nicole and Gaspard Boucher along with Jean and Mathurine Guyon, had come as witnesses. Both agreed. Etienne Fortin had already cleared a path from the chapel to *L'Auberge Oie Bleue* to bolster his business in the inclement weather, and today had drawn a respectable crowd.

The entire group but Françoise ordered ale. "I'll have Calvados," she announced, "Maybe it will help young Elisabeth finally sleep tonight."

Once drinks arrived, Gaspard broke the ice, "Have you heard anything about the Iroquois?"

"I haven't," Noël reported, "I haven't even been to the docks in weeks." Looking to his other neighbor, "What have you heard, Jean? Now that you are on the Council, you must have some information."

Jean Guyon was one of the four men chosen for a committee now referred to as the Council of Québec to replace the defunct Committee of 100 Associates. "Things seem slow," he reported, "I think because of the brutal winter, but there have been a few small raids around *Trois-Rivières* and Richelieu, also two in Sillery, but nothing major. Governor Montmagny hopes to call the tribes together when the weather breaks—to see what can be done."

CHAPTER 10

Fleuve Saint-Laurent Valley: Early spring, 1645

His name was _Piskaret,_ an odd name even for an Algonquin. Taller than most and braver—some might say more foolhardy—he and six companions had taken the Richelieu River south and entered the long narrow Lake Champlain. Paddling close to the swampy shore, they encountered a line of fishing nets and hid themselves in nearby bulrushes. This was Iroquois country, but it was what he was seeking.

Lying low in their canoes, they waited patiently as the sun cleared the horizon. Eventually, two Iroquois canoes, each crewed by eight braves, came to check their nets. _Piskaret_ and his men waited for the right moment. Standing suddenly, they shot all eight in one canoe. They pushed out of the reeds to overtake the second. After a brief battle, they had killed all but three Iroquois whom they took as prisoners and headed toward *Québec*. Along the way, one of the prisoners stole a knife and attacked one of the Algonquin. As he attempted to cut the man's throat, *Piskaret* put an arrow in his heart. Three days later, they arrived with the two remaining prisoners at a small Algonquin camp near Sillery.

Outside the camp they encountered a Jesuit missionary who, fearing what might occur, persuaded them not to allow the tribal members to *caress* the prisoners—an odd term for various types of Algonquin torture. Rather, he secured the two remaining unfortunate Iroquois and sent word to *Québec*.

Three days later, Governor Montmagny called Noël to his office. He gave him a summary of the encounter and capture of the Iroquois, adding, "I went and interviewed these two men. They both are Mohawk, and I would like you to take them to *Trois-Rivières.*" Noël was a bit surprised Montmagny would take the prisoners from near the large fort at *Québec* back to the smaller fort nearer Iroquois country, but remained silent until the governor explained, "We have three other Mohawk imprisoned there, taken from a skirmish last summer." Handing Noël a letter, he instructed, "This is for Commandant Champfleur. I am instructing him to return three of the men—one of these and two of those in *Trois-Rivières*—to their tribe, asking the tribal leaders to come meet with us in good faith in the hope we can trade the remainder of the prisoners on both sides and put a stop to these shenanigans." He added, "I don't know this new Champfleur well, but I hear he is a reasonable sort."

Two days later, Noël left port with Bergeron, two soldiers who were to remain in *Trois-Rivières* and the two

Iroquois captives. In addition, he had permission to bring Jacques-Henri. Following an uneventful voyage, they arrived in *Trois-Rivières* greeted by Commandant Champfleur and Pierre Boucher. The two prisoners joined the three tribal members under Champfleur's guard and Pierre explained the details of the exchange. Two men— one from each group, would remain in *Trois-Rivières*. The other three would be released. Upon their return with other tribal members to negotiate a peace, they would all be free to return home.

That evening, Pierre and Noël dined with the commandant who, with some misgivings, agreed to invite Jacques-Henri as well. "I am a career officer, Captain Langlois. I will certainly abide with the orders of my superior. However, I am mystified by the details. For instance, how do we know these men will return?"

"Iroquois have loyalty," Noël responded. "They also want the other two men back."

"You think they are that loyal?"

Noël smiled, "I also think they want a part, if not all, of the beaver trade."

"Well," Champfleur added, "as I said, I am not about to question the governor's orders." Finishing his third glass of Calvados, he looked at Jacques-Henri whom he had ignored all night. "And what do you think, sir?" Jacques-Henri thought for a minute, deciding this man would not be moved by his opinion, so gave an Indian shrug and remained silent.

The next day, they released the prisoners and the shallop headed for home. Once they were away from shore, Noël asked Jacques-Henri, "What did you really think about the commandant's question?"

His native companion smiled, "Question not what Iroquois will do, is what Huron and Algonquin will do."

Two Months later:

His name was *Kiotsaton*. He was tall, handsome and chief of his Mohawk tribe. Standing on the prow of the small sailboat, he wore strips or belts of varying sizes decorated with beads and shells—called wampum. Stepping ashore as soon as the boat touched the dock of *Trois-Rivières*, he waited impatiently to be greeted. Along with him were the three former Iroquois prisoners and a bedraggled Frenchman in native dress.

Having just learned of the arrival, Commandant Champfleur hastened to the dock followed by Pierre Boucher. Champfleur welcomed him in French, and Pierre translated to Iroquois before Pierre went to get the Frenchman, bringing him to the commandant. "This is Guillaume Couture," Pierre explained, "who worked with the Jesuits and was taken with some of them about three years ago." Champfleur had Couture taken to the barracks to rest and bathe.

He then ushered the four Iroquois into his office where they were seated Indian fashion on the floor and given pipes of tobacco. Champfleur assured the chief they had nothing to fear and were as safe as they would be in their own home. *Kiotsaton* responded in Iroquois for Pierre to interpret.

"He says to tell you that you lie," Pierre said.

As Champfleur stood speechless, the chief spoke in good French, "No man goes to the camp of an enemy and is as safe as in his own home, Commandant." Champfleur was flabbergasted. Clearly, this *savage* was much more civilized than he had anticipated. He soon dispatched a message of this meeting to the governor in *Québec.*

Once Montmagny had the news of the meeting, he called Noël and assembled a few officers, city leaders, and Jacques-Henri to sail immediately to *Trois-Rivières.* As usual, the mid-July weather was spectacular as they sailed upstream. Bright sunlight brought out the deepest blue of the *Saint-Laurent* and the brightest green of the forest. While wildlife came to the banks as if to visit, André Bergeron came to the helm. "Captain, it is hard to believe there is anything amiss in the world on a day like today."

Noël only nodded, "I hope you are correct, André." Two days later, they docked at *Trois-Rivières.* The usual calm of the port had turned to pandemonium by the arrival of multiple factions: Iroquois, Huron, and the various divisions of Algonquin as well as missionaries and voyageurs. Each of these divergent cultures keeping to their own.

As he stepped from the shallop into the cultural whirlpool, Bergeron declared, "I ain't seen confusion like this since the last time I sailed from *Dieppe,*" referring to the chaotically busy French port. The next few days were filled with small but wild camps of divergence: eating, drinking, dancing around campfires and the occasional fight—generally involving members of the same faction. Eventually opening day of the talks arrived.

Governor Montmagny had arranged everything as well as one could in such a field of bedlam. Noël had known the man since his arrival in 1636 and each year became more impressed by his abilities. Montmagny knew a good deal of the native customs and how each group viewed each other.

He had gained respect from all the tribes. Even the Iroquois had given him a favored name, *Onontio.*

Standing in the center of a great clearing chosen for the talks, the governor explained to representatives of each faction. "Each group will have its own place. My people will be here, next the Jesuits, Iroquois over there where the ground is covered with the pine branches they favor, next the Algonquin with the various divisions, then the Huron. In the center are two posts with a line to hang wampum."

Kiotsaton would speak first. He arose and took center stage. Taller than anyone but *Monsieur* Bergeron, he was an imposing figure. Pierre Boucher would interpret, but *Kiotsaton's* skill was such he spoke Iroquois, Algonquin and French. Walking to the Jesuits, he extended his hand to Guillaume Couture, who had cleaned up considerably. "This man had been my prisoner, but in the interest of peace, I returned him to his people." *Kiotsaton* removed wampum from his rope belt and attached it to Couture's arm. "I escorted him back so he would not be harmed on the way."

He then went to the Iroquois and took the hand of one of the freed prisoners. "This man, my brother, was a prisoner as well. When the French saw fit to set him free, they let him find his own way back, and he suffered harm, as he had no protection." He gave this man wampum as well. The next wampum belt was for others to withdraw their war parties and another for slain Iroquois. Additional belts were to clear the way to peace. Another belt was that the French and all Indian tribes become friends. Eventually he called for celebration. All groups took part, singing, dancing and feasting.

Two days later, Montmagny accepted the peace but demanded the French and their Indian allies be unmolested.

Even the Algonquin warrior *Piskaret* pledged peace. That evening the head Jesuit, Father Vimont, gave the ambassadors of each tribe a sack of tobacco.

The next day the tribes prepared to leave. All agreed a larger group must gather to fix the truce permanently. A September council to finalize the peace was planned as *Trois-Rivières* returned to a quiet outpost.

<u>*Trois-Rivières*: September 1645</u>

As autumn approached, the leaves began to turn and the parties returned, beginning as a trickle of Montagnais braves, then a steady flow of the other bands, Atticamegue, Nipissing, Ottawa and Algonquin. Finally, a flotilla of Huron arrived with sixty canoes. All tribes came with great stores of furs. Camps appeared everywhere and trade was abundant. Evenings were alive with dancing, feasting and speeches. Halfway through the month, Montmagny called Noël and Jacques-Henri to his temporary quarters.

"Where are they?" he asked about the Iroquois with a concern in his brow. "If they don't come soon, the others may leave."

Jacques-Henri walked outside the door with his nose in the air. Returning, he simply reported, "Tomorrow."

With Indian precision, a canoe arrived the following afternoon, carrying four prominent Iroquois, charged to speak for their people. The next day talks began with gifts of wampum and endless speeches, but in the end, all agreed. Following dances, feasts and celebration, the tribes left for their camps. A beam of hope was seen when Guillaume Couture agreed to spend the winter with his former captors.

After the tribes had departed to enjoy what would be the most peaceful winter in memory, Noël, Bergeron, and Jacques-Henri pointed their shallop, loaded with officials, toward home. The first evening was clear with a fine breeze and bright moon, so as the officials went to their cots, Noël elected to continue sailing. Around midnight, with the bright lunar rays bouncing off the *Saint-Laurent*, Noël asked his native friend. "Just between you and me, Jacques-Henri, do you think this will succeed?"

Staring at the bright globe, he answered, "Why not? Has never worked before."

Appreciating his friend's sarcastic humor, Noël smiled, querying, "But why?"

Continuing to stare at the moon, his friend answered, "Do not forget, Iroquois is five tribes, Mohawk just one of them." With a pained look, he concluded, "Still, is not Iroquois, is Algonquin and Huron. In end, they not share this trade."

With this bit of wisdom, Jacques-Henri moved to the front of the shallop, forward of the mast and sails, where he sat quietly, contemplating the wonders of nature as only an Indian could.

Noël remained at the helm, watching the stars and river for navigation, while contemplating his enigmatic native companion. A few years Noël's senior, Jacques-Henri had been born to privilege. His grandfather had been chief and his father a person of rank in the tribe. At a young age, Jacques-Henri attended one of the first Jesuit mission schools where he excelled. Along with religious training, he learned mathematics and science and became proficient in several languages. He could communicate in all the regional native tongues as well as English and Dutch. His French was frankly better than many of the colonists, but he had learned as a lad the importance of not appearing superior. Although he occasionally spoke well around the Langlois family and a few others, he generally used a pidgin dialect common to less educated natives.

While the moon lit the way, Noël knew he was fortunate to have this man as a companion.

CHAPTER 11

Québec, Taverne Terre Sauvage: March, 1646

Winter had seemed calm with no tales of significant Indian violence. Noël and Abraham Martin had braved the end of winter coming to the docks to check the boats and plan for the season. Entering the tavern, they were surprised to see their old voyageur friends, Benoît and Bernier. Ordering drinks for himself and Noël as well as the two backwoodsmen, Abraham asked about the Iroquois.

"For the most part," Benoît began, "things been right quiet." Downing his shot and sipping some beer, he went on, "Was one scare out of _Trois-Rivières._ Seems there was this old priest there, _Anne de Nouë_—funny damn name. Anyway he's getting' pretty long in the tooth and short in the smarts if ya catch my drift. So he goes with two soldiers and an Indian to Fort Richelieu. Colder than a witch's tit it was, but the old boy wanted to go hear confessions. Course

I don't know what the hell you'd have to confess living in that God-forsaken place." Bernier made a sound that could have been a giggle before his companion went on. "Took sleds across the ice. Stopped and camped for the night. In the mornin' he was gone. It took 'em a few days to find him, dead in an ice hole. At first, they thought he had been killed by Iroquois, but when they dug him out looks like the old boy just got up, wandered off and froze." He signaled for more drinks before continuing, "Then there was a raid on a Huron Camp close to *Montréal*. Seems Iroquois come in, stole their furs and killed a few Huron including two little kids."

Bernier sipped his beer, mumbling an incoherent word, while Noël asked, "Isn't that breaking the treaty?"

"Well, Captain," Benoît answered, "Ya see, this wasn't them Mohawk Iroquois, was one of them other four tribes." The voyageur concluded, "Anyway, that's all we heard. We come back early this season. Have enough furs, and we wanted to be here when them Iroquois arrive and see how things goes." Noël and Abraham went about their business and headed home. Françoise had told her husband she was pregnant a few days earlier, so he decided it would be a mistake to discuss the tales of the voyageurs with her.

A few weeks later Benoît and Bernier canoed to *Trois-Rivières*. "I hear the Iroquois are comin' to trade," Benoît told Abraham Martin, "Wouldn't miss it for the world." One week later eighty Iroquois canoes, overflowing with pelts, came up the Richelieu River and headed downstream to *Trois-Rivières*. Upon arrival, their leader went to the headquarters. Commandant Champfleur had taken Pierre Boucher to discuss a different matter with the local Algonquin chief, so his second-in-command, newly arrived from France, attended to the matter.

"We here to see chief—start trade," the Iroquois translator told him. Unsure what to do, the soldier went to see a Huron chief who had come to the fort the previous day. He explained the situation, asking what he should do.

Seeing his opening, the chief instructed the soldier, "Tell them they are to first sell them to us and then we will trade with the French." The young officer returned with that message. The Iroquois translator relayed the news to which the chief threw a stick he was carrying at the soldier's feet and stormed out to his canoes and his furs, heading back down the river toward Lake Champlain.

Upon his return, Champfleur heard the news. Overwhelmed with anger, he berated the young officer even though he realized he had not properly briefed the man.

Taverne Terre Sauvage: May 1, 1646:

Abraham Martin had just returned from a trip to Fort Richelieu and was meeting with Noël. "As we suspected," Abraham began, "things are really getting hot upriver. The Iroquois have raided Huron villages by all three forts. They have also staged raids way to the west, well into Huron country. Now it's more than Mohawk—some of the other Iroquois tribes are joining."

"What's to be done?" Noël queried anxiously.

"I hear Montmagny has a plan. He is sending the engineer, Jean Bourdon, along with Couture and a couple Algonquin, into Lake Champlain to see if they can negotiate. He's even sending that Jesuit missionary, Isaac Jogues, with them."

"Isn't he the one that's all beat up?" Noël questioned.

"That's him," Abraham replied, "Lots of scars and a gimpy hand."

"Why does he get hurt so much? Shouldn't he be more careful?"

"I certainly would," Abraham asserted, "but I have a crazy theory about the Jesuits."

Sitting back in his chair, Noël chuckled, "And I have a feeling I am about to hear it."

"When I was in school in France—long time ago, we had this Dominican teacher who taught us about the early church. It seems back then they believed to get to heaven you must suffer to the point of death—be a martyr. So they didn't object when the Romans threw them to the lions."

"Seems weird to me," Noël told him.

"This Dominican," Abraham continued, "told us after the conversion of the Romans, no one would abuse them to that point anymore, so they tried new ways to get abused, even did it to themselves. At that time it was the only way to become a martyr."

"So what does this have to do with the Jesuits?"

"Well," Abraham concluded, "It seems they go looking for trouble and getting into situations where they are having the shit beat out of them and they don't mind dying—at all."

"Still seems weird to me," Noël said, "but I do know we need to get to work on our schedule."

CHAPTER 12

Québec backcountry: June 1646:

Young Robert Langlois was first to see the landmark, "Jacques-Henri, is that it?" he shouted, almost dropping his paddle.

"Yes," the Indian smiled, "but not so loud, chase away all game—even fish." *It* was the highest peak in the north range. Still holding a layer of snow at the summit, it remained many miles away and even more majestic than the four boys had imagined when Jacques-Henri first described the voyage. "We stop up at next clearing," the Indian instructed, "spend night."

Landing in the clearing, the four fathers stood by as the four lads pulled the two canoes ashore. Their fathers had assured them that part of the cost of this trip was doing much of the work. Once the canoes were secure, Jean Guyon ordered, "All right, lads, this is the third night. You had better know the drill." They broke out with military precision as they collected water and firewood, set up the small tents, and began to clean the fish caught that afternoon.

The fathers sat on a long log, enjoying the event, and the level of confidence their sons had achieved. Jacques-Henri's son, Henri-Makya, was youngest at 12, only a few weeks younger than Robert Langlois. Jean Guyon's boy, Michel, was next at 13, and Galleran Boucher, son of Marin was oldest at 14. Once the fish were fried on the open fire—that improved with each camp, the men and boys stood for grace. Tonight was Robert Langlois' turn. "Thank you, Lord, for your bounty and bless this food. Also thank you for bringing us to this wonderful new world and putting our fathers in a position of privilege. Amen."

"Let's eat!" hollered Michel Guyon, and the feast began.

In the past the boys and dads had made short one and two-night trips, but this was special. The men had explained to the lads that in this busiest season of farming, they were able to come only because their fathers were blessed to be among the first Frenchmen in *Québec*. This gave them the advantage of having *engager* and tenant farmers to farm their land. Their fathers also stressed, this privilege came with great responsibilities and did not absolve one of hard work.

Following dinner, they sat around the dying flames as Jacques-Henri told an old Indian fable of a woman who had lost her children in a storm. One of the Indian gods had turned her into a she-wolf who wandered this part of the world in search of new children. Having heard it many times, the boys were scared at first. Tonight it was only a favored part of the trip. June nights in this part of the world were nothing more than periods of dusk, and the boys found this more frightening, as shadows and sounds never disappeared into total darkness. However, they never admitted it.

Jacques-Henri told the boys daybreak was signaled by the first call of a special north woods hawk. No one had heard of this before the voyage, but it seemed to work, and the hawk, instead of the sun, which barely set, gave the signal. The boys knew the drill and prepared breakfast. At the same time, they broke camp. Up to now, most of the day had been travel and fishing. "Today, last day before real hunting starts," Jacques-Henri declared.

"Will we get to the snowy peak?" Robert asked. The Indian laughed, "Would need month—or more." This morning was the most arduous, with long portages up steep slopes filled with rapids and giant pieces of granite. They were tired at lunch and exhausted at dinner, but the camp setting was worth it all. At the end of the rapids, they found a lake, ringed by granite peaks and cliffs, peppered with small beaches, conifers and a gentle waterfall just across a short sandy cove. After pulling his canoe onto a small beach where they would make camp, the fatigued Jean Guyon told the boys, "Surely, this is what heaven is like."

"Tomorrow we hunt," their guide instructed, "Walk—no canoe, fathers take guns, sons take bows." Jacques-Henri preferred the native weapon, but when the mothers heard of the planned voyage, they raised concern about the ongoing *Iroquois problem*. The men assured them there were no Iroquois in this area, and they always brought some guns. When the settlers first came to the new world, Jacques-Henri had taken some of the fathers and older boys on a shorter trip. At camp, a giant bear had appeared and was undeterred by Jacques-Henri's arrows. Only young Pierre

Boucher holding his father's musket saved the day that was now a local legend.

In the morning, the boys were up before the hawk called and ready to go. After breakfast, they set off, following Jacques-Henri up to a plateau with a spectacular view of the landscape. Here he broke them into two groups and gave each their directions. They had decided early on to have each father and son spend one day with Jacques-Henri and today was Robert and Noël's turn. Soon they were back in the woods following seemingly non-existing trails. Jacques-Henri showed Robert how to travel in dense woods. "Don't look at trees, only spaces." This seemingly obvious advice worked quite well as they continued with Jacques-Henri explaining how to distinguish the tracks of each animal.

Two hours into the trek, they heard an almost imperceptible soft crack. Jacques-Henri held up his hand and sniffed, pointing to the east. Robert peered into the trees, and then he saw the prey! It now seemed impossible that he had not noticed this enormous male caribou as big as two cows. Both Robert and Henri-Makya had bows and their fathers had told them how to take down even the largest animal with the correct technique—of course, they had never done it. Henri-Makya nodded to his friend indicating he go first. Robert's arrow was on target in the neck of the creature causing it to back up. Then Henri-Makya landed a shot in the rear changing its course to forward. They continued until of eight spent arrows, five had hit their mark, and the hapless monster staggered and fell.

The ecstatic lads began to move forward, but Jacques-Henri stopped them, cautioning them to wait. The caribou rose once, staggered and fell. Jacques-Henri then moved them in for closer shots on critical areas. Eventually the majestic beast quit. Only then, Jacques-Henri led them to their kill, saying an Indian prayer for the animal before helping them bleed and gut it while staying away from the legs. Once this was over, he ordered them to search the woods for their three wayward arrows, which took some time. Afterwards they tied the creature to large branches allowing them to haul it back to camp where they set to finish skinning and cleaning. Soon their mates arrived with two deer and three turkeys—all in all a grand day.

The following afternoon, the fathers allowed the sons to do all the gutting and cleaning. When they arrived back at camp, covered with animal blood and excrement, Jacques-Henri looked them over. Holding his nose, he declared, "Only one cure." Leading the way, he took the entire entourage along the shore of the shallow sandy cove ending at the bottom of the waterfall. The boys were familiar with Montmorency and its thunderous flow. Their mothers warned them, "Never go under it!" This flow, however, was gentle as a spring rain as Jacques-Henri disrobed and entered. The boys followed. Robert went first, screaming, "It's freezing! Like a snow bank!"

The Indian laughed, pointing to the snowy peak. "Was snow—once."

That night when Robert crawled into his blanket next to his father, he announced, "When I'm old enough, I'm going to live here. I'll be a backwoodsman and will live on that snowy peak."

The end of the third afternoon brought a violent but brief thunderstorm. Even this could not dampen the spirits of the boys and their fathers. That evening, they packed their bounty of meat preparing for the trip home. When Robert helped his father move their canoe, he groaned, "How are we going to portage this all that way with all this meat?"

"We will manage," Noël reassured his son, although he secretly harbored the same fear.

Morning broke clear, and after a brief breakfast, they launched the canoes into the lake. Marin Boucher pointed his east, toward the river of rapids that brought them. Jacques-Henri, however, whistled and pointed west. They followed him for a short distance to the source of another stream also flowing south. Wider than the stream that brought them, it was deep and calm. The gentle current flowed at a perfect rate, pulling the crafts downstream toward the *Saint-Laurent*. Rather than watching for rocks and rapids, they enjoyed the sight of mother deer bringing their young to drink, and the occasional hawk or eagle diving for a fish dinner, even a mother bear bathing with her two cubs.

From time to time, the stream narrowed and the current increased its power. There were even occasional rapids that pushed the boats along at an exciting pace but remained controllable, without portaging. When they pulled onto shore at the end of the day, no one was exhausted. Robert asked Jacques-Henri, "Why did we not take this stream in?"

The Indian only gave his trademark shrug, "Too easy."

After dinner, they sat watching the river, lit by the full moon as Marin Boucher played his Jew's harp. "My father took me fishing once," Noël told the boys. "He was a carpenter, like me. He had done some work at one of the manor houses and the lord of the manor invited him to fish in his lake. We only caught one fish, but it was a memory. In France, rich men owned all the lakes and fishing streams." He lit his pipe before continuing. "Here, in

Canada—nobody owns it. It belongs to everyone. My God, I wish my father could have seen this!"

Robert came and sat by him. "I am glad *my* father got to see it."

All seemed right with the world, and the Beaver Wars seemed a lifetime away.

Two days later the two canoes entered the *Saint-Laurent* at the same place they had left it several days before. The combination of traveling downstream and avoiding the vicious rapids had greatly hastened their return, and it was not quite midday when they landed by their homes in Beauport, greeted by their families. The excited boys all related their stories before helping the fathers move the meat and fish to Jacques-Henri's camp where they helped to prepare it for consumption or storage.

The families agreed to dine at home that night and have a picnic after mass on Sunday. Once Robert had retold all his tales and all the Langlois children were in their lofts, Noël asked his spouse, "I notice no one said anything about local news today."

"We decided to wait until the children were in bed," his wife replied. Going to the cupboard, she returned with two cups of Calvados, which they took to the rockers on the porch. "Several weeks ago, I think around Ash Wednesday, there were three Algonquin families gathered at the small Jesuit chapel in *Trois-Rivières.* They just disappeared. No one knew if they had left for the Algonquin camp or had run into foul play. Only a couple weeks ago two of the women arrived way down in *Ville-Marie*—in very poor condition, at the home of Madame d'Ailleboust."

"She is the wife of the temporary governor of *Montréal*, is she not?" he questioned.

"Yes," Françoise answered, taking another sip. "Apparently a group of Iroquois raided the chapel and took all three families. They went all the way to the far end of *Lac Saint Pierre* before they stopped at a small camp. There they tortured the Algonquin terribly. They killed the men—skinned them alive!" She began to sob.

"You don't have to tell me the rest," he told her.

"No, I need to get it out," she said, wiping her tears with a handkerchief. "They abused, then killed one mother—then the other children…" She wiped her tears again. "They took the baby and…burned it alive! Finally these last two women escaped." She collapsed in tears as he embraced her. Once she was composed, she added, as if to change the subject. "I guess Governor Maisonneuve's father died in France and he had had to leave. They made Madame d'Ailleboust's husband temporary governor. Now the poor woman has to deal with—this." Looking up to her husband, "What is to become of us? Why can't people get along?"

Taking her in his arms he only whispered, "I don't know—I just don't know."

Reality had returned.

CHAPTER 13

<u>*Québec*</u>: Sunday, July 1646

The tolling bells dismissed the *Québec* population into the bright sunlight of an early July day. Following the traditional socializing outside the Jesuit chapel, the five original families of Beauport left for home and a neighborhood picnic. The men led the charge to the carts as the women, filled with gossip, brought up the rear with the throng of 28 children in tow.

"The new church looks nearly finished." Françoise noted, pointing across the market square to the large stone structure close to the ashes of the old church.

"Marin says it will be ready for occupation by Christmas," Perrine Boucher added. "And the Augustinian nuns are now in their new convent at the *Hôtel-Dieu*."

"My Pierre says they will be much safer there," Nicole added.

"Doesn't it worry you," Mathurine Guyon asked, "to have him at an outpost the way *things* are?"

"Some," his mother replied, "but he stays near the fort and is with the military."

"Ladies!" scolded Xainte Cloutier, the elder stateswoman of the neighborhood. "My Zacharie said we are not to talk about the *trouble* today or we shall have to leave the picnic."

"Well," began Perrine Boucher, doing her part to change the topic, "did you hear about what Madame Poitier was found doing in their barn?" Once the entourage discussed the improprieties of Madame Poitier, they boarded their carts and headed to the *Riviére Saint-Charles* Bridge and home.

What had been densely forested woodland only twelve years earlier, Beauport was now a pleasant riverbank of farms. Each of the original five Beauport families still owned and occupied their original several hundred feet of frontage, each stretching miles to the north like wide ribbons. Where their small cabins originally stood, stone homes, rivaling Normand farmhouses, now guarded the waterfront. The massive acreage of each was steadily being divided into smaller tenant farms tended by new citizens who paid rent to the original owners. In addition to the newer tenant farmhouses, there were many small cabins occupied by *engager*, single men who helped work one farm or the other.

The five original Beauport settlers were tradesmen, not farmers, and today the tenants and *engager* did the farming. As more families came to tend the seemingly limitless land, the original owners, called *sous-sieur,* became wealthier, but as the men had told their sons on the hunt, this came with more work and responsibility for the owners.

The families gathered on the riverfront of Noël Langlois whose home sat between that of Jean Guyon to the west and Gaspard Boucher to the east. Next came the farms of Zacharie Cloutier and Gaspard's older brother, Marin. Jacques-Henri and Félicity-Angel came down from their camp with their two children. The boys started the fire in the large fire pit and began to cook meat from the hunt, while the girls prepared salad and vegetables from their kitchen gardens. A keg of ale produced by one of the tenant farmers served as beverage along with the ubiquitous Canadian apple cider and some of its famous and notorious by-product, Calvados. The women gathered to discuss the news from town, mainly whose children were courting whose and selected gossip of the few new women, some married and some eligible *filles à marier* who had arrived on the latest ships from France. The men discussed business and politics, both groups avoiding the forbidden topic.

Following the feast, the boys began a game of lacrosse. Jacques-Henri's oldest son had tutored the older boys in the fine points of the game before leaving to guide for the military. Marin played his Jew's harp and his brother his fiddle while the others danced. Ultimately, dusk descended and the women and children headed for home, while the men took the Calvados to the canoe dock on the bank to drink, smoke and discuss the one topic they no longer considered taboo in the absence of the families.

"Jean," Noël asked his neighbor, "you are on the council, what have you heard of this party *Sieur* Bourdon took to the Iroquois country?"

Jean Guyon looked around as though he feared snoopers, and then closed in to speak quietly, "We received information only yesterday, brought from *Trois-Rivières* by a courier. Apparently, the group included Bourdon, two soldiers, two Algonquin and that Jesuit, Isaac Jogues. They made their way down the Richelieu to Lake Champlain and all the way into Dutch country on Lake George. We heard the meeting went well, they exchanged gifts, and Bourdon left optimistic. At the last minute, however, the Mohawk retained the two Algonquin and told Bourdon to go—this was not his affair. He left with the soldiers and Jogues. When they reached the Richelieu, Jogues went on his own. They expect Bourdon back here in the next few days."

"What does this all mean?" Gaspard questioned.

"We are not certain, but the governor suggested we wait for Bourdon, remain hopeful and not do anything unless further trouble arises." The men discussed possibilities into the evening until they were out of ideas—and Calvados before leaving for bed.

Beauport: September 1646

As the canoe approached the docks at Beauport, Noël was contemplating what to tell his wife. Having just returned from *Trois-Rivières* and Fort Richelieu, he had all the local gossip about the Mohawk and it was not encouraging. Raids had become common. Although currently confined to raids on Huron villages rather than the French towns, he knew it would upset her, particularly as she entered the final month of her pregnancy. Robert brought the craft expertly to the dock. Since the trip up north, Noël's oldest son had become obsessed with hunting, fishing and canoeing and had convinced his parents to allow him the craft to ferry himself and the younger children to school each day. Noël managed to catch a ride home as well when it fit the schedule.

As the boat touched land, the younger children scampered off while Robert secured it. "Pa, can Henri-Makya and I go hunting this weekend?"

"What about your chores and studies?"

"Oh, I'll have them all done. They say the fields above the meadow are filled with pheasant." Noël looked skeptical and his son said, "Please, I'll have everything done—and more."

"Well, all right," he said as he took the front of the canoe.

"I'll get that, Pa," the boy said, taking the line from his father.

As Noël approached the house, he worried his son's outdoor interests were eclipsing his academics. The younger children had already been through and were off to their chores when he entered the house to find Françoise at the table. "Have you been crying?"

Drying her eyes, she replied, "No—yes. Oh Noël, they're moving!" Before he could reply, she continued, "Pierre Boucher was given an important promotion and it includes a large tract of land in *Trois-Rivières*. It already has tenants and *engager,* but Pierre needs someone to manage it, so they are all moving."

"Well…"

She continued, "I know Nicole wants to be near him, but she was the first friend I ever had—my best friend."

"Well…"

She arose and dried her eyes, waddling over to the kitchen. "Never mind, they are coming over tonight to tell us all about it. I don't want to rain on her happiness, but I'll miss her." She resumed sobbing.

After dinner, the children retired to their lofts and studies as the neighbors knocked. Gaspard entered with a bottle of Calvados, not the local brew but the real thing from France! "I brought this with us in '34. I thought this might be the time."

They retired to the rockers on the porch to take advantage of one of the last warm evenings of the year. "Pierre just informed us of this," Gaspard continued, "the opportunity for him and for us is too good to turn down. We will have a large parcel that has tenants. There is not much for us to do, and I can help with the growing construction in *Trois-Rivières.*"

"What will happen to your *concession* here?" Noël inquired.

"It is all taken care of," Nicole responded. "There is a couple newly arrived this year. They are our age with a family. He was going to start as a tenant but has the means to buy our place. We should do very well. He is going to keep all the tenants but work our farm. He is a beef merchant and will be raising and butchering cattle."

"Where are they from?" Françoise asked.

"*La Rochelle.*"

"Not Normand?"

'No, sorry, they are *Poitevin*" Nicole told her. Then with a smile, "Let us not forget, you are *Parisien*. Their name is Badeau, Jacques and Anne-Ardouin. They are coming by tomorrow. We will have everyone over to meet them." They discussed more plans before the Bouchers took their leave.

Once she had closed the door, Françoise began to sob. "From *La Rochelle*—probably Huguenots!"

Noël put his arm around his very pregnant wife and took her to bed, pleased he had not mentioned the Mohawk.

The following afternoon, Nicole and Gaspard arrived with their buyers. Françoise had convinced herself she would not bond with them but soon lost her resolve. Jacques and Anne-Ardouin Badeau were nearly the same age as Noël and Françoise. They brought their three children. François was one year older than Robert. They and the three boys from the hunting trip immediately left to explore the shore. Jeanne was seven; exactly the age of Marguerite Langlois and Jean-Jacques was five, the same age as Jean-Pierre Langlois. Following introductions, Jacques explained he had been a beef merchant in France and was anxious to follow the same trade in the new world expanding to raise beef as well as process it.

Worried they might be among the converted Huguenots from the region of *La Rochelle*, Françoise carefully inquired about their church. Anne-Ardouin assured her when she told them they were from the parish of *Saint-Sauveur* in *La Rochelle*. As they met the other three couples, it became apparent they would be an excellent fit in the community. Nicole set out a small picnic, and soon after, Robert came to his mother. "Can Henri-Makya and I take François out back to show him the woods?" As she frowned, he added, "We asked his mother and she said we could."

"Very well," she replied with misgivings, "be back well before dark." The excited threesome headed to the back. She did not know they would stop by Jacques-Henri's camp for bows. As the afternoon progressed, Françoise continued to watch the woods for the return of the boys. Relieved when she saw the threesome coming through the trees, her relief was diminished by their appearance. Covered in mud, they carried not only the bows, but also a string of rabbits, two pheasants and a turkey.

The hunters came directly to their mothers. François proudly showed his mother the rabbit he had shot while extolling the wonders of the woods. Françoise told Robert, "Take François to the river and clean up." Turning to his mother, "I apologize, I…" Anne-Ardouin interrupted, "It's no trouble, Madame, we came to be in this wild new land—and boys shall be boys, *n'est-ce pas?"*

Once they returned home, Noël broke out in laughter, "I loved the look on your face when you saw the rabbits. I thought you would have the baby right there."

"But," she retorted, "in company? It's your fault for taking him on these hunting trips."

He came and embraced his wife, "As the lady said, my dear, 'we *all* came to be in this wild new land—and boys shall be boys, *n'est-ce pas?'"*

On the last day of September, Marie Langlois was born. Named for her late sister, the family would call her Mariette. Two weeks later amid hugs, tears, and promises to visit, Gaspard and Nicole Boucher moved their family to *Trois-Rivières,* and Françoise cried herself for sleep for the next two weeks, mourning the absence of her best friend.

Québec, lower town: Six weeks later

Pulling his coat against the chill of November, Noël Langlois brought the shallop to the dock where *Monsieur* Bergeron hopped off with the lines. "I'll see you tomorrow, André," he told the mate. "I am going to the office to do the paper work—too cold out here." Crossing the square, he saw an unexpected face sitting alone outside the *Taverne Terre Sauvage.* "Jean Guyon!" he exclaimed in surprise, "What are you doing here, especially in this cold?"

"Waiting for you," his friend replied, pulling out a chair. "Have a seat." While Noël sat, his friend called to the waiter, "*Garçon! deux Calvados, s'il vous plait.*" The waiter brought two cups of *Québec's* worst Calvados and Guyon began, "We had a meeting of the council today and received some information I thought you should know. I did not, however, want to upset your wife—with the baby and all." Drawing closer to maintain secrecy, he said, "You remember the committee *Sieur* Bourdon took to the Iroquois in the spring?"

"Of course."

"Well, it did not go as well as we hoped, and things have been deteriorating between the Mohawk and the Huron— and the French." He took a sip and grimaced. "This summer, the Jesuit, Isaac Jogues, went back to the Mohawk camp with a young Frenchman, Lalande." Noël sipped his drink, which he tolerated better than his neighbor, and Guyon continued. "They stayed the summer as Jogues continued to try to negotiate a peace, but the Mohawk were having none of it. Never one to give in, Jogues continued to press the subject. I guess the Mohawk got tired of it and began to torture both men. I do not know how this Lalande took it, but Jogues was never one to back down—no matter what. The Indians tried other things but that does not matter. In the end, they chopped off their heads and put them on pikes in front of the camp." Guyon finished his libation with one heroic gulp and concluded, "I know this will get out soon, but I wanted you to know before Françoise."

Pushing away from the table, Guyon added, "You know, I just can't understand that man—what did he expect?"

Noël finished his drink and looked down the square, "If you have a minute, I see my partner, Abraham Martin, coming. He has an interesting theory."

CHAPTER 14

Québec: Christmas Day, 1646

"I remember how many Christmases we were not able to attend mass due to the weather," Françoise told the children as Noël headed their cart, converted to a sleigh, along the road to the upper town. "Thank goodness, today is so fine."

"The improvement of the roads and the sleighs has also helped," her husband added.

"Oh, my goodness!" she exclaimed as they made the turn approaching the newly opened *Notre-Dame de la Paix* church. "Look, Agnes-Anne, have you ever seen anything so beautiful?"

"No, Mama," her oldest daughter replied, trying her best to feign interest.

As they unloaded, Françoise stood and sighed. Although she, and all of *Québec*, had been watching its development over the past six years, on this bright Christmas day, it finally seemed real. Entering, even the children were impressed by the size—length, width, and particularly height—especially compared to the cramped Jesuit chapel where they had prayed for most of their childhood. Once seated, they could visually explore all the fine features of the structure, particularly statues of the Virgin and Child, Saint Joseph, and, of course, Jesus, peering down from the crucifix into the deepest recess of each soul in the congregation.

Eventually the bells rang and Father Vimont walked down the aisle for his first mass in the building. Typical of Christmas, the high mass was long. Noël felt the Father could have given a homily with less fire and brimstone on Christmas Day, but everyone was smiling when they exited into the sunlight. Many headed to a meal at *L'Auberge Oie Bleue* where Étienne Fortin had once again enlarged his upper town facility to accommodate the growing population.

Filled nearly to capacity, the eatery even had tables for each of the convents. Jean Guyon was pleased they sat a comfortable distance away so the good sisters listening did not dampen their Christmas fun. Once served, Mathurine Guyon asked, "Has everyone heard about the show at the fort next week?"

Anne-Ardouin replied, "No, what is it?"

"Well," Mathurine answered, "It is what they call *un pièce de théâtre*. People on the stage perform a story."

"Yes, I heard about those. I think they had them from time to time in *La Rochelle*, but I never went to one. They were for the rich."

Perrine Boucher stepped in, "The good news is, in *Québec* they are for everyone. I guess we are all rich enough."

"Oh?" their new neighbor questioned.

"Yes," Perrine answered, "it is free for everyone. The governor has built a large building by the fort, mainly for military training, but they have put up a stage and a group will perform. It is on December thirty-first, the day before the feast of the circumcision."

Françoise asked, "Who performs this *pièce*?"

"I heard," Perrine continued, "it is a few people from Paris and some from here. I have no idea what it is about, but we are definitely going. It is called *Le Cid.*"

"Françoise," Xainte Cloutier asked, "you lived in Paris. Did you see any of these?"

Françoise knew her neighbors were aware of her checkered past and simply replied, "I had been by many theaters. This is where they perform. I only went, however, to beg and pick pockets."

Anne-Ardouin Badeau looked shocked. Perrine touched her arm, "Do not worry. In *Québec*, we have no secrets."

One week later the weather remained calm, and the adults of the five Beauport families loaded two of the sleighs and made their way to the fort. "The governor is fortunate to have clement weather," Xainte Cloutier declared. "Yes," Mathurine Guyon agreed, "especially because he spent a lot of money, and Jean said much of it is from his personal funds. I heard some of the actors actually came on the last ship from France this year."

Making their way through the upper town, they took the road through the Saint-Louis Gate leading into the grounds of the *Citadelle*, as the fortress was known. "I have never been up here," Anne-Ardouin Badeau told them, "I imagine the view is very nice."

"Oh," Mathurine answered, "you must see it, I believe we have time." The men parked the two sleighs among others by the new building where the *pièce* was to occur and took a walk up to an overlook on the wall. When they reached the top, Anne-Ardouin exclaimed, "My God! I had no idea!" Aided by the clear day, one could see what seemed to be forever. "Down just below," Mathurine explained, "you can see the upper and lower towns out to the docks. To our left is *Riviére Saint-Charles* and Beauport. You can even make out some of our houses. To our right is the tip of *Isle d'Orléans* in the center of *Fleuve Saint-Laurent.* On the northern channel is Montmorency Falls, it only freezes in the dead of winter, but some flow generally continues all year."

As they surveyed the wild beauty of Canada from on high, Perrine Boucher announced, "It looks as though they are opening the building. We should go." As they entered the new structure, Françoise said, "Look, there is Madame de la Peltrie."

"It is good to see you, my dear," Madame told her, "what with winter and all." She then added, "I see all your children are excelling in the convent school."

"Thank you, Madame. May I introduce my new neighbors, *Monsieur* and Madame Badeau." De la Peltrie took their hands and greeted all the other couples, asking, "Do you know about this *pièce*?" Françoise shook her head, "No, Madame." De la Peltrie explained, "It is a French work by Pierre Corneille from Paris. It is a *Tragi-Comédie* and takes place in *Castile.* I have not seen it but hear it is quite good." Looking up, she said, "Oh, I believe these soldiers want us to take our seats."

The two men ushered them in. There was comfortable seating in front for religious personnel, officers, prominent families of the upper town and the Beauport *Concession* owners. Most citizens sat on benches, and standing room in back was for *engager* and non-officer military. They faced a temporary stage with makeshift curtains. With everyone seated, the governor took the stage.

"I welcome you to our first attempt at theater," he began, pleased to see how many people turned out in the dead of winter. "It is our hope that we can have many such events in the future to bring *Parisian* culture to Canada." Looking at notes, he continued, "*Le Cid* is a work by Pierre Corneille from Paris. I met him there on the opening of his *pièce* just before I sailed to *Québec*." Looking again at the notes and realizing he had nothing more, he finished abruptly, "I hope you enjoy it" He took his seat and the curtain opened.

Three hours later, after the final curtain closed, the audience cheered and began to filter out. "I am glad they had this early," Noël said. "Even in December we still have time to stop at *L'Auberge Oie Bleue*." The friends agreed and they took the sleigh back to the upper town.

When seated, Xainte asked, "What did you all think?"

"I have never seen a *un pièce de théâtre* before," Jean Guyon admitted, "I guess it was good."

"I am not sure I understood it," Marin Boucher added.

"Well," his wife explained, "It was a story of two families. A story of love gone bad that triumphed in the end. I think a lot of *pièces* are like that."

When the others had given what opinions they had, Françoise told them. "I don't think that was what it was about. I think it was about Canada—I think that is why the governor brought it."

Noël took the risk of questioning his spouse, "Were we at the same *pièce*?"

"Yes," she retorted, "Think about it. It begins with two people, a man and a woman, in love who wish to be married." She sipped her Calvados before continuing, "But one of the fathers insults the other, and suddenly everyone wants to fight to the point they are going to fight each other in a duel—to the death! Eventually in the *pièce*, there are fights and bloodshed, but in the end they find a solution." Seeing little reaction to her theory, she continued, "In Canada the French and the Indian were friends, but now one tribe has insulted the other—like the fathers. They both want the same thing, but just cannot agree—like the families. We must find a solution." Beginning to see her point, the group began discussing potential solutions to the Indian problems without arriving at an answer.

Finally, Marin said, "It will be dark soon, we should head home." On the way home, winter arrived with its usual vengeance, and by the time they reached the bridge, they could scarcely see. The Badeau family was nearly hysterical, but their new neighbors assured them this was nothing. (Perhaps this was not reassuring). They arrived in Beauport intact, however, retiring to their homes.

When Noël and Françoise were safe inside, he asked, "When did you become a philosopher?" Slipping out of her dress, she responded, "While you were sailing your boat." They crawled into bed and held each other as the blizzard began to reach full rage.

CHAPTER 15

Québec: March 1647:

"I apologize for sending you men out so early," Montmagny told Noël as he and André Bergeron prepared for their first long voyage of the season. "We know the ice broke up early, and the last voyageurs through reported the river was remarkably clear for this time of year."

"We should be all right, Excellency," Bergeron told him as he hoisted boxes of supplies.

"The problem," Montmagny added, "is along with the favorable ice report, they said things with the Iroquois are not so favorable." Handing a paper to Noël, "This is a list of raids on the three posts over the winter and only contains the raids the voyageurs heard about." Noël nodded, handing the paper to Bergeron while the governor continued, "These other papers are the list of the soldiers we are sending, and who is assigned to which post." Noël looked over a list, much longer than any he had handled before, as Montmagny added, "Can you accommodate this many men?"

"Yes, sir. Should be no problem," Noël replied, hoping he was correct. "This is our largest shallop." When the supplies were stowed, they assembled the soldiers, assigning berths wherever possible.

"Well, Captain, it looks as if you are ready to go."

"Just one more thing, Excellency," Noël said, pointing down the dock.

"Oh, yes, your Indian man, I nearly forgot."

Jacques-Henri boarded with some last minute supplies. Noël had insisted he accompany them as he had more experience traveling in these conditions than anyone. Taking Jacques-Henri and Bergeron aside, he instructed them, "I want each of you to take one soldier, who has been down the river before, and stand watch in front, on either side, to call out ice floes. I would like to get back in one piece." As the weary governor watched them sail around the bend, he hoped privately this would be his last year in Canada.

When they were clear of *Cap Diamant*, Bergeron came around to the helm. "These two men on watch are pretty sharp, Captain, and if the south-east breeze holds out, we should be good. The ice is pushed to the north bank, and we can continue this course without too much tacking."

"I hope you are correct, André. We shall see how it goes, but I am still inclined to stop before dark halfway to *Trois-Rivières.* Ice floes and darkness do not mix."

"Amen to that, Captain."

The weather did hold and Noël went as far as he dared before making the prudent stop for the night. The anchor was set by nightfall while the weather continued fair and unseasonably warm. With a bright crescent moon illuminating the deck, the soldiers talked and laughed. Some played harmonicas as Bergeron served supper. Looking over this idyllic sight, Noël could not help wondering, *"Do any of these men know what they are getting into?"*

The weather continued to be their friend as they hoisted the anchor at sunrise, arriving at *Trois-Rivières* ahead of schedule. Commandant Champfleur and Pierre Boucher met them at the dock. They ordered two of their men to assign the reinforcements to quarters and billet the other men for the night. They then invited Noël and Jacques-Henri to the office.

After Noël reported on their voyage, Pierre told him, "Our weather has been about the same as you report. The last voyageurs through *Lac Saint Pierre* reported it was relatively clear, but you know how the ice can hide in that place."

Noël nodded, "Good, we will be careful. What do you hear about the Iroquois upstream?"

Champfleur reported, "We have not had any communication directly from either fort this winter. We have had a few skirmishes in nearby camps, but nothing in town. The voyageurs who have come through report similar situations upriver. They seem to see the most action at *Ville-Marie*. Still, mostly at the Huron camps, but a few small scuffles in town. The problem is they do not have sufficient military to withstand anything of significance, should it occur."

"That is unfortunate," Noël noted. "It seems the governor has sent the fewest men to them."

"I don't understand that," Champfleur replied. "Fortunately, Maisonneuve is back from France. Don't get me wrong, I feel Commandant d'Ailleboust is highly competent. It is just Maisonneuve seems to have the religious zeal they require."

When business was complete, Pierre said, "I promised my mother that I would bring you to dinner tonight if possible. She will be doubly pleased to see Jacques-Henri. We can go now, and I will have you back before daybreak."

The reunion at the new Boucher *concession* began with hugs, tears and laughter. Gaspard gave a tour of the place with as much remaining sunlight as he had, ending with a grand dinner and visit. Eventually they retired, and as predicted, Pierre had them up and out before daybreak with promises to stay in touch and visit *Québec* when possible. The weather was unchanged, and soon they were entering the wide *Lac Saint Pierre*.

With the exception of the occasional random ice floe, the trip was uneventful, and they approached the Richelieu River ahead of schedule. As Noël looked out, he ordered, "*Monsieur* Bergeron, bring me the glass!" When Bergeron returned with the telescope, Noël trained it on their destination, "Dear God!"

"What is it, Captain?" the mate inquired. Noël remained silent, handing him the glass. While Bergeron peered out, Noël whispered, "Smoke and ashes." Jacques-Henri came for a look, and as they neared the fort, they saw a canoe approaching. Jacques-Henri looked through the glass, "Algonquin canoe." Noël breathed a sigh of relief as his friend helped one of the Indians aboard while his canoe-mate paddled beside them.

The two natives sat on the deck by the helm as they conversed in Algonquin. The guest spoke rapidly with grand gestures. Although his Algonquin was nothing compared to his wife's, Noël did know that these two traits generally meant the message was grave. Ultimately, Jacques-Henri returned to the helm. "I know this man," he began. "He is known to be honorable." Noël signaled for Bergeron and the ranking soldier bound for Fort Richelieu to join them.

"He tell me," Jacques-Henri continued, "this winter see only few small raids in north, near Huron Country. Commandant Durocher post men on both banks of river—near fort—to warn of approaching Iroquois. Two nights ago, they come at full dark, no warning, set many fires. Eventually break down gate and enter, kill with arrows—and guns! Guns from Dutchman they think. By sunrise, fort burned, some dead, many missing, Iroquois gone."

"Where did they go?" Bergeron asked.

Jacques-Henri shrugged, "Back upriver, I guess." When they arrived at the fort, the damage was more severe than Noël had imagined. Even the dock had burned. Anchoring near shore, they ferried the men ashore by canoe as Noël and Jacques-Henri went in search of Commandant Durocher.

Walking through the ruins, they saw most of the palisade was in ashes, along with half the buildings. A few men wandered around picking up debris, while a few corpses lay on the ground, apparently where they fell, some killed with arrows, others with bullets. The air remained heavy with smoke as some areas of the former structure continued to smolder. Finally, Noël saw Durocher, sitting on an ash-covered chair by half a desk where his office once stood. He remained covered with soot as he sat aimlessly, attempting to polish a gun.

He looked at Noël as through a fog. Noël remained silent, and finally the commandant spoke. "They came from nowhere," he whispered. After a pause, "I was asleep when I heard the ruckus. When I came out to the yard, they were coming over the walls and through the gate they had smashed down. The sentries were already down, and fires were beginning everywhere. Our men began to shoot them, but faster than they fell, more arrived. Our men shot a few, but were overwhelmed. They had guns! Better guns than ours!" Looking at his feet, he added, "I don't even know when it ended."

When Durocher appeared to be improving, Noël asked, "What of the guards on the river?"

"I sent a contingent out this morning…" He stared at the ground as though looking for an answer. "They said they were all dead…" He repeated with a whisper, "all dead."

Noël began to look around and found Jacques-Henri examining something on the ground. "What is it?" he asked.

His friend stood, holding two arrows. Showing the first, he told Noël, "This Iroquois arrow."

"Yes, I recognize it." Jacques-Henri had taught him how to identify them several years ago.

"Mohawk arrow."

Noël nodded, "Yes."

He displayed the second, "This Iroquois." Noël nodded and Jacques-Henri added, "But not Mohawk." Pointing to a few subtle differences, "This Onondaga!" Noël nodded, wondering how this made a difference, when his friend continued, "Onondaga has been good friend of Frenchman." Looking off in the distance, beyond the charred and collapsed wall, he declared, "This bad—this very, very bad."

Noël put the men to work clearing the debris. By morning, Durocher was stable and had his fort functioning. Among the few dead soldiers lay many dead Algonquin, several scalped or otherwise mutilated. Jacques-Henri found two braves who spoke enough French to carry the story to *Québec* and sent them in one of the few remaining canoes to deliver the bad news. After three days Noël had not planned to spend here, he loaded the shallop with the recruits for *Montréal* and headed upstream, wondering what awaited him there, while thinking, *"I guess now these men know what they are getting into."*

For as many times as Noël had made this trip, today he carried a frightening premonition. If most of the fighting had been in *Ville-Marie,* what was he to expect there? The foreboding worsened as the wind shifted violently to the southwest. This, along with the strong head current, slowed the boat severely. His hopes to reach the island of *Montréal* before nightfall went by the wayside as the setting sun forced him to drop anchor before he was halfway to the destination. To make matters worse, as darkness fell, the sky was again illuminated—by lightning. Multiple strikes hit close to the shallop. Bergeron said he saw one hit the mast. Then came the pelting rain, a deluge of freezing water. Down below was hardly better as the rain began to penetrate the deck and frigid drops found their way into every corner.

By morning, everyone was drenched and shivering. The sun remained covered by heavy clouds, but the rain had slowed to a drizzle and the headwind had diminished. Weighing anchor, they began to make slow progress toward their destination. As the day progressed, conditions improved and before long, they could see the island of *Montréal*. The solitary officer from the small group of soldiers came to the helm. "I don't see a town, Captain."

"You won't for a while," Noël explained, "until we turn around that sharp point ahead. I only hope we can make it before dark or we will not be able to land tonight."

Dusk was approaching as they made the turn. Noël had to strain his eyes to see if the village still stood, but as they came closer, it appeared to be unaltered from his last voyage at the end of last season. By the time they tossed the docking lines, it was dark. As the men began to disembark, Noël heard, "Welcome, Captain, we had begun to fear you had perished."

With a small amount of moonlight beginning to appear, Noël could recognize Louis d'Ailleboust. Holding out his hand, Noël said, "Thank you, Governor, we, too, had some doubts."

"It is no longer governor, Captain. Thankfully, Governor Maisonneuve has returned from France. Once your boat is secure, I will take you in to get warm and dry, and we will take care of the men for you." As Noël turned, he felt a cold nose. Looking down, he saw Pilot, the Indian-dog, still playing dockhand. With a grin, he said, "This is the first time I have smiled on this voyage."

D'Ailleboust took him to small quarters in the fort. "Get warm and dry, Captain, and we shall meet with the governor in the headquarters and have something to eat." Fortunately, Noël's sea bag had protected his change of clothes and there was a fire burning in the main room. By the time they reached headquarters, he felt nearly normal.

Paul Chomedey de Maisonneuve was tall and handsome with an authoritative manner that made all men treat him with respect. "Welcome, Captain, we had begun to worry, but fortunately our prayers were answered." As Noël took his hand, Maisonneuve added, "I must say, however, we had hoped you would bring us more men than this."

"Well, Excellency, this is what they sent."

"Oh, I know it was not your choice," said the governor with an understanding air, "sometimes I worry *Monsieur* Montmagny doesn't care for us." *Sometimes?* Noël thought to himself.

"Please sit down, we have prepared a nice hot stew for you," Noël and d'Ailleboust both sat as the governor gave an overly long blessing.

While the men dined, their discussion was limited to polite inquiries about the health and status of common friends and acquaintances in *Québec*. Not until coffee, did Maisonneuve get to the real topic of interest. "Our winter was typical," he began, "a bit colder than usual. Our missions worked with the friendly tribes, and we had little involvement with the Iroquois, an occasional sighting and a few rare injuries to citizens and property."

Signaling to his porter to bring a flask of local wine, he paused before beginning, "The real issues are with the Huron. The hostiles have been relentless in their raids against them. Almost every small Huron camp in the area was burned and its people slaughtered." He took a generous sip before continuing, "We tried to help where possible, however, there is little we can do with our current resources." Lowering his voice, he continued, "In fact, just between us, I can't see our settlement surviving the year."

On his return voyage, Noël stopped at *Trois-Rivières* to report the situation at *Fort Richelieu*. When he began his report to Champfleur, the commandant stopped him. "Let me get Lieutenant Boucher, I value his opinion." As he went out to get the young man, Noël reflected on the amazing level of prominence the lad had obtained. When the two returned, Noël gave the full report.

"Thank you for the warning, Captain." Champfleur told him. "I will increase our guard. Of course, we are better prepared than Fort Richelieu *and* farther from the Iroquois country."

Noël then reported the concerns and pessimism of Governor Maisonneuve in *Ville-Marie*. Pierre spoke up, "Governor Montmagny has never fully approved of this settlement being on the island of *Montréal*. I am not entirely certain why. However, I do believe, Captain Langlois, he holds your opinion in high regard. Perhaps you should discuss this with him."

Later, upon arrival in *Québec*, Noël reported promptly to Montmagny. He related his long trip as well as his opinions in detail. The governor listened calmly until he was finished.

"Nothing here surprised me, Captain," Montmagny began, "I always feared we did not possess sufficient manpower to hold the Iroquois from coming up the River Richelieu, and I never favored the location of *Ville-Marie* on the far off island of *Montréal*. I offered these people *Île d'Orléans* before they arrived. It is much more suitable and *totally* more defensible—they, however, turned down the offer. I believe we only have the ability to guard our interests east of *Trois-Rivières*."

Going to a map of the area where he had drawn the lands of the various tribes, he pointed out, "Most Huron camps are entirely north of the *Saint-Laurent* river basin and well west of the island of *Montréal*—far out of our control." Sitting, he concluded, "I am pleased to tell you," he announced, "I have received information that I am to be replaced at the end of the year and returned to France for a long-needed retirement. Perhaps my replacement will possess magical skills I do not have."

Noël left the governor's office in an unsettled mood. Going down to the docks, he ran into Abraham Martin who had just returned from Tadoussac in the east. Stopping at *Taverne Terre Sauvage,* Noël related his recent voyage along with all his concerns. When Noël finished, the old mariner sipped his beverage and replied, "When I first came, in 1619—my God that was nearly thirty years ago. Anyway, we thought we would merge cultures with the natives. We knew there were some hostile tribes to the south but did not think it would affect us. Who would have thought this creature that is nothing more than a large rat with a flat tail would cause so much trouble?"

"I believe that *rat* has become the primary source of wealth in the new world," Noël replied.

Abraham laughed, "Yes, well, it has certainly caused us to take heed of the hostile natives. Montmagny has had a grand run at governance, but in the end, he is still a *Parisian*—and thinks like one. What we need is someone who thinks like a real Canadian. Now that you tell me he is leaving, it gives me hope. In addition, our new council is made up of Canadians instead of *Parisians* like the old Company of 100 Associates." Standing, Abraham concluded, "Do not fear, my young friend. We shall prevail—*courage!*" Finishing with a smile, he said, "You may pay the tab." Noël left a few coins on the table and headed to the docks where he found his children coming from school for the canoe ride home.

As always, Françoise was anxious to hear of the voyage, "I was becoming concerned you were gone for so long." Noël blamed the weather and did not discuss the details. That evening he sat on the porch with his son who was filled with tales of hunting and fishing. Retiring to his bed, he reflected that maybe Robert was to be a *true Canadian* and not just a Frenchman living in a new world. He spent the next three days visiting tenants and dealing with the business of his *concession*. When he returned at the end of the third day, it was evident the news from the frontier had reached *Québec*.

"Why didn't you tell me...?" his wife began. He explained he did not want to alarm her and all the problems were far to the west.

"The problem is between the Iroquois and the Huron," he explained. "We will not see any of it here." Fortunately, he was accurate, and although tales of skirmishes continued to arise, it was generally west of *Trois-Rivières*. Things were relatively normal in *Québec*, and as usual, the leaves began to turn and the snow began to fall.

CHAPTER 16

<u>*Québec*</u>: June 1648

Approaching *L'Auberge Oie Bleue,* Noël saw his wife waiting at the table. With the older children in school and Félicity-Angel watching the two youngest girls during the day, Françoise had time to volunteer two days a week at the Augustinian Hospital. "I feel just like a lady of privilege," she told her husband who merely replied, "You are."

As he sat, she was reading a paper. "Look at this," she told him with excitement, "I received a letter today—in the post that came on one of your small shallops." Showing him, she announced, "It's from Nicole Boucher." Setting it down, she added, "I believe this is the second letter I have ever received. The first was from you in France—when I was working at the convent in *Mortagne.*"

"So what does she say?"

"Well, let's see, I just started." Slowly perusing the several pages, she reported, "It looks as everyone is doing well... Oh my! Their Madeline was married this winter... To an Urbain Beaudry... he is from *La Flèche.* That's north of Tours in France. She says he is a tailor. I guess that's good, she won't have to go naked." Laughing at her own joke, she continued to read. "Oh my goodness! Pierre was named Post Commissioner. That's a big deal, right?"

"Yes," he answered, "especially for his age."

"Maybe he will be the new governor." She continued to read, "Oh, dear, she says... let me see... there was a big battle. The Algonquin, two tribes, went west trapping. When they returned Iroquois ambushed them... she says it was a big battle but the Algonquin won. She says everyone sees this as a good sign, and Pierre told her it could mark the end of the wars!" Finishing, she folded her letter and tucked it in her bag. "This is all good news. Let's have a good wine with lunch."

When lunch arrived, she asked, "Do you think Pierre *could* be governor?"

He shrugged, "Maybe someday."

"Who do you think the new governor will be?"

He finished chewing before answering, "I don't know, but I heard it was to be announced soon. Abraham went to *Montréal* with the large shallop. He might know something when he returns. In fact, he could be back today if things go well."

Following lunch, they strolled down to the lower town and the docks. On arrival, they saw the large shallop. "That's him," Noël told her, "let's go see what he knows." When they reached the dock, Abraham was coming off with a distinguished looking gentleman. "That's Louis d'Ailleboust," Noël explained. "I told you about him."

Walking up they greeted the two men. Shaking hands, he introduced d'Ailleboust to Françoise.

Following the greeting, d'Ailleboust told them, "You must excuse me. I am due at the Fort."

As he headed to the upper town, Martin suggested to the Langlois, "Let's go to *Taverne Terre Sauvage*. I'm buying."

Crossing the road, Françoise noted, "We are certainly being good to *Monsieur* Fortin today."

Abraham Martin ordered. Leaning over to be private, he whispered, "I have not been told for certain, but the talk is, *Monsieur* d'Ailleboust is to be named to replace Montmagny."

"Is that good?" Françoise queried.

"I think so," Abraham told her. "He has the will and foresight to adequately fortify *Ville-Marie* and all of *Montréal* as well as *Fort Richelieu*." Taking a generous sip of Calvados, he added, "And suddenly that is *very* important." Looking around for eavesdroppers, he added, "I saw our old friends, Benoît and Bernier, in *Trois-Rivières*. They came from far west in Huron country at the large village of *Teanaustayé*. The Jesuits have a mission there they call Saint-Joseph. It is probably the largest of Huron villages with two or three thousand residents—I should probably say *was*. A short while ago, the Iroquois came *en masse*. It was terrible—the worst! Benoît says they slaughtered every soul, burned the palisades, the church and the buildings—left everything in ashes."

"Oh dear God!" Françoise gasped.

"It's worse. Benoît reported from there they went to other villages with the same result."

"How could they have been that strong?" Noël asked.

"Guns," Abraham replied. "Benoît said they all had new Dutch muskets. Apparently the Dutch sold them the whole lot."

"What could be worse?" Françoise whispered.

"I'll tell you what," the old mariner replied, "With those villages out of the way, the Huron are all but finished, and that leaves *nobody* between the Iroquois and all the French towns."

Finishing their drinks, they left for their respective residences in a decidedly more somber mood. As their canoe approached home, Françoise broke the long silence. "It may be a bad time to tell you, but I am pregnant."

Québec: August 20, 1648

Despite fears of Iroquois penetration following the fall of the Hurons, the summer had remained calm east of *Trois-Rivières,* and today found the five Beauport families heading two carts toward the *Citadelle de Québec* and the grand ceremony to install Louis d'Ailleboust de Coulonge as Governor of New France.

"Things are going to be better now," Jean Guyon explained. "We learned at our council meeting that the *Conseil du Roi* in Paris has created a law to establish order and surveillance in Canada. They will form a council composed of the Governor of New France, the Superior of the Jesuits and the Governor of *Montréal*. They said this council will control everything from the fur trade to the general interest of New France." He lowered his voice as though the birds were spying, "Best of all, Montmagny has promised to go to the court in Paris and obtain the means and funds to adequately arm the colony all the way to *Montréal* and beyond."

Reaching the *Citadelle* early, they had time to socialize, discussing their views of the future with the other colonists. Although theories varied widely, they were all positive for the first time in a while. Ultimately seated, the Beauport families and all other landholders took seats in the front along with the military officers, clergy, and residents of the upper town. Next were the tenant farmers on benches, then the *engager* standing. In the far back was a large group that had the greatest interest in the event, the many Algonquin who had thrown in their lot with the French.

Father Lalement gave an overly long invocation, following which he introduced the engineer and now *Procureur Général,* Jean Bourdon, who gave a short introduction of each man. Both also gave a brief and optimistic speech after which Bourdon and the priest ordained Louis d'Ailleboust the official Governor of New France. Following the usual conversations discussing the ceremony, the landowners headed for *L'Auberge Oie Bleue* and the tenants for *Taverne Terre Sauvage*. The Algonquin departed for their own celebration at the nearby village.

The five families took their usual position at the upper town bistro, discussing the future with guarded optimism. "Unfortunately, the military reinforcements will not arrive from France until next season." Marin Boucher told his neighbors. "We can only hope for a winter too cold for the Iroquois."

"We will be ready for winter," announced Xainte Cloutier, changing the subject. "We have started burning coal."

"They had coal in *Mortagne*," explained Perrine Boucher, "but only the lords used it in their manor houses."

"Well," Xainte continued, "I guess we are the new lords." After a giggle, she added, "*Monsieur* Guillaume Pelletier—he came from *Perche—Tourouvre*, a few years after we did. He was a carpenter with my Zacharie until he got into this coal business. Now he has a shop in the lower town. You can go there and load it in your cart or he will even deliver it to your home. It is easy to use, much warmer and you don't need enormous stacks of wood. When it's done burning, there is almost nothing left to clean out." Finally, the older couples discussed children and who was to marry whom.

When the Langlois arrived home, Françoise told her husband, "I'm happy Agnes-Anne is not old enough for marriage. I want her to get as much education as possible."

"This is Robert's last year in school," her husband noted.

Suddenly his oldest son entered the house with Tutu, their aging Indian-dog close behind. "We did great, Ma. I got two big turkeys, three pheasants and a big wild boar. Henri-Makya did even better." Carefully putting his rifle, a birthday present from his father, safely in its place, he added, "They're on the porch. We cleaned and gutted them all at Henri-Makya's. I'm going to the creek to wash up."

As the door closed, his mother noted, "I'd say something about all this hunting, but he brings it home ready for the fire. It is almost as easy as going to *L'Auberge Oie Bleue*."

"I agree," Noël added, "He is doing well in school. When he finishes in the spring, he can begin to help me manage the property." Then looking at the fireplace, he told her, "I think I'll stop by Pelletier's shop next time I'm in town."

Monday found Noël and Abraham Martin doing their schedule at *Taverne Terre Sauvage*. "Things keep getting busier," Martin noted. "We will need more pilots next season and you and I will only be doing the long trips."

"I hope I don't have many more to *Montréal* until things improve," Noël replied.

"Well, his Excellency Montmagny isn't leaving until next month, so we will not see relief until at least next season."

Finishing their business, Noël rose, "I'm going to see a man about some coal." Walking across the road, he came to the building with a sign written with black soot.

Guillaume Pelletier et fils
Marchand Charbonnier

The typical structure of a town merchant, the shop was below, and above sat the home with a large porch overlooking the road and *Taverne Terre Sauvage.*

"Ah, *Monsieur* Langlois, I hoped to see you here someday."

Noël had met Guillaume Pelletier in France many years before and had seen him from time to time in Québec. He was married with one adult son who worked with his father. Noël asked about the coal, and Pelletier, a born merchant, explained the fuel and all its wonders. "You can cart it yourself or we will deliver for a small fee."

"I guess you can deliver it."

"Fine," the shopkeeper said, "I will have my boy, Jean-Claude, bring it over tomorrow. I will send enough to last a few weeks. If it does not suit you, there is no charge. If you like it, the next time we will bring enough to last the winter."

When Noël arrived home the following day, a fit-looking young man in his early twenties was unloading the coal behind the house. "Jean-Claude Pelletier," he introduced himself and proceeded to demonstrate the use of coal to Noël and his wife.

Noël thanked him and went inside, "Seems like a nice boy." Françoise noted, "Very helpful." They retired to the rockers on the porch and enjoyed a glass of wine while watching *Fleuve Saint-Laurent* flow to the sea.

An hour later, their son, Robert, joined them, holding an apple. "What is the coalman doing out back?" he asked.

"He was delivering coal." Françoise responded.

"Looks to me," their son noted, "like he has been talking to Agnes-Anne for the past hour."

Standing, Françoise said, "Well…"

"It's all right, Ma," Robert said, "he's being real nice to her."

"Yes, but she's only twelve…" Suddenly it struck her how many of the young ladies had married at that age, and how she once declared by the time her daughters were that old, marriages would occur later in life.

Robert took a bite from his apple, "It's okay, Ma, lots of the girls are getting married at twelve."

Françoise walked out to the back trying to appear calm. Agnes-Anne was talking to the young man at a respectable distance, smiling, giggling, and twisting her hands. "Oh, Mama," the girl called, "This is Jean-Claude Pelletier. I have met him at church. His father sells coal and they are from *Perche*." Françoise smiled and said hello, realizing her daughter had just reviewed his credentials and pedigree at the same time—all perfectly acceptable.

Jean-Claude Pelletier tipped his hat, "Well, I must go. It was a pleasure to meet you, Madame Langlois."

While the cart pulled away, Françoise said, "Agnes-Anne, that boy is…"

"Oh, Mama, I was just being polite. I was not going to have sex with him."

"Sex! What do you know of sex?"

"Oh, Mama, I do go to school. Anyway, I must go set the table."

As her eldest daughter walked away, Françoise put her hands on her abdomen, realizing she was carrying her unborn youngest child, who would be entering a new world.

On September 23, 1648 Charles Huault de Montmagny, now a private citizen, sailed to France, never to see the new world again, while *Québec* began to prepare for winter.

CHAPTER 17

Huron Country: March 1649

A small camp by Huron standards, its small Jesuit chapel was equally meager. Most of the Huron camps had been raided and abandoned last fall, but this one, on the outskirts of Huron society, had remained intact. When the two men visited in early winter, they believed it was too insignificant and remote for the Iroquois to bother, but its store of pelts was growing so the two men hoped it would provide enough trade for a good season, especially in these desperate times. When they returned in late winter, however...

"Dear God!" whispered the shorter man. "Look at this ground." Kicking it with his heel, it barely showed a dent. "It's not frozen—it's filled with dried blood!" His partner only nodded as they inspected the few remaining bodies. All were in stages of decomposition, what flesh they had, remained only due to preservation by winter cold. These Huron natives had obviously been tortured, evidenced by long strips of flesh peeled away. None retained their hair. The two women remained spread-eagle on the ground with stakes through their hands and feet, holding them in position for violation. Even though the flesh was falling from their faces, they still seemed frozen—timeless in screams.

The small chapel was nothing but ashes. In front of what was once the door were two pitiful corpses, still tied to posts. The remnants of cloth told they were Jesuits. One burned to death, the other skinned—with a poker, probably red-hot on insertion, pushed down his throat. Beyond here was nothing but bare ground leading to the woods.

Walking slowly back to their canoe, the shorter man said, "Nothin' here fer us, let's get out." As he pushed the craft into the river, his large silent friend turned and uttered one of his infrequent words. It was not a soft mumble as usual, but a mighty shout that echoed through the wilderness, "BASTARDS!"

Bernier entered the canoe with tears in his eyes and spoke no more.

<u>Beauport: The same day</u>

Entering the room, Noël commented, "This one is certainly a good eater."

"Sister Marie-Forestier told me the last child is usually the best at nursing," his wife replied. "But she said it was more because the mother is less anxious."

"How do you know it is the last one?"

117

"Félicity-Angel told me. She said it is because of my age, my glands, or something. Anyway, I think nine is quite enough for any woman in one lifetime."

Noël pushed back the youngster's unusually long hair. "Well, you had to have that many just to give me three sons out of the lot." Françoise swatted his hand. Born five days before Christmas, Jean-Louis Langlois was proving to be not only the biggest eater, but also the largest child.

Noël went to the table and poured a glass of cider. "When I left the docks today, I walked by Pelletier's store—you know, the coal merchant."

"Of course, I know," she replied with a slight air of irritation.

"I saw his boy, you remember, the one who brought our first load."

"Yes," she replied, "the cute one who talked to Agnes-Anne."

"Yes, well, he asked for my permission to call on her."

She sat up abruptly, interrupting her new son's meal. "What!"

Jean-Louis began to protest as his father told his mother, "That is usually how it is done."

"Yes, but she is only twelve, and still has a term of school remaining."

Noël sat by his wife, attempting to be calm. "Twelve is not too young in *Québec*, and the school term shall soon be over."

"Yes, but…"

"But this young man," Noël interrupted, "is of *Percheron* heritage, has some education, and his family owns a thriving business to which he is the only heir."

"But what if she doesn't want him?"

"Then she can turn him down," he countered, "but I think she does fancy him."

Sitting upright, she asked, "How do you know this?"

"I asked her."

Françoise rose to return Jean-Louis to his crib. "Before you asked me?"

He shrugged, "Well..."

Now returning to the table, pouring her own cider while sitting across from her man, she began, "We can ask him over and interview him with Agnes-Anne present, and then we shall see what his prospects and plans are."

"That's good," Noël answered "—he is coming over tomorrow night."

Françoise was rendered speechless.

Later that day, Françoise gathered the family for a rehearsal. "Robert and Agnes-Anne will remain with your father and me until the *young man* leaves. The others will be excused after you are introduced. Either go outside or to your loft—but you *must* remain silent!"

The youngsters nodded, but Agnes-Anne interrupted in an uncharacteristic fashion. "Mother...," she began, she had never before referred to Françoise as *Mother,* and Françoise was at a loss as how to interpret it. "Mother, he does have a name. It is..."

"I know what it is, Agnes-Anne. It is Jean-Claude." Françoise continued, "Robert, you speak only if you are addressed, or if you have something pertinent to say—and I mean pertinent."

Agnes-Anne asked, "What if I have something *pertinent* to say?"

Losing patience, her mother replied, "Keep it to yourself!"

"Mother?" the daughter asked, "Did you have to do this when you met Pa?"

"No, dear, first of all, I was not twelve years old, and my family didn't... do things like this."

"Lucky you," was her daughter's sarcastically tinted response. Suddenly the thought of marrying off Agnes-Anne was taking on an allure for Françoise. She discussed details of seating and menu, while the other children wandered off physically and Agnes-Anne wandered mentally.

The next day, Françoise was frantic with details as she and Agnes-Anne arranged the seating and the food while continuing mental sparring.

That evening, Jean-Claude arrived exactly on time, "I took my Pa's canoe," he said, "I don't take it often." He was as handsome as they remembered, and he and his clothes were clean—even his hands showed only mild signs of the coal industry.

When they were seated, Marguerite broke the first rule. "When did you come to Canada?"

"In 1641," he replied, "I was 13."

"Agnes-Anne is only 12," the sister announced as she caught her mother's glare.

"I know," he said.

Françoise quickly introduced, then excused the children who all retreated to their lofts to listen. She served a plate of cookies and punch while her husband took the reins. Françoise had thought she would do most of the interviewing but was pleased to see Noël do it so well. When he had visited the amount of time his mother had told him was appropriate, Jean-Claude excused himself but asked, to everyone's relief, if he could call again. They set a date and took him to the door where Françoise said, "Robert, why don't you help him out to the canoe dock?"

As they exited, Agnes-Anne said, "I'll come with you," and was out the door before her mother could grab her.

As she paced, Françoise asked, "What could they be doing?"

Noël replied, "I suppose the usual. Robert and he have tied her down so he can rape her."

Snarling, she said, "You're no help—not even funny."

"Calm down," he told her, "This is only the first daughter to be courted." Looking up to the loft, where the younger siblings had been stifling giggles all evening, he added, "I pray to God it is not the last one."

Eventually her two children returned, laughing, with Agnes-Anne holding her brother's arm. "Well?" Noël asked, "How did it go?"

"Fine," his daughter responded, "Robert invited Jean-Claude to go hunting with him and Henri-Makya this week."

"He's never been," her brother reported and launched, to his parents' astonishment, into an analysis of what a fine brother-in-law Jean-Claude would be. The following day, Noël left on his first long voyage of the season, upriver all the way to *Montréal* and *Ville-Marie*.

The overnight hunting trip went well, and the boys returned with a collection of turkey, geese and pheasants along with several rabbits. That night at dinner, Robert reported, "Jean-Claude did pretty well. We helped him with his musket and he was pretty good after the first day. He never shot a bow before, but we told him we would help. Next week we're going fishing."

Agnes-Anne had been listening quietly and finally asked, "Did he say anything about me?"

Swallowing his mouthful, her brother replied, "Never came up."

Looking soberly at her plate, she whispered, "Oh."

Then laughing, he told her, "Agnes-Anne, he never stopped talking about you. Henri-Makya and I considered leaving him in the woods."

"Really?" she asked.

Putting his hand on hers, he answered, "Sister, dear, if you want this guy—he is yours."

She sat up straight with a muted smile and returned to eating, while her mother, absent her spouse tonight, sat silent and astonished. Her two eldest children rarely spoke other than to argue or criticize each other. She was pleased at the tone, but unsure of the subject. She decided, however, to remain silent and let this wild new world take its course.

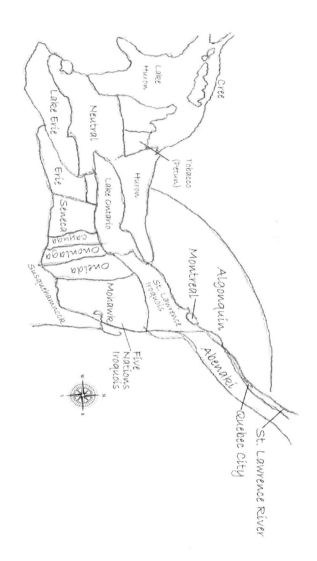

INDIAN NATIONS 1649

123

CHAPTER 18

Fleuve Saint-Laurent: The next day

"Pretty nice day for beginning of April, Captain."

"Yes, it is, *Monsieur* Bergeron." Noël replied, as they approached the docks at *Trois-Rivières.*

"First trip of the season upriver is always a worry," Bergeron declared. "Hope we don't see too many surprises from the natives."

"You and me both, André." Noël had heard rumors from a few voyageurs who had already landed at *Québec* and knew there had been some difficulties upriver, but he would not know the real situation until he visited each post. The first ships from France had yet to land in *Québec* and the citizens remained uncertain as to how much help, if any, would be coming from the homeland this season.

When secure at the dock, Noël hopped off and headed to headquarters where he met Commandant Champfleur who sent immediately for Pierre Boucher.

As soon as he arrived, Champfleur announced, "Pierre is now *Captain* Boucher." As they sat, Champfleur continued, "I am being recalled to France, probably on the first ship of the year. We are uncertain of my replacement and Governor d'Ailleboust has taken the precaution of naming Pierre Captain of the village, which gives him a good deal of leeway and responsibility."

Pierre unrolled a map of the village and explained, "From the beginning, the arrangement of farms in *Trois-Rivières* was haphazard, not at all as organized as the ribbon farms of *Québec*. This makes the protection of our properties difficult and confusing. We are now rearranging properties as best we can to make an arrangement similar to yours which will enable us," demonstrating on the map, "to enclose the farm houses in a palisade."

Going to a larger map of Canada stretching to the Great Lakes of Ontario, Erie and Huron, each named for an Indian Nation now threatened by the Iroquois, he explained, "From what we have heard, the Huron are all but gone. Those surviving have sought refuge near this large bay in the north of Lake of the Huron going up to this isolated island they call *Manitoulin*. The Wenro on Lake of the Ontario are all but conquered, and the Erie, Neutral and Tobacco nations are all severely threatened. Beyond this, it is only the broad northeastern expanse of Algonquin, who remain. If we cannot turn this around—and soon—we will have no friends left among the natives." Rolling up his maps he added, "Now I am instructed to bring you home for dinner and a little surprise."

Boarding a small military cart, Pierre told him, "We have sent a few troops out to inspect the area. I hope to hear back in a few days. My brother, Nicolas, has joined them." When they reached the Boucher *concession*, Nicole and Gaspard greeted Noël. Entering the home, he found a young native woman who was vaguely familiar. "Do you remember *Ouébadinoukoué?*"

Before Noël could answer, the young woman told him, "I am also called Marie-Madeleine."

"You were the girl at the Ursuline Convent," Noël replied.

"Yes," claimed Pierre, "Now, she is my wife, Marie-Madeleine Boucher. She came some time ago with Madame de la Peltrie who was here looking for another convent site. When we met as adults, we fell in love and were married the first of the year." Noël related to their old friends the courting of Agnes-Anne, and they had a grand time discussing the past. For a short while, they could forget the ominous clouds on their horizons.

The situation was no less ominous at Fort Richelieu, which was no longer an actual fort, but a simple outpost at the mouth of the river. "As of now," Commandant Durocher told him, "we have no funds in hand or in sight for a fort. We try as we can to guard the river, but with little success. Unless we get aid from France, we may soon have to abandon the location altogether."

Ville-Marie was not much better, "The Iroquois have made regular penetrations inland," Governor Maisonneuve told Noël, "and we are helpless to stop it. Our sources tell us the hostiles will soon control everything to Lake of the Huron." Looking off in the distance, he continued, "When

126

we came, we only wanted a mission. I was foolish not to take more help from *Québec*. Now I realize the voyageurs were correct. To control and protect the friendly natives, we must make this the center of the fur trade and protect it with a proper military fort."

As Noël headed for home, he had heard the same questions at each stop. "Was help coming from France? How much and what kind would it be? Will it arrive on time? And will it be adequate to the task?"

When he arrived home, Noël had decided to leave the details of the trip for the officials and only tell his family the happy news about Pierre. They, in turn, related the tales of hunting, fishing, and the boyfriend. As he crawled into bed, Françoise told him, "Jean-Claude is coming to call again this week. I think it is serious." He expressed his approval and she slept soundly—he did not.

CHAPTER 19

<u>Beauport: April 1649</u>

Jean-Claude was again punctual and well groomed. He and Noël discussed the hunting and fishing excursions with Robert as well as his father's coal business. Eventually Jean-Claude took a deep breath and the big step. "Sir, I would like to ask you for your daughter's hand." Her parents hid their glee while Noël asked about his life intentions.

"Well, sir, I can continue to work with my father, the business is doing well and I will inherit it."

"Where would you live?" Françoise asked.

"Well, Madame, we could live with my father. He has expanded the store and built a second residence above the addition. Or, if we wanted a farm, we could live on the *concession* in Beauport."

"Here?" Noël asked.

"Oh, no Sir, it is a bit of a story. When we came to *Québec*, my father's brother, Antoine, came with us. He was single, and he acquired a *concession* in Beauport just west of Montmorency Falls. He married a *Québécoise* woman. Soon after the marriage, he went out in a small boat and was trapped under the falls and drowned. She remarried and I inherited the *concession*. Therefore, you see I am blessed with options: live and work in *Québec* or live on the *concession* by the falls. I would do whichever my bride desired."

Both of Agnes-Anne's parents had the same silent thought—*brave man.*

Françoise's older friends had counselled her that she should defer a decision at this point, but she decided to ask a few questions. "You know she is still in school?"

"Yes, Madame, we talked about... I mean I heard about that. We would wait until after her school term and marry before Christmas."

"And you know she is still quite young?"

"Oh yes, Madame," he answered, "but she is very mature and... well, of course I would be sensitive to that."

After a few more volleys, they agreed, shook hands and kissed on the cheek before they showed him to the door. "Agnes-Anne, I suppose you may go say goodnight, but stay on the porch and come right back."

When the door closed, Noël said, "If I had known this, I might have ordered coal sooner."

His wife chuckled, "It is good he is the sole heir, but it would be nice if he had a few younger brothers."

Eventually Agnes-Anne returned and went to her loft. Her parents poured cups of Calvados and, in spite of the cold weather, went out on the porch to celebrate.

Three weeks later, Noël came home to an empty front room. "I'm home," he announced, "with good news!" Looking into the bedroom, he saw his wife sitting at a small table. He noticed the paper on the table before he realized she had been crying. "What is the matter?" he said softly as he sat next to her.

"This," she replied handing him the note. "It came in the post. I picked it up on my way home from working at the hospital." Before he could read it, she took it back. "It's from Nicole in *Trois-Rivières.*" Looking at the paper, she read, "Weeks ago some local men went with a few soldiers to scout the Iroquois..."

"I know," he reported, "Pierre told me, Nicolas went with them."

Looking back at the paper, she continued, "She says that. She also says his band did not return at the same time as the others."

"Maybe they took a different route," he suggested. "That happens a lot."

"That's what they thought." Turning to the next page, she read, "They finally sent a search team and found them—two weeks ago today. They were along the river about ten miles upstream." Setting the paper back on the table, she began to sob, "Dead, all dead—even Nicolas." Sobbing harder, she ended, "Nicole wrote, 'you don't want to know how they died'."

He sat on the bed, putting his arm around her as she collapsed into his embrace, sobbing. A while later, she stood, taking a taking a deep breath for resolve, before suggesting. "Let's go out on the porch. The children will be home from school soon." As they stepped out into a lovely spring day, she asked, "What was your *good news?*"

Putting his arm around her, he reported, "I went to the docks today, and discovered Abraham went downstream three days ago to guide in the ships from France. Apparently, they have arrived, and it is not one but three ships. They should be here in three or four days. D'Ailleboust says this is a good sign—a very good sign."

Three days later, they received word the ships would be in port early the next day. As usual, a number of local residents were in town the following morning to watch. Ships from France always drew a crowd, but today's arrivals held even greater interest. Françoise came with some Beauport neighbors, but Noël had been at the docks since late last night to help organize. Most deliveries from France involved one ship at a time, but today all three large vessels were arriving together, straining the local docking capacity.

As soon as they appeared around *Isle d'Orléans*, the crowd began to cheer in anticipation. It would seem like an eternity, however, until they were docked and ready to disembark. Finally, the first gangplank connected the first ship to a dock. Jean Guyon, in his capacity on the council, had some idea who was who. The first to exit were religious people: a few Jesuits, Augustinian nuns for the hospital, Ursuline nuns for the school, and Dominican nuns for *Ville-Marie*. Finally, two priests wearing unfamiliar robes stepped off.

Next in line was a small group of prosperous looking men and women. "I suspect these are government officials and their spouses," Guyon reported. Then came a small throng of ordinary looking people, first came families, then single men, and ultimately a few apparently single women. Once the humans were ashore, a group of farm animals

131

came next, followed by farm implements and other equipment.

By now, the second ship was unloading, beginning with another group of official-looking souls followed by soldiers: first officers, then enlisted men, marching with as much precision as they could muster after two months at sea. The crowd began to cheer, and one could feel the beneficial effect it had on the men who, to a man, stepped onto land smiling. Trying to keep count, Jean Guyon announced with excitement, "This is already more men than we had hoped for, and the third ship is just mooring!"

The third ship held a few citizens and more soldiers. Finally, military equipment and armaments began to appear from the holds of both vessels. Governor d'Ailleboust came from behind and put a hand on Guyon's shoulder. "My friend," he said, "I believe France has just saved Canada!"

As the crowd began to disperse, the Beauport residents adjourned to *L'Auberge Oie Bleue*. Noël met them briefly. "I cannot stay," he reported, "Abraham and I have a great deal of work to do. They are sorting out who and what goes where, and we need to decide how to transport them." Putting his arm on his wife's shoulder, he added, "I may not be home before tomorrow."

Lunch arrived and discussion ensued about the newcomers. "Who were the two priests in odd clothes?" Perrine Boucher asked.

"I heard," Mathurine Guyon replied, "They are an order from France called Sulpicians and will eventually take over *Ville-Marie* from the Jesuits. I understand the people there do not get along with the Black Robes."

"I never heard of Sulpicians," declared Xainte Cloutier.

"I believe it is a new order," Mathurine answered, "I think they started at a church in Paris called Saint-Sulpice."

132

"I know that church," Françoise said. "It's an old parish. In central Paris, Royalty goes to Notre-Dame, rich people to Saint-Germain l'Auxerrois, and the remainder to Saint-Sulpice." Then with a grin that all her friends now understood, "It was the best church for picking pockets when I was a street urchin."

Three days later, Governor d'Ailleboust called a meeting of his provisional council to improve military protection throughout the colony. It included *Monsieur* Bourdon, the military heads of each unit, the four-man council of *Québec,* and a few other military leaders as well as Noël and Abraham Martin. "These two river captains," he explained to the newcomers, "have traveled these routes and visited the areas of interest more than anyone in Canada."

Going to the wall displaying three maps, he began, "These are the three areas that will receive the most attention today. Each is a post along the *Fleuve Saint-Laurent,* the great river many of you have been on for several days." At the first map, he explained, "This is *Trois-Rivières,* at the mouth of *Rivière-Saint-Maurice* as it enters the *Saint-Laurent.* It was once the main highway of the fur trade. The town is of respectable size and the fort is well built and equipped. However, the farms and businesses are scattered and do not lend themselves to adequate fortification. The residents are currently arranging a situation where many businesses and homes will be inside a palisade. This work is ongoing, and you will be asked to participate. The military protection here is better than the other towns—although they have had recent difficulties. The smallest group of reinforcements will go here."

At the second map, he explained, "The post at the Richelieu River was Fort Richelieu. Unfortunately, the Iroquois have just recently burned it to the ground. The small settlement here is only a few cabins with few people. The fact this previously good fort was unable to withstand an attack is discouraging. The Richelieu River has always been the Iroquois highway to the *Saint-Laurent*. Here we are going to rebuild only a small-fortified post, but we shall eventually place smaller posts to the south along the Richelieu as far as Lake Champlain, to observe and control the native traffic to the north—as best we can."

At the final map, he announced, "Here is the most important and difficult of our three challenges. The town of *Ville-Marie* on the south shore of *Montréal*, one of Canada's largest islands, began a few years ago as a religious colony and Indian mission. Its founders underestimated the potential of Iroquois attacks— something they have come to regret. They began with a moat around the town. Frankly, I call it a ditch. It is totally inadequate. Recently they have embarked on construction of a palisade but it is still far from secure. Our first job is to adequately protect the town and build a proper fort."

Standing away from the map, he continued, "My wife and I lived in *Ville-Marie* for a few years and I served as temporary governor, so I know it and its challenges well. Our largest group will go here, not only to build proper structures, but also to form a defensible community. It is my opinion that this will become the heart of the North American fur trade, and a critical city in Canada."

Stepping back he concluded, "I shall be here all evening if there are questions. Captains Martin and Langlois are here with rosters of who goes where and when."

134

Rather than stepping down, Governor d'Ailleboust paused to look at each map, then picking up the glass he had brought to the podium, he turned, holding his drink up to the blue and white *fleur-de-lis* flag of *Québec* and shouted.

"Vivre la France! Et vivre le Canada!"

CHAPTER 20

<u>Beauport: November 9, 1649</u>

As *Québec* grew, marriages at home became more common, either to relieve the church building of the increasing number of ceremonies or simply to avoid traveling to town in bad weather. Plans for a chapel in Beauport were discussed, but the massive work to fortify the outpost communities took precedence. A remarkable break in the early winter weather allowed the Langlois family to invite their neighbors to their ceremony on the riverbank.

The young priest and his younger server stood at the makeshift altar on the front porch while Jean-Claude and Agnes-Anne stood below, flanked by their sponsors, Marin and Perrine Boucher. The absence of a church, along with the age of the cleric, made for an abbreviated service, and soon he declared the couple husband and wife. As they kissed, Henri-Makya released a pigeon to fly over the couple, and drinks were served while Jean Guyon and Marin Boucher began to play their fiddles.

"Very nice service, Father Villard," Noël said, handing the young cleric a cup of Calvados. "Was it your first in

Québec?" A young Jesuit, Ambrose Villard, had arrived on the last ship of the season from France. When the Beauport people heard he was from *Perche*, he became an instant celebrity.

Blushing, he admitted, "In truth, Captain Langlois, it was my first alone anywhere."

"Well, Father, it was excellent," touching his cup to Villard's, Noël said, "*a votre santé!*"

As he sipped the beverage, the young man's eyes widened. Clearing his throat, he whispered, "This is the real thing."

"Almost," Noël responded, "we have the finest apple cider here, but we have yet to find someone who can distill it into perfect Calvados."

Wiping the tears from his eyes, Villard declared, "I have not had it in over three years. As you can imagine, it was not on the menu at the seminary." Looking about, he continued, "I must say I have been impressed at how modern Canada is. I had expected total wilderness." Bravely taking another taste, he added, "I had also expected savages everywhere. The man who brought us in the small boat—canoe, is it? He seemed very civilized, his French was surprisingly good."

"Jacques-Henri is not your typical Algonquin. He speaks three European languages and every native dialect of the area—and there are many."

"I am also a little disappointed at the weather, I heard winters were frigid. In truth, they seem just like back home." Noël only smiled.

At this moment, the ladies descended and began to monopolize the young priest, allowing Noël to circulate. He headed for Guillaume and Michelle Pelletier, parents of the groom. "Excellent ceremony, Captain," Michelle declared, "and such a wonderful day."

"Not likely to last for long," Noël warned.

"No, but it is so lovely here. We have this farm by the falls that belonged to Guillaume's brother and we rarely get out there. I hope Agnes-Anne will not be bored living in town."

"I think it will work out," Noël responded, thinking, *it will be good to get her away from her mother for a while.*

"I believe it will be best, with her so young and all. They can always move to the country if it suits them." Lowering her voice, Michelle continued, "Isn't it grand? Here we are, simple artisans from *Perche*, now talking as we were lords of the manor."

Noël smiled, "It is good to be among the first."

Soon the Pelletiers moved on to the priest, while Jean Guyon and Zacharie Cloutier took their place. "We have scarcely seen you since the first boat of the season, Noël. Tell us what is happening on the frontier."

Noël poured more drinks before beginning, "We have been enormously busy bringing men and supplies to the three posts. I think Abraham's boat today will be the last for the season other than canoes. To tell the truth, I am astounded—pleasantly astounded—that things are as quiet as they are. There continue to be raids on various Indian villages, but nothing enormous and nothing of much note at the three outposts. I hope the Iroquois have been frightened by the new forts being built and the increasing number of men and supplies we are putting into them." Taking a generous sip of his drink, he added, "Unfortunately Abraham Martin is of a different mind."

"How, so?" Guyon asked.

"Abraham thinks they are just lying low, waiting for the right moment to do something outrageous." The discussion lasted until the wives began to drag the men home. Guillaume Pelletier came to Noël and Françoise. "Lovely wedding but we think we should put the newlyweds in our cart and head home. The sky is ominous."

Finally, Jacques-Henri convinced the young priest it was time to go. As they walked to the dock, the snow began. Soon after they pushed off, the winds approached gale force and visibility was ending. "I suspect," Noël told his wife, "the priest is soon to change his attitude about the weather. Let us get inside."

Taverne Terre Sauvage, Québec: Late April, 1650 (four months later)

"I guess that about does it," Abraham Martin said while closing his log. "Looks like a busy year—hopefully not as busy as the last. With two new shallops and more pilots, you and I will only be getting the long trips and mainly the ones upriver—unless those Iroquois bastards move into the east as well."

Noël closed his folder, "I was thinking last night, it's been forever since we saw Benoît and Bernier."

"Let me see…" Martin began counting on his fingers, "I think it has been at least two years. You are correct. We usually see them much more often. I can't imagine anything happened—they are so crafty, but I guess no one lasts forever." The two men parted as Noël left for his shallop and his first trip of the year.

"Never know what to expect on any trip, but always beware on the first voyage of the season," Bergeron told him as they readied the log and checked the supplies. "Especially nowadays."

Warm for April, there was not much remaining ice, and they made *Trois-Rivières* in two days. As they docked, they saw a familiar face, "Pierre, what's new?"

"A few things," he replied, "first, let's go up to the office to meet the new commandant."

"Actually," Noël told him, "I believe I met *Monsieur* Leneuf two years ago. I was surprised at the announcement. I thought it would be someone from France."

"It is unusual," Pierre reported. "However, I believe he is a very good choice. He is more businessman than soldier and has extensive experience in the fur trade, which seems to be of the utmost importance *these days.*"

As they entered the office, the man behind the desk stood. About Noël's age, he was short, thin and well groomed. "Jacques Leneuf," he said, extending his hand. Noël shook it—it was soft. "I believe we met two years ago at Robert Giffard's in the upper town."

"Yes, I recall," Noël responded.

Remaining standing, Leneuf said, "Let us go to Captain Boucher's office to see the maps." As they walked, he told Noël, "This job would be hell without Pierre. I could not do without him."

In the office, Pierre unrolled maps. "You can see how we managed to design a palisade to encircle a number of the homes. Unfortunately, their farmland is outside the walls. In the future all new homes are to be situated as seen on *this* diagram. In the event of a raid, we can sequester almost everyone within an hour or so. In addition, with our new military personnel we can effectively hold the palisade against an attack. Most importantly, we can now facilitate a fur market inside the walls where it will be safe." After walking the grounds, Pierre told Noël, "And now, as always, you are invited to dinner." It was only a short stroll to Gaspard and Nicole's home next to Pierre's now both inside the enlarging palisade. As usual, Nicole greeted him with extreme enthusiasm. Taking him by the hand to Pierre's, he saw Marie-Madeline nursing an infant. "This," announced Pierre, "is Jacques Boucher, my first son."

The following afternoon the shallop landed at the site of old Fort Richelieu where a new but smaller fortification was being constructed. Commandant Durocher, who was in much better condition than during their last meeting, greeted him. "Even though this is smaller, it is more defensible. We cannot accommodate many people, but our civilian population since the attack last season has dwindled to almost nothing." Unrolling a map, he pointed out, "We have small posts at each of these sites along the River Richelieu. They are more for reconnaissance than battle. So far, it is working, but most of the action is well upriver of here. I'm afraid you will find the real action around *Ville-Marie*—and beyond."

The next day, when Noël made the turn around the point of *Montréal,* he saw considerable construction going on in *Ville-Marie*, however, no signs of battle. Governor Maisonneuve greeted him at the dock with more enthusiasm than he had shown on earlier visits. They went directly to the construction of the new fort where Noël could see a greatly enlarged and better-fortified structure taking form. "We hope to have the entire community sheltered here," the governor told him. "I hope to have it nearly completed before winter." Taking Noël to his new office, he showed him an area map before he began his report. "Right now, there are more raids going on than we have seen in the past. However, most of it is well upstream." Going to a map of the lakes and Indian territories, which Noël had seen elsewhere but never before in *Ville-Marie*, the governor explained, "The Huron, who once controlled this entire area north of the Lake of the Ontario, are entirely gone—and I mean entirely. Those still breathing have fled way up the lakes to two islands in the north of the Lake of the Huron." Pointing to the map, he explained, "This smaller of the two was named Saint-Joseph by the Jesuits, and this larger island retains its Indian name, Manitoulin."

Pointing again at the map, Maisonneuve continued, "West of the old Huron country are the Petun, also called the tobacco tribe due to their famous crop. They are nearly wiped out. To the south are the Neutral, but they, too, will not last long. Below the Lake of the Ontario are the Wenro, also nearly abolished, while below this are the Erie. They persist, but who knows for how long?" Rolling up the map, he finished, "All of these tribes are related to the Huron, and they all speak a type of Iroquois dialect. This makes it easier for the Mohawk to take hostages and blend them into the society of the five nation Iroquois tribes. In conclusion, soon there will be no one in our corner but the Algonquin to the north and east. If this trend persists, soon there will be no one but Iroquois for trading."

Noël already knew much of this. However, wishing to encourage the governor whose knowledge of such matters was finally blossoming, he said, "Thank you for the briefing, sir. It gives me a better grasp."

Beauport: May, 1650

Two weeks later, Noël was off visiting his tenants and managing the *concession*. He had brought Robert along, still hoping the lad might be able to take over some of these duties in the near future. Things had been quiet in *Québec*, and the only Indian problems were reflected in reports from upriver, well past *Montréal*. Arriving home, they found Françoise nursing young Jean-Louis on the front porch. "Thank goodness you are home." His wife exclaimed, "A soldier from the fort was here not two hours ago. He said when you return, you and Jacques-Henri are to go to the fort post-haste—for an emergency meeting with the governor."

As this sort of urgency was uncommon, he replied, "I'm going. If I cannot be home for dinner, I will send word," and headed to the canoe dock where Jacques-Henri was waiting.

Aided by Jacques-Henri's excellent canoe handling, they were at the *Québec* dock in less than an hour and at d'Ailleboust's office soon after. "Thank goodness you are here," the governor told them, "I have urgent need of either you or Captain Martin and he is making deliveries downstream in Tadoussac." Inviting Noël and Jacques-Henri to sit, he began, "Two days ago a courier arrived with an urgent message from Governor Maisonneuve. He reports *Ville-Marie* is in dire straits."

"Things seemed to be under reasonable control two weeks ago when I was there," Noël reminded him. "They did not seem to be in imminent danger."

D'Ailleboust rose and looked out his window. "Unfortunately, this is all the information I have. I need you two men to take the fastest shallop with the few

143

soldiers we can spare, along with Lieutenant Charron to find out what is going on. I have already called your Mr. Bergeron who is readying the shallop, as we speak. I hope you can leave immediately. I will send a man to inform Madame Langlois."

They all stood as d'Ailleboust concluded, "Jacques-Henri, I have come to realize how valuable your wisdom is and why the captains rely on it so heavily. I sincerely hope you can help put some sense to this." Jacques-Henri merely nodded, but Noël could see his old friend was pleased.

When they reached the docks, Bergeron had the shallop ready. "All our supplies and the soldiers are already onboard, Captain. We have full moonlight for the next few nights and it promises to be fair weather."

"Do you think we can sail throughout the night?" Noël questioned.

"Perhaps," the old seaman said. "Worst thing that can happen is we drown." Then smiling, "Of course, that's always true when you sail."

Once they were away and around *Cap Diamant*, Noël asked Jacques-Henri. "So what does your *wisdom* tell you about this?"

Jacques-Henri rarely smiled, but he did now. "Iroquois want all fur trade. Must defeat all tribes— kill or *adopt* the defeated. They can trade some pelts to English and Dutch, but most furs are in French lands. They will threaten French and may kill some, but they need French market to succeed." As always, his native friend's wisdom never ceased to impress Noël.

144

Ville-Marie: Three days later

Noël brought the shallop to the dock in expert fashion. "Well, *Monsieur* Bergeron," Noël announced, "I believe we have a new record, slightly less than three days." Looking into the village he added, "I don't really see anything amiss. Hopefully this is only bad nerves on the part of the governor."

"I don't know, Captain. He never struck me as the type with bad nerves."

As soon as they were on shore, Noël, Jacques-Henri and Lieutenant Charron from the military hastened to Maisonneuve's office. "Praise God, you men have made it. Since you left, a short time ago, the savages have gone to full attack. They have nearly eliminated the Wenro, Neutral and Petun-Tobacco tribes, either killing them or taking hostages who must promise to be their slaves. Even the Erie are beginning to fail. Every camp that was to trade with us this year has been assaulted, including those small camps right on our island. They have totally blockaded us."

"We didn't see any sign of blockade," Noël told him. "We sailed in with no problems. We have not seen a single hostile."

"They are not blockading us from you," Maisonneuve tried to explain. "It is the trade they have blockaded. They are lying in wait upstream along the *Fleuve Saint-Laurent*. When any of the other tribes bring canoes toward us, they are attacked, their pelts stolen and if they are *fortunate*, they escape with their lives. We have not had a single pelt brought in to our market. Not even from the Algonquin to the northeast. We understand they, too, have been frightened away."

"I don't know if I understand this, Excellency."

Maisonneuve tried to calm down, "You see, Captain, we can now only obtain furs for our market from the Iroquois, not our old friends and historic trading partners who have been devastated by these attacks—any pelts they had have been stolen. And if we refuse, the Iroquois will take them down Lake Champlain to the Dutch and English markets."

That evening Noël and Jacques-Henri spent the night on the shallop. Noël told Maisonneuve it was to protect the boat, but it was really to gain some native insight on what appeared an insoluble problem. Following a small meal, the two men sat on deck in the cool moonlit night.

"Need pipes." Jacques-Henri began. Lighting two, he handed one to Noël, "Iroquois tobacco—but from Petun tribe, the best."

Noël took a puff, careful not to inhale too deeply, wisdom he had garnered in his early days in Canada. "I don't see a solution here, my friend," Noël began.

"Is solution," Jacques-Henri replied, "just not good solution." Taking a puff much larger than Noël would dare, he blew the smoke high in the air, rising through the moonlight. "*Ville-Marie* need more fighters—many more. Algonquin could help, but will not. Too far away, and not enough French soldiers. Must have more soldiers."

"So what do we do?" Noël asked, hoping there could be an answer.

"Must move market closer to *Québec*, maybe *Trois-Rivières*. They said they would have market *inside* the fort this year. Then French and Algonquin can protect trade. Iroquois would need to move far downriver, near *Trois-Rivières*. Huron and other tribes would move back here. Then Iroquois caught in middle." The two men talked into the night, eventually abandoning the quagmire of the fur trade and reminiscing on hunting, fishing and times when they were younger.

In the morning, Noël met with Maisonneuve and told him the situation as he saw it. Obviously disappointed, the governor said, "I was planning a trip to France soon. I will go to Cardinal Mazarin. Perhaps he can help. I realize you are correct, I need more soldiers and more civilians—many more."

On their way back to *Québec*, Noël stopped to see Pierre and LeNeuf, who were in agreement with moving the *Montréal* trade closer in and holding it inside the *Trois-Rivières* fortification. Two days later, near dusk, the shallop landed in *Québec*. Going immediately to the fort, he met with d'Ailleboust, discussing his less than successful venture and the thoughts of both Jacques-Henri and Maisonneuve. D'Ailleboust took notes and said he would consider the options but thought Jacques-Henri's plan was likely the best. As Noël left the fort, he asked a guard, "Is that smoke in the upper town?"

"It looks like it, sir," the soldier at the gate said.

Noël looked more closely into the dark only penetrated by the glow of flames, "It looks like the convent!" Turning to the soldier, he ordered, "Go get every man you can to come to the upper town. Tell them the convent is on fire!" Noël began to run along the road to the upper town.

Arriving first, he saw Noël Morin also approaching. Langlois told him, "Go alert every man you can and begin the bucket brigade, this is a disaster!"

Morin ran to the square and Langlois went to *L'Auberge Oie Bleue* for more help. Soon a line formed, taking water from the well in the square and passing it on to the inferno. As he looked up at the upper level of the convent, Noël saw a gowned figure. *Marie de l'Incarnation* was throwing books and documents to the ground below as fast as she could. Soon a sizable crowd had gathered and the brigade began to work well.

Three hours later, the flames had been reduced to smoldering, but much of the wonderful stone convent was in ruins. *Marie de l'Incarnation* had come down and was feverishly picking up documents from the yard. When Noël went to help, she told him, "These are all the records of the convent—and much of *Québec*. They are priceless. I pray we have saved most."

Two days later, Jean Guyon called for a meeting of all the building artisans on the part of the Council of *Québec*. "Marin Boucher and I have toured the ruins. Fortunately, because it was built of stone, it is not totally destroyed. We are drawing plans with the help of *Sieur* Bourdon and hope to begin reconstruction soon. With the help of all of you, we believe we can have the convent and school habitable before winter." Following the meeting, he walked to *L'Auberge Oie Bleue* with Noël and Zacharie Cloutier. "I remember in *Mortagne*, sometimes I would get bored—in *Québec*, life is *never* boring."

CHAPTER 21

<u>*Québec*</u>: October, 1650

Coming down from a meeting with the governor, Noël saw Marin Boucher coming out of the Ursuline Convent. "Looks like your work is coming along nicely, Marin."

"Thanks, Noël. Everyone has been working as hard as possible. Fortunately, the original stonework was quite good and we were able to salvage a great deal of it. We are putting more stone work in, hopefully to prevent a similar disaster."

Nodding, Noël added, "I hear *Marie de l'Incarnation* is taking similar precautions with the records."

His friend looked puzzled, "What do you mean?"

"I was just meeting with the governor who told me *Marie de l'Incarnation* made the head Jesuit decree that copies of all records will be kept in duplicate—for now, one set kept at the fort and the other set at the parish churches. Once we have a church of the Archdiocese, it will keep the set from the fort. That way if one burns, the other still has copies of the documents."

"I hope with the work we are doing at the convent," Marin said, "it will never burn again." As they headed into the upper town square, Marin asked, "Where have you been the last few days?"

"Upriver, as usual. If you have time to stop at *L'Auberge Oie Bleue*, I'll bring you up to date."

As they took a seat outside under a sea of autumn leaves, Noël began. "Things remain tense in *Ville-Marie*. There have been a few minor Iroquois raids, and the tribe has prevented *all* fur trade in the area. Fortunately, they have not caused any *major* damage to the people of *Ville-Marie*. In the countryside, however, it is a different story. The Iroquois raids on the outlying tribes have nearly wiped out the Neutrals and have severely damaged the Erie."

"Is there *any* trade upriver?" Marin queried.

"Most of the tribes still in the area have been trading with *Trois-Rivières* inside their new fort," Noël explained, "but it is a far cry from the old days. The Algonquin continue to come to Québec, and that is probably the most active trade in the area. Still, I cannot see how this whole thing will end other than badly."

When they finished their drinks, Marin told him, "I had better get back to the convent."

"I need to leave, as well," Noël replied. "I haven't been home for several days, and tomorrow my son and I must go visit the tenants of the *concession*."

Three days passed before Noël and Robert had finished their business on the *concession*. The following morning, Noël headed into town and his other job. Holding the logbook, Abraham Martin was waiting for him at the docks. "Come to the office where we can sit," he told Noël, "we have quite a lot to do."

With the growing population and increasing river traffic, complicated by the Iroquois interference, what had begun as a part-time venture was turning into an industry. As the sun was high in the sky, Abraham closed the log. "That's enough for now. Let's go over to *Taverne Terre Sauvage* for something to eat." With a grin, he added, "and perhaps something to drink."

They sat outside where each gust of late October breeze brought down a few of the last colorful maple leaves of the season. Brushing the leaves from the table, Abraham said, "Good God, look across the way!"

Noël looked across the ever-enlarging courtyard of the lower town tavern. "I guess they are not dead—I knew no one could do in that pair."

They began to walk to the table, but before they arrived, Benoît had already stood. "Well, if it ain't the captains, I was just tellin' Bernier, I thought we might see you." Ever silent, Bernier rose and shook hands. Noël had forgotten Bernier was as large as he was quiet.

"Where the hell have you been?" Abraham inquired.

"Well, yer honor," Benoît began, "couple years ago when things started to get bad, we was out in Huron Country—not much left there. Anyway, we seen some awful sights and decided to head south awhile—kinda like the King goin' to the Loire Valley fer the season. Except we ain't got a chateau."

Bernier stifled a mild giggle while Noël asked, "Why go south?"

"Well, ya see, Captain, when we first come here—a little after old Champlain hisself—we spent some time down there tradin' with them Iroquois and sellin' to the Englishmen and Dutchmen, especially when the English chased old Champlain out in '28." Taking an impressive swallow of beer, he continued, "This time we's wonderin' how things might have changed. Also thought we might get some idea what went wrong to have all these wars now."

Becoming interested, Abraham ordered another round of shots and beers before he asked, "And what did you learn?"

"One thing, yer honor, things is sure as hell changed down there—changed a bunch."

"In what way?" Abraham questioned.

"Well, sir, when we first come, things wasn't too different anywhere from anywhere else. The two businesses was codfish in the east and furs in the west, and there was lots for everyone—was also lots of land. Now the French is doin' it like always, we got some towns and posts along the way, but most the land is still wild fer trappin' and fishin'. Most the folks comin' ta Canada is still single men. In fact, I seem to recall the captain here tellin' us a while back, the big problem was not enough women and families."

Finishing his beer and ordering more, Benoît added, "Problem down south is different. See, them English and Dutch don't have much land in Europe, so they got lotsa folks lookin' to get out. They also got some problems with religion and they got people wantin' to come to git away from persecution. They wants their own religion so's they can be the persecutors." Bernier stifled another chuckle.

"You should see it down there now, yer honor. It's farms all over, far as you can see in some places, and the places with room—why they's movin into them as soon as new folks git off the ship. And they's boatloads comin' all the time—and not single men, but families with lots of kids, ready fer farmin' and needin' more space." Taking a

152

breath, followed by another gulp of beer, he concluded, "Them beaver didn't just get trapped out by voyageurs. Hell, they got run out—by farmers." Pushing back from the table, he went on. "There's this book, *The Art of War*." Noël recalled Abraham had told him he suspected Benoît was well educated. "Book was written a while back—fifth century B.C."

Bernier whispered slowly, "Long time ago…" as his partner continued, "Chinaman—Sun Tzu wrote it. Long book, but what he says is ta do well in war you must know yer enemy—and know yerself." By now, Benoît's interest had shifted from beer to books and pointing to Abraham, he asked, "Here's a question. Who are we?"

"France," Abraham replied.

"Good so far, yer honor, now who is our enemy?"

"Iroquois?"

"Why?" the voyageur asked.

"Because they attack us," Abraham declared.

"But does they attack us or just attack some tribes who been our friends?"

Abraham responded with a decided lack of confidence. "Well, kind of both."

"So who's our enemy?" Benoît returned.

"Shit, I don't know, this is too damn complicated." Abraham called for another round.

"Unfortunately," Benoît returned, "no one involved has read the book. But let me throw out an idea."

Defeated, Abraham said, "Go for it."

"I believe," Benoît began, recovering his interest in beer. "England's the enemy—of everyone here—French, Iroquois, and everybody else. Rumor has it that even the Dutch is plannin' to leave the continent. England's takin' up all the land, and chasin' the natives off. It's clear they got no use for the Indian and they considers any dead Indian a good one. As far as the French go, I think everyone had enough history to know where France stands with them English."

They all sat silently until Benoît concluded, "Say or think what you will, but before this is all over, I believe you will see France and *all* the natives linin' up against England. Might be a while, but we will see it!"

As Noël and Abraham made their way to the docks, Noël asked, "What do you think of all that? Do you think there ever was a Chinese guy like this?"

Abraham Martin lit his pipe, "I don't know, but I guarantee you, he never knew an Englishman, Frenchman, or an Indian—and he sure as hell never knew a voyageur."

CHAPTER 22

Beauport: April 1651

Noël slowed the cart to a near stop as Robert hopped on. "How are the Dumas?" his father queried.

"Pretty good, Pa, Madame is pregnant again. She never misses a year. She's about as regular as the moon, and this is going to be her eighth. She says she's prayin' for a girl, the last five were boys." As Noël headed to the next *concession*, his son continued. "The cows both had calves and they got six new pigs, I can't begin to count the chickens." Smiling, he added, "This is the most fertile farm in Canada."

"These are the folks we want, son. The old man always has things in order and pays his fees on time each year."

Visiting the tenants was a critical part of running a *concession*, and Noël had been teaching his son the ropes since before he finished school. They tried to visit each tenant and each *engager* every month or two, but the most important times were in early spring, following the brutal *Québec* winter, and in the autumn, to tally the harvest. That was also the time to collect the fees. Noël kept some and passed the balance to Robert Giffard who, after taking his share, gave the remainder to the government.

As they approached the next farm, Robert told him, "Henri-Makya and I were talking. We'd like to take off after the fall harvest is in and spend some time up in the high country."

His father pondered for a minute and merely replied, "Oh?"

"Yes, sir, I've been thinking. I am probably going to take on some of this business, then get a wife and a family... and this is probably the best chance I will ever have to do it. I mean, look at Agnes-Anne and Jean-Claude. They don't even have children yet, but he couldn't take off like this. If I wait, I'll miss my chance."

As Noël pulled up at the next farm, he said, "You see the Bérards, and I'll go up and visit old Croteau."

Before his son jumped off, he asked, "But how about my plan?"

Noël tried to be nonchalant, "We'll see when we get closer to fall. You will need to see the rest of the tenants yourself after today. The first ship from France is already in the *Saint-Laurent*, and I have to go downstream tomorrow to bring it in to *Québec*."

"Yes sir!" he answered as he hopped off.

After dinner, Noël and Françoise sat by the fire as the young children attended to their studies and Robert and Henri-Makya were out checking fish traps. "Henri-Makya and Robert want to go into the high country this fall," he told her.

Putting down her knitting, "Oh, Noël, do you think that's a good idea? The high country is dangerous enough, and with all the Iroquois problems…"

"I suppose we need to let him go sometime. There haven't been any problems that high up, and Jacques-Henri has trained them well. I might see if he will go with them for the first few days."

"Yes, but do you think it is safe?"

Sipping his evening cup of Calvados, he replied, "Nothing is safe out here. It's a wild new land—but then again, isn't that part of why we came?"

Standing, he finished his drink and announced, "I'm off to bed. I need to be in early. We always have a meeting before greeting the first ship of the season."

Most such meetings involved only the captain and a member of the governor's staff, but when Noël entered the office, he was surprised to see Jean Guyon, Abraham Martin and Governor d'Ailleboust. With everyone seated, Jean Guyon brought the meeting to order, "This is a particularly important ship that you are going to meet, Noël. The council members just heard about it last night. The governor has all the particulars."

D'Ailleboust rose, "Due to the native hostilities, it has not been made public knowledge that I am returning to France. My replacement arrives on this ship." Taking out notes, he put on his spectacles, "The new Governor of New France is Jean de Lauzon. A *Parisian*, he is a man of great skill and experience. I have met him in France and can attest to his capabilities. He was a member of the old Company of 100 Associates and has a significant knowledge of the colony. A widower, he is bringing his

157

three adult sons—all unmarried." Smiling, he added, "So you should all guard your girls."

Following the laughter, he continued, "He owns interest in the islands of *Montréal* and *Île d'Orléans,* and has considerable knowledge and interest in agriculture, the fur trade, and most importantly, the Iroquois Nation. I must sincerely say that he is the most qualified person to hold the post." D'Ailleboust went on to thank everyone for their work and express other pleasantries before adjourning the meeting and sending Noël off to his shallop and crew.

Once the shallop was away, Bergeron came to the helm. "So I hear we are getting a new governor, Captain, what do you know about it?"

Noël smiled, secrets were short-lived in *Québec.* "Yes, André, as I suppose everyone in Canada knows. It is Jean de Lauzon, a *Parisian* and from what I'm told, a very capable man."

"Capable enough to solve the Indian problems, Captain?"

"I hope so, André, but sometimes I think God alone could solve those—and it would take him a while."

Bergeron laughed, "I guess you are correct, Captain. I must say, however, I'm happy to be sailing downstream for a change instead of upstream to Richelieu and *Ville-Marie.*"

"I believe we should look on the bright side, *Monsieur* Bergeron. The Ursuline Convent is due to be entirely completed this month, and I understand the fur market inside *Trois-Rivières* was successful."

Bergeron looked over the rail at the river, "I guess, Captain, but I saw a couple of voyageurs I know the other night, they said it was all right, but nothin' like the days of the open market before them damned Iroquois started

158

comin' around." Noël had also heard this from very reliable sources, but he remained silent, while Bergeron got on with his job.

Three uneventful days later, they landed at Tadoussac. The sea captains familiar with the eastern portion of the *Saint-Laurent* generally made it this far inland. From here, however, the river became narrow and the navigation considerably more difficult. Here the river captains more familiar with the waterway, such as Noël and Abraham Martin, took over.

Arriving at the dock, it was apparent the ship from France had yet to arrive. Noël went to the office to report while Bergeron and the crew visited the pub. They had only to wait a few hours until the ship appeared, coming around the bend. Bergeron then took the crew and shallop and headed back to *Québec,* while Noël and one of the new river pilots watched the larger sea vessel dock. Once secure, a lone man walked down the gangplank. "Captain Dubois," he introduced himself while shaking Noël's hand. "Governor de Lauzon has asked that we proceed without delay. He is quite anxious to reach *Québec*." Noël simply agreed. He was happy to proceed, but not giving a brief shore leave to the passengers who had been several weeks at sea was rather unusual. It did provide Noël, however, some early insight into the nature of the next leader of New France.

As he stepped onto the ship, Noël was personally greeted by de Lauzon who accompanied him to the helm. Once they were away, the governor said, "I will leave you to your work, Captain, but when we stop for the night, I will await dinner in my cabin for you." Noël had been piloting ocean ships up the river for more than 15 years. In 15 minutes, he had seen two *firsts*.

When nightfall made navigation unwise, Noël dropped anchor and joined de Lauzon. Entering the elegant cabin, he was served an excellent dinner. "I brought my personal chef to cook for me on the voyage," he explained. Telling Noël a little of what he had heard of New France, along with a few personal facts, he spent the remainder of the evening seeking Noël's opinions. Noël tried to be frank as well as helpful. He even revealed a few of Benoît's unusual thoughts.

The voyage continued uneventful with fair weather for April. By the end of day two, Noël felt he knew more about the new chief and his ideas and goals than he had known about any other leaders by the end of their entire tour. On the third morning, when Noël was bringing the ship into the northern channel around *Île d'Orléans*, de Lauzon came to the helm and told him, "I must say, the weather here has been nothing like I had been told. It has been delightful—especially for April." Noël remained silent, and in the next hour, the wind shifted to the north, and an hour later, it began to snow, as the wind continued to build.

In spite of deteriorating weather, Noël managed to bring the snow and ice-covered ship into the port of *Québec* just before nightfall. Equally as impressive, the new governor had tightened his coat and stood with him at the helm the entire day. Once the ship was secure, Noël began to work his way down, but de Lauzon stopped him. "If possible, Captain, can we remain up here while the other passengers disembark? They have had a difficult voyage, too."

Noël agreed, and finally, it was their turn, after the last *engager* and before the few farm animals. De Lauzon was slightly taller than Noël and of average build. His long, curly hair and well-trimmed goatee and mustache were all encased in frozen white.

"This will be wonderful," Françoise declared as she paddled the front of the canoe, "like going with friends before we had children."

"It is different," her husband replied as he guided the canoe toward the *Québec* canoe docks. "I'm anxious to see his property, too. They must be ready, I see them waiting on the dock."

Jean-Claude took hold of the front of the canoe, while Noël held the dock from the back. Agnes-Anne handed a large basket to her mother. "I made a picnic, I hope you like it, Mother."

"Oh I'm certain we will," Françoise replied as she took a center seat to allow Jean-Claude to paddle from the front. There was no doubt Françoise was the superior canoeist of the foursome, but as always in early French Canada, sexism prevailed.

Proceeding northeast, the downstream current overpowered the mild headwind, helping them quickly to their destination. Approaching Montmorency Falls, they could hear its roar a considerable distance away, but the massive spray hitting the mild headwind obscured the falls from view. Jean-Claude pointed to a flat area on the bank where two canoes were stored. "We can land there."

Before hitting the shore, Jean-Claude hopped out in knee-high water, pulling the canoe onto the land. Noël knew he could have easily beached the craft without any wet feet but was sensitive enough not to comment on his son-in-law's technique. Heading inland, the flat bank soon rose as it did at the Langlois *concession*, but the rise here was higher—considerably higher. "We can use the granite slabs as steps," the young man explained, as he led the way up.

Twenty minutes and a few short rest stops later, they arrived at a long, wide plateau with a moderate stone cabin. "This was my uncle's home before his death. Now I let it to a man named LeBlanc. He and his wife were tenants of the *concession* before she died—about the same time as my uncle. We convinced LeBlanc to move to this home and manage the *concession* in my absence. If we do move back here, he will return to his old place, which is just upstream."

Walking over to the stone building, he explained, "We can go in. He does not mind and is never home during daylight. He is always working." The interior was simple and neat, with almost no furniture. "As I said, he is rarely here."

Françoise and Anne took a tour. "This could be lovely," Françoise began, "with a little work." Pointing up in the rafters, she dropped an unsubtle hint, "Your father could easily put lofts there for children."

As they exited, Françoise stood on the porch, "This must be the most beautiful view in Canada," she exclaimed. "On the right you can see all the way to the city, and straight ahead, all the way across *Île d'Orléans* to the southern channel and the mainland."

Jean-Claude told them, "Let us take our picnic and hike up to the top. It's not too difficult."

"I once did it when Governor Montmagny first came," Noël announced. Looking at his wife, he said, "I suspect we can still do it."

One hour later, they arrived at the top. "See, that was not so difficult," Noël declared, gasping for breath. "I do believe, however, it is higher than it was 15 years ago."

162

"Look, Agnes-Anne," her mother said, "you can see way beyond the south bank of *Fleuve Saint-Laurent* well into the mainland, and up and down the river—almost forever!"

"Look how fast the water flows up here," her daughter exclaimed, going to the edge, "and how it thunders at the bottom."

Her mother instinctively grabbed the tie of her apron, "Not so close, dear."

"My father," Jean-Claude began, "knows a man who arrived from France a year ago who ran sawmills. He believed he could put one right up here. He said it would outperform anything in France!"

Jean-Claude took them a short distance further to where they could enjoy their meal with an unmatchable view of the falls. Eventually they descended to the canoe and returned the young couple to town.

That evening, Françoise and Noël sat enjoying their own view from their rockers. "I think the children are doing splendidly," Françoise told her spouse.

"Yes," Noël replied, "I wonder when she will start her family."

"Well," she said, coming closer for confidentiality. "She just told me today that she went to Sister Marie-Forestier who told her girls who have children before the age of sixteen have a greater chance of losing the child—or the mother!"

"So does that mean they aren't…?"

"No, dear," she told her husband, "she went to Félicity-Angel who gave her a special root. The Indian women chew it in between their monthlies if they do not wish to conceive."

"But…"

"Agnes-Anne told me," Françoise interrupted, "she is going to use it until she is sixteen." Noël looked astounded, "Didn't you ever wonder, dear," she added, "why Indian women have so few children. I think it is highly responsible of her."

"Well," he began again, "I was hoping to hear pattering feet around here again."

Françoise stood to look out at the river, putting her hands on her abdomen, "You needn't feel deprived, dear."

"You!" he said in astonishment, "You said that Félicity-Angel told you that you could not…"

"Well dear," she broke in, "I guess Indian women are not *always* correct."

CHAPTER 23

Québec: July 1651

Noël had met with Governor de Lauzon a few times, always in small groups. Today was the first time they met privately. "I have been told you took other new governors on their first tours of Canada in your shallop, and they all seemed to have found it highly valuable. I would like you to take me on such a tour soon. I have interviewed several people in the capital, but I am now ready to move into the frontier. We should plan to leave in two days."

Noël agreed. As he stood to leave, de Lauzon added, "I understand you have an Indian man who is helpful. We should include him as well."

That evening on the rocking chairs, he discussed it with his spouse over a glass of Calvados and the quiet view of _Québec_. "The man is meticulous in his research, and I think he is going to be a fine leader," he told Françoise. "Unlike the other *Parisian* officers, he seems to intend to build a family in *Québec*. He has brought all three of his sons, and one already has a marriage planned. He has interviewed almost everyone in town," he reported, before adding with a smile, "He even had the nerve to interview Abraham Martin."

His wife chuckled, "So what are you worried about?"

Noël stood, gazing at the river, "I still don't think he realizes how bad things are upriver. I've been three times this season, and each time it seems worse..." Finishing his drink, he concluded, "I suppose I shall just wait and see," and took her hand, leading her inside.

Noël, Jacques-Henri, and Bergeron arrived at the shallop early on the appointed morning of the trip. Shocked to see de Lauzon and two other men already at the dock, Noël asked, "Is something wrong, sir? You are quite early."

"Not at all, Captain, I just like to rise early on fine mornings such as this." Turning to the two men, "I suspect you know my secretary, *Monsieur* Petit, and Lieutenant Charron?"

"Yes, sir," Noël answered, "and this is André Bergeron, first mate, and my good friend and guide, Jacques-Henri."

"Yes, good to meet you," de Lauzon replied." Noël could not help notice the governor's reaction when he introduced Jacques-Henri as *good friend*.

The captain and crew quickly did their pre-checks and set sail. Once they had rounded *Cap Diamant*, Noël went to do paperwork, while Bergeron took the helm. The governor soon addressed Bergeron, "Looks like a beautiful day, *Monsieur*."

"I hope, Excellency. You know in Paris the weather comes off the sea. Here, our weather comes off the land— not so predictable."

De Lauzon smiled, "Ah, yes, I recall my day arriving in *Québec* when it went from spring to blizzard in moments." The governor continued his discussion and in less than an hour, he knew a great deal about the first mate. Then he got serious, "So what do you make of this *Indian affair, Monsieur?*"

"Tough subject, Excellency," Bergeron replied, while keeping his eyes fixed on the horizon. "You know, it is *their* land." Jean de Lauzon began to feel he was to learn a great deal on this trip.

Eventually he made it to the front of the shallop where Jacques-Henri was organizing lines. His attempts to join the Indian in a conversation initially met with grunts and shrugs, but the governor persisted, and Jacques-Henri, realizing this man was serious in his inquiries, began to answer. By the time the sun was setting, Jean de Lauzon likely knew more about the Indian and his culture than did any governor since Champlain.

At sunrise, they weighed anchor and headed to *Trois-Rivières.* "Give me your read on this place, Captain," de Lauzon asked, "I've heard a lot from the council, but I'm coming to value your opinion."

"Well, sir," Noël began, as he steered around a rocky outcropping, "it is a very old settlement, once the heart of the fur trade, when the furs came down the *Rivière-Saint-Maurice.* However, the beaver are now gone from that area, so trade was coming from further up the *Saint-Laurent*, well beyond *Ville-Marie.* That was the most active trading outside of *Québec* until the Iroquois went on the warpath this winter, essentially ending trade in *Ville-Marie.* The fortifications at *Trois-Rivières* improved things, and there was a trading post inside the walls. It was small but successful. They have just welcomed a new governor of *Trois-Rivières* from *Bretagne*, a Guillaume Guillemot, I have not met him."

After a moment of consideration, Noël went on, "There is another man there, Pierre Boucher. He is quite young, but I know him well. He was made captain of the village when the last governor left."

"Yes, I heard of him in *Québec*. Everyone's opinion was sterling."

By early afternoon, they came into sight of the docks, where two dockhands were ready to take their lines. Stepping ashore with de Lauzon, Noël said, "I don't see Pierre. He is usually out to greet us."

One of the dockhands told him, "Beggin' your pardon, Captain, but Captain Boucher is in the fort office with the governor." Lowering his voice for Noël, he concluded, "I'd be careful, sir, they seem to be havin' a bit of a shit fight."

Overhearing, de Lauzon said, "Perhaps we should go see what it is about." Turning to his secretary, he added, "You come, too, *Monsieur* Petit, I may need notes for this."

As they walked up to the fort, Noël observed, "This is unusual, Pierre is not one for heated arguments." As they approached the office, a tall man exited the building, slamming the door and proceeded into the compound. Entering the office, they found Pierre behind a desk reading documents. He rose to attention when he saw them. Noël introduced de Lauzon and Pierre shook his hand. "Governor Guillemot has just left," he said. "I will go find him."

"Sounds as though you had somewhat of a disagreement," de Lauzon noted.

"Yes, Excellency, we had some trouble outside the fort, and we were discussing a solution. I should get him before I give you my thoughts."

As Pierre left, de Lauzon told Noël, "Quite a mature attitude, most men would like to give their own view right away—make a note of that, Petit."

Noël replied, "As I told you, Governor, Pierre is not *most men*."

When the two combatants returned, introductions were made and Guillemot reported, "Two days ago we had an incident outside the fort. We found ten Frenchmen dead, obviously slaughtered by Iroquois. Pierre knows the details."

"They were only a short way from the palisade," Pierre began, "We identified two as men from *Trois-Rivières*, two more seemed to be voyageurs and the other six were mutilated beyond recognition."

Guillemot stepped forward, "Excellency, I was commander of the *flying column* in France. I would suggest we form such a unit and attack these rascals head on. Eliminate them for good!"

The governor looked to Pierre, "Captain, you seem to have more experience in this venue, how do you see it?"

"Well, sir," Pierre began calmly, "I have never commanded a *flying column*, but it seems to me to be a battlefield tactic. We are not a battlefield, we are a wilderness—one where the enemy has enormous experience. The Iroquois way is not head-to-head—it is stealth. There may seem to be a frontal attack, but they always have others in reserve. You *never* know where. I believe we need to wait until we have more manpower."

"How much more?" de Lauzon asked.

"I fear a great deal more, Excellency. If you have seen these people in full attack, you would understand."

Clearly, Guillemot was not persuaded, and de Lauzon concluded, "We will be here a day or two. I'll give you my opinion when I leave, but in the end, it will be the decision of your military."

During the following two days, de Lauzon spoke to many people. He then examined the fort as well as the outlying wilderness, including the sight of the recent attack where evidence of the Iroquois ferocity was still evident. As he left, he told Guillemot, "You are in charge, sir, but if you want my opinion, it is to proceed with caution." Turning to Petit, he ordered, "Make a note of that."

The following morning the shallop set sail to Fort Richelieu. Once they were away, de Lauzon sat on the foredeck with Jacques-Henri. "How do you view Governor Guillemot's plan, sir?" Jacques-Henri looked up at the gathering clouds. "Suicide," was all he said. De Lauzon would not need a note to remember that.

That afternoon they saw the mouth of the Richelieu River and landed at the small outpost—a remnant of old Fort Richelieu. Commandant Durocher greeted them before giving a summary of their slow progress and recent experience, "We still have almost no citizens apart from the military. We have deflected a few minor raids, but I think the real problems remain farther upstream at *Ville-Marie* and beyond. Trappers who have been through have tales of progressive destruction of the Neutral and Erie tribes, but I'm certain you will find out more yourself at *Ville-Marie*."

The morning was dreary with persistent drizzle as Noël pointed his shallop upstream. "If we don't get more wind," he told the governor, "the current will carry us back to

Québec." By noon, the storm began and in spite of the drenching downpour, they began to make good progress to the big island. As they docked at the improved landing facility at the much-improved Fort *Ville-Marie*, Maisonneuve himself greeted them. "Captain, I am pleased to see you are still not hindered by a little moisture." Disembarking, Noël began introductions, "No need, Captain," Maisonneuve declared. "Jean de Lauzon and I were together at school in Paris—some years ago as I recall."

The sailors left the shallop for the dry refuge of the new fort, where Maisonneuve poured drinks for all. Noël thought to himself of the days when the man was not so welcoming. Shown to quarters, Noël, de Lauzon, Bergeron and Jacques-Henri were invited to dine with the governor once they were settled.

Accompanied by friendly conversation of two old school chums reliving the past, dinner was often amusing. Only after dishes were cleared, did Maisonneuve get down to business. "Unfortunately, gentlemen, things continue to deteriorate in spite of our improved facility. I have arranged to leave for France next season, and I am promised a large unit of men and supplies for my return. Until then, unfortunately, we are in desperate straits. Our sources report the Erie, Petun and Neutral tribes are hanging on to their last. The Huron are entirely gone from their home. Now they are living—or should I say subsisting—on islands in the Lake of the Huron. We had no fur trade this year and attacks on the outside have made it too dangerous. I am insisting all citizens remain within the walls unless they have specific permission from me." The conversation continued, but at the end of the evening, it was clear there was no relief in sight.

Noël retired in poor spirits only saved by a pleasant dream of his love, when he was awakened by shouting. "Fire! Fire in the hospital! The *Hôtel-Dieu* is aflame!"

Everyone rushed to the enormous plume of smoke and formed a bucket brigade. A few hours later, the fire was extinguished, but the hospital was all but gone. The nuns reported deaths of a few patients and two of their order. As they examined the ruins, Noël said, "We have had fires like this in *Québec*, at the church and convent, sometimes it is the fireplace, sometimes lightning…"

Jacques-Henri walked around the periphery picking up sticks. "This not lightning, or stoves," he declared. "This is Iroquois!" He then proceeded to show the evidence—how they entered the palisade and how they set the blaze. The throng returned to a sleepless night with fear of things worse than bad luck.

The men made it back to *Québec* without further incident. The towns upriver continued to be vigilant but saw no more major events. Winter descended, hostilities declined and Robert, Henri-Makya and Jacques-Henri headed north as planned.

CHAPTER 24

Northern Canadian wilderness: November 1651

"The mountain has more snow than the last time we saw it," Robert exclaimed to Henri-Makya as they beached their canoe on the large lake they had fished and hunted a few years earlier, "a lot more."

"Last time in June." Jacques-Henri reminded them at as he beached his much smaller canoe. Joining the two boys, he pointed to the opposite shore of the lake. "Gulley in red rock cliff is where we find river—big river to north. Get there tomorrow—if we get up before sun."

The boys had been this way twice since their first trip in 1646, both times with the fathers, and both times in the summer when sunlight was not at a premium. Françoise had finally relented at the end of the harvest and agreed to allow the two boys to take this epic voyage, but only if

Jacques-Henri accompanied them until he and they felt confident.

Landing across the large lake in the waning sunlight, they unloaded equipment needed to camp, leaving the rest in the canoe. Apart from ample warm clothes, and the Indian snowshoes that the French called *raquettes*, they had each brought bows and arrows. At Françoise's insistence, however, each brought a rifle as well. Jacques-Henri, of course, favored the bow. "Can always make arrow in wild—bullet and powder, not so easy."

Once the fire was hot, they cooked the fish caught earlier and sat against a large granite rock to eat, watching the remaining sun disappear. In the light of the fire, Jacques-Henri drew a map in the sand, "This route above lake—is all river for few days, *always* take fork to west. We come to mountains in one week—then up. Make sure you have landmark at bottom of mountain to find way home. Then, sun and stars are guides—like I teach you. First plateau of mountain is Algonquin village. You will be all right, but make sure you have this." He showed the amulet around his neck. He had made one for each of the boys. "It shows you are friend of my tribe. No one else up here but Algonquin...maybe some Mi'kmaq from east— but they friends." Although they had heard the instructions every day for two weeks, they still listened intently.

The boys were up, fed and ready to go as the first rays showed on the horizon. The lake was calm, allowing them to make good time all morning. By midday, the sky turned dark and a moderate north wind slowed their progress. The snow began two hours later and was heavy for a short while. Eventually it subsided, and they made their destination across the lake by sunset. As he began to set camp, Robert realized, in spite of the weather, he had not been cold. As Jacques-Henri had told them, "Hard work keep you warm, fear also help."

It was morning before they could clearly see their route. The opening in the red cliff was about twenty feet wide and the river flowing through it about ten. It was evident from the terrain that at times the river filled the canyon. "One difficult portage in river," Jacques-Henri warned, "and it is today."

Around midday, they came to a series of rapids. Obviously, this had to be portaged, but the portage was not apparent. Jacques-Henri led them to the western bank of the rapids where a thin path wandered slowly uphill. The boys each carried an end of their canoe, while Jacques-Henri hoisted his smaller craft over his head and led them up the narrow path. The left side was a sheer granite wall and the right, a violent flow of falls and rapids, the path between was less than three feet wide. Reaching the end, Robert was soaked in sweat, but his level of fear had diminished with the work effort. Happily, the narrow path became a wide expanse into a small meadow where the stream was wide and seemed almost tame. Launching the canoes, they paddled on.

Three days later, they came to a falls that rivaled Montmorency. From almost one-hundred feet up, the wall of water came crashing down to become the wide and gentle stream. "We leave canoes here," Jacques-Henri instructed and he took them to a thicket where a cave sat, made to order for canoe storage.

"Will they be safe?" Robert asked.

"This Algonquin country," Jacques-Henri replied. "Steal canoe worse than steal woman."

Making camp for the night, they rose to a bright, chilly morning. Packing their goods to carry, they suddenly realized they had brought too much. After some discussion, they put the less essential items back in the canoe and proceeded on. The path up the mountain almost seemed man-made, a wide track that snaked up and around the grand mountain. Robert wondered when they would reach the snow. It was sooner than he had expected. What began as strolling suddenly became drudging through the fluffy white. Soon they had to use their *raquettes* to walk on the deep snow.

Three days later, they came to a plateau where there was indeed a small Algonquin village. To the boys' surprise, the tribe greeted Jacques-Henri like a long-lost friend. Later he explained, "I was born here, but my father left to work with Jesuits when I was young. My family and I went with him." The tribe greeted the boys warmly and began to prepare a feast. Dancing and smoking went into the night. In the morning, Jacques-Henri was gone.

Beauport: Four days later

"My God, Félicity-Angel! Is nothing happening?"

"No, Miss Françoise. Baby not come."

"But it was small and early, my water broke hours ago— and, my God, I have delivered nine others. This one should fall out on the floor."

"Nothing happening, I send Marguerite for Sister Marie-Forestier two hours ago. She come soon. Maybe she know."

Soon the girl returned with the nun, and Félicity-Angel told her what she knew. "There are only a few things I have seen cause this," the nun replied. Putting her hand in Françoise's vagina, she said, "Félicity-Angel, push down on her abdomen, where the baby seems to be." The Indian pushed, the nurse probed and the patient screamed. "Wait," Sister Marie-Forestier said, "I feel something, maybe…oh, dear!" She pulled her hand out and softly told Félicity-Angel, "I thought I felt a foot, that is bad, but it was an arm—that is even worse."

"What we do?" Félicity-Angel asked.

The nun stepped away, motioning to the Indian to follow. "I have only seen this twice and heard about it a few times, the leg, or worse, the arm comes out first and the rest of the baby is hopelessly stuck in the womb."

"Then what?" Félicity-Angel asked. "What we do?"

"Pray." was the answer. "In all cases, both mother *and* child died."

Félicity-Angel stood with resolve. "Miss Françoise not die!" Motioning to Marguerite, "Come." Then she told the nun, "We be right back."

A short while later they entered the room with two large packages. The frantic nun told them, "She is starting to bleed more!"

Félicity-Angel put the packs on the bed and pointed to the side while she told Sister Marie-Forestier, "You stand here."

Then she took a small cloth and poured a liquid on it. The odor filled the room. Handing the cloth to Marguerite, she instructed, "Put over mother's mouth and nose, like this. After you breathe two times, take away, after you breathe two more, put back. Keep repeating."

The young lady nodded while Félicity-Angel took a large knife to the fireplace and held it over the flame. Returning to the bed, she handed two large cloths to the nun. "You hold down when I cut." She nodded to Marguerite who put the cloth on her mother's face while Félicity-Angel cut fearlessly down the midline of her

177

protruding abdomen. Sister Marie-Forestier pushed hard to stem the hemorrhage, and the Indian cut further.

A short while and great deal of blood later, she handed a small but active, blood-soaked infant to Marguerite. "Wrap in towel and hold, throw breathing cloth outside."

She then had the nun hold both sides of the wound while she took four hooks and pulled the uterine sides together. Then she applied a potion and put three hooks in the skin. Now she placed a number of cloths over the wound and began to wrap long strips around Françoise's abdomen with the help of Sister Marie-Forestier. "Must bind tight—stop blood."

As she watched in amazement while Françoise continued to breathe normally, the nun asked Félicity-Angel, "How often have you seen this?"

She gave an Indian shrug, "Never seen, mother told me once."

Marguerite had attended to the cord and washed her brother whom she was now rocking in the chair. "He's hungry. Should I go get one of the women in the *concession* to nurse him?"

Félicity-Angel said, "Bring him to his mother. She asleep—but ready." Marguerite brought him over and placed him at their mother's breast. "See," Félicity-Angel declared, "he know what to do."

Soon Françoise began to stir, as she opened her eyes, she realized where she was. "Dear God! What has happened?"

Sister Marie-Forestier came to her and gave a mild version of the event. "You poor thing," she concluded, "You must be in pain."

"Actually I'm not," Françoise replied.

Félicity-Angel came over and said with as much of a smile as she ever had, "Don't worry—is because of potion. You hurt plenty good in two hours."

The trip had exceeded the boys' wildest expectations. The association with Jacques-Henri's tribe had made it easier than they expected, and certainly safer than their mothers had feared, but they soon realized they had learned more and accomplished a great deal more the first week with the tribe than they would have done alone all winter. They had formed a special relationship with Mingan, a young man their age, whose name meant gray wolf. He and some of the other young men of the tribe accompanied them on short trips through the high country, teaching them hunting, trapping, exploration and basic survival skills while significantly improving their fluency in Algonquin.

When they inquired about a trip to the high white peak that had captured their attention some years before, Mignon's father advised them, "This is difficult venture—can take many weeks even months. In deep snow, best to take dogs."

The boys told him they had experience with their own sled dogs in *Québec*. Therefore, with the man's blessing the three boys planned the great adventure to end the trip. Just before they were to leave, Mignon's father came to them. "I have given this more thought. If you wish to learn well the outback wilderness, take Nixkamich, my father. He is also the master of the dogs."

The boys agreed, and later, when they were to meet, Mignon told them, "My grandfather is a great chief, but you will find him odd. He is very old and speaks his mind, but you will learn from him." Then he added, "The name Nixkamich means *Grandfather*. I do not know if anyone still knows his real name."

They went to the old man's hut where Mignon called him. The deerskin curtain opened as the withered face looked out before he stood. More than a head shorter than the shortest boy, his height was further compromised by a bent and crooked spine. His legs were bowed, his hands gnarled and his skin hung loosely from his frail skeleton. His white hair straggled to his shoulders, leaving his crown bald. Smiling, he showed only four well-worn teeth. When Mignon asked if he would accompany them, he merely nodded and returned to the warmth of his tent.

The following morning the boys were ready at daybreak. Aside from the bows and arrows, the old man allowed them to bring only one of the rifles with the understanding they were not to use it without his permission. They were to bring adequate clothes and other necessities but no food. "We go to get food," he explained. Each of the proposed two sleds held one seated passenger and the equipment. The second man stood on the back to control the six dogs per sled. When the boys arrived, they found Nixkamich reclined beneath the blankets of deerskin. When Mignon asked him where they should head, he pointed at the white mound, "Up," and pulled the skin blanket over his head.

Along the way the boys stopped a few times to shoot game. Although they encountered three small bands of deer, they were uniformly unsuccessful. As the sun began to set, Mignon suggested, "We had better make the shelter." Once their small tent was erected, Nixkamich crawled inside.

"I guess we go hungry tonight," Robert moaned. As they entered the small tent, they found their teacher chewing on a piece of meat from home. As they looked silently at his feast, he declared. "I say *you* cannot bring food." Finishing he threw his bone far into the darkness and crawled under two of the four skin blankets. The three neophytes huddled together with the remaining two.

The boys broke camp in the early morning, while Nixkamich dined on another piece of meat. "Today," he decreed, "go west. Better hunting."

Indeed, it was, and they shot two elk. Making camp, they skinned their kills. After cutting and storing most of the meat high in a tree, they devoured the rest. More satisfied than the night before, they sat by a small fire made entirely of items scavenged at camp. The old man said. "Now have enough food for three days—and more covers. Tomorrow, travel—only hunt if game come to us."

As the week played out, the lessons continued while the boys acquired more backwoods wisdom—how to travel and survive in brutal winter wilderness. When they made the summit of the domed mountain, the day was clear and cold, the wind but a breeze. The 360-degree view of the surrounding mountains was unimaginable to anyone who had never been, and for the first time in his life, Robert began to appreciate the total majesty of this land into which he had been born. That night, for the first time, the old man actually arose and walked about, going to each corner of the summit, singing a chant. The young men were soon chanting with him, chanting to a mystical force they had not previously known.

Snow began at night, and by morning, visibility had ceased to exist. "Must stay," the old man told them. "This why need two or three days food." The following morning was clear and Nixkamich showed the boys how to determine the side of the mountain to which the prevailing wind brought less snow. Here trees, rocks and caves were evident, and they could see how this could be used to their advantage. Eventually they started down. Each day was a textbook of lessons in the northern wilderness, its wonders and its evils.

Several days later, they began their final descent. The weather had improved and the boys were beginning to feel safe and competent in this wilderness. They stopped a bit early for the evening and Henri-Makya and Mignon began a fire, while Robert cleaned the small elk shot that day. Nixkamich lay in a layer of pelts on the sled.

The roar shook the earth, as the boys looked up in disbelief. A bear—not black but brown, with a giant head—twice the height of any they had seen near *Québec*. Robert moved slowly to his sled and put his hand under the cover to get the rifle. It was not there! He then took his bow and began to back up, looking in panic at Nixkamich, who sat quietly looking at Robert. The old man slowly pointed his finger at the bridge of his nose.

Robert took the clue, pulled his bow back, and let the arrow hit the beast exactly between the eyes. The monster roared. He was clearly not dead, but it did seem to confuse him. As it stood to nearly twice Robert's height, the old man pointed to his left chest. Robert took the shot straight on and succeeded in making the bear even more ferocious. This ballet continued with Nixkamich giving direction and Robert taking shots. He recalled his father's tale of the black bear in *Québec*, brought down only by Pierre Boucher's rifle. Finally, the beast fell and Robert stepped forward. The old man, however, cautioned him to stop. He then picked up and threw a rock, hitting the animal on the head without a response. Nixkamich rose slowly from his sleigh and retrieved Robert's rifle from under his cover. Handing it over, he said calmly, "Do not need rifle."

CHAPTER 25

Beauport: Early April 1652

"It looks like he is coming around to normal size," Noël estimated as he stroked the dark hair of his new son and namesake.

"Well," Françoise began, as she handed young Noël to his father and stood to stretch. "He was a better eater than even Jean-Louis—in spite of the difficult birth, but I knew he'd be a fighter if I named him for you."

"Took long enough," her husband complained as he carried his son over to an open window and looked out. "Speaking of sons, I hope our oldest gets home soon. I need him to work the *concession*." Opening the door, he stepped out on the porch. "Going to be a warm spring, I think." Looking around the back, he said, "Well, speak of the devil!"

Françoise came to look and screamed as she rushed to her first born, almost knocking him over with an embrace. Pulling back, she looked him over, "My God, what did they do to you?" He had gained considerable weight, entirely in muscle, and had long straggly hair with a matching beard. Robert simply shrugged, as his mother pulled his hand, "Come. Meet your new brother."

Going up the porch, he called, "Hey! Pa."

"I'd shake your hand," Noël told him, "But this guy's becoming a handful."

"You didn't name him another Jean-something, did you?"

"No," his father answered, "she finally named one for me. But come on in, we want to hear all about it."

"Ok, Pa, but first I got something I brought for you and Ma. I have to get Henri-Makya to help me carry it up."

As he ran back, his mother wondered, "What in the world...?"

Soon the two boys came struggling with the mammoth bundle. Once they were up on the porch, Robert said, "Oh good, it will fit through the door."

When they had the fur in the main room, he announced, "I think it will fit in here," and they began to unroll the bearskin. When it was open on the floor, it did take up a considerable space. "It's a bear, but a brown one, not a black one." When Nixkamich had helped the boys skin the monster, he also showed them how to keep the enormous head attached. Four-year old Jean-Louis, the only child apart from the newborn not at school, cautiously touched the monster's head. "Is it real, Robert?"

"Yes, Jean-Louis, maybe you can come with us someday." The boy stroked the fur, "Really?"

"Who shot it?" Françoise queried.

185

"I did, Ma," he told her, bursting with pride.

"See?" she said triumphantly, "Aren't you glad you brought the rifles?"

"I didn't use a rifle, Ma, I got it with arrows."

"Impossible!"

"It's true, Ma."

His mother took his hand, "Come sit at the table, I'll make tea and you can tell us everything." Just as they were seated, his siblings burst in from school. Pandemonium reigned as they hugged their brother, examined the bear, all asking questions at the same time. "Everybody!" Françoise shouted as she stood. "Sit down and be still! Robert will speak and then you can all ask questions."

Conversation blended into dinner and after, sitting around the fire. As the younger children retired to their lofts, Noël told his eldest son. "I hope you're not too tired. I need you to start visiting the *concession* with me tomorrow, because the following day, I must take the first shallop run upriver to *Ville-Marie,* and you will need to finish."

Three weeks later, Noël landed back at *Québec* and headed straight for the fort. Governor de Lauzon wanted his reports immediately. "I don't like hearing news from town before I hear it from my men," he explained. The governor's secretary, *Monsieur* Petit, met Noël at the office entry.

"Oh, good!" Petit exclaimed. "His Excellency has been waiting to hear from you. He is in a meeting with the council, but I am to interrupt him." Smiling, he added, "He feels your report is more important."

The governor exited the room almost immediately and hustled Noël into his private office. "Well, Captain, how bad is the news?"

Noël shrugged as he was seated, "Nothing totally unexpected, Excellency. The people in *Trois-Rivières* are staying close to the fort and seem to be all right. There have been a few minor attacks on the periphery, but no reports of deaths of citizens. Unfortunately, the governor and Captain Boucher continue to be at odds. Guillemot continues to plan for an attack by his *flying column,* and Boucher remains skeptical."

"I have given this a good bit of thought," de Lauzon replied. "Guillemot is in charge and who knows? He may be correct. At any rate, I cannot second-guess every decision by the authorities in the countryside. I'm going to let it play out."

Noël did not agree but moved on to other issues without comment. "The post at River Richelieu remains understaffed. They have not had any major issues, but Commandant Durocher fears they miss a number of hostiles coming downstream to the *Saint-Laurent.* As before, *Ville-Marie* is the most precarious. Maisonneuve continues to restrict citizens from leaving the fort without permission and has suffered a few losses among those who have gone outside. The word is the Iroquois have killed or chased off all Huron from the island of St. Joseph in the north of the Lake of the Hurons. Those that fled have gone to Manitoulin Island and are barely surviving. Governor Maisonneuve did tell me he will come to *Québec* on one of the late summer shallops in time to take a ship to France to try to raise more soldiers and citizens."

"I pray he is successful," de Lauzon replied. "More soldiers will be critical. I, too, am sending requests for aid and reinforcements."

Noël left for the canoe dock and home. There was some information he had not passed on, as he believed it was personal. Upon arrival, he was greeted by the Langlois hoard. The children were filled with stories of school, Robert had a detailed report on the *concession*, and Françoise revealed young Noël's new skills. Following dinner, he told the children to clean up and go study while he took his wife to the porch for a glass of Calvados on a clear, but chilly night.

"I'm afraid I have some bad news from the Boucher family. Pierre's wife, son and mother have all died."

Obviously stunned, Françoise only uttered, "What…?"

"There was an outbreak of measles in the fort. Among those affected were Marie-Madeline, young Jacques and Nicole."

"Oh my God! How could Nicole…?"

"Gaspard said she thought she had them when very young. I guess she was incorrect."

His wife sobbed for a while, then moved close to her husband as they sat silently, contemplating the dangers of the wilderness and the precarious nature of life.

Québec: Late August 1652:

Coming up to check the ship logs, Noël was surprised to see Abraham Martin at the *Taverne Terre Sauvage* with none other than Benoît and Bernier. "Abraham," he called, "I thought you were still upriver."

"Got back last night, been up meeting with de Lauzon, now I'm meeting with these two."

"How was it?" Noël asked as he sat.

"Not good, my friend—not good at all. You will hear about it soon, might as well get it from me." Noël signaled for a beer as his friend proceeded, "It seems there have been a few raids at Cap-de-la-Madeleine, that small post

188

across the *Rivière-Saint-Maurice* from *Trois-Rivières*. Well, our friend Guillemot decided to take action and took a band of soldiers and citizens out looking for Iroquois. They found them—and how! His flying *whatever* was absolutely slaughtered. Twenty-two soldiers and citizens as well as his Excellency—all dead. Apparently, a member of almost every family was involved. There is even talk about abandoning the town."

"What about Pierre Boucher?" Noël questioned with a very worried look.

"He didn't agree with Guillemot's plan and stayed back with a few men—damn good thing. He is upset, but says he is going to give it a go. I think de Lauzon will make him governor. About time if you ask me."

"What do you men think?" Noël asked the two voyageurs.

"Like I said before," Benoît began, "know your enemy, and until somebody shows them damn Iroquois it ain't the Huron, or the French, but the damn English, this ain't never going to get solved."

"One good thing," Abraham added, "I brought back Maisonneuve, and he's getting on the ship to France due in a couple days to go get more help."

Three weeks later, Noël returned home from visiting the *concession* with Robert. "I received a post today," his wife announced, "it's from Gaspard Boucher." Reading slowly she told him, "He says Pierre has remarried, a local girl named Jeanne Crevier. Her parents are Normand—from Rouen. They came in 1639 to *Trois-Rivières* and her father owns a *concession*. Pierre's new wife is just sixteen years old, and Pierre was named governor of *Trois-Rivières* as

189

you predicted. Gaspard says he has a great deal of issues, but knows Pierre can handle them."

"I suspect he can," Noël replied. "I have some news as well. Today, Robert told me he wants to return to the northern wilderness again this winter. I asked him about help with the *concession*. He suggests I let Jean-Pierre handle it. He may be correct. Jean-Pierre does seem to have more interest in it than Robert."

CHAPTER 26

Québec: November 1, 1652

Bringing his tea to the porch rocker, Noël sat to enjoy a cool autumn morning as the sun began to peek over the horizon of *Île d'Orléans*. His real reason, however, was to watch Robert and Henri-Makya at the river, loading their canoe with the equipment for their winter excursion north. Accepting that Robert was determined to abandon land baron for backwoodsman, Noël had given the task of assisting on the *concession* to Jean-Pierre. Although the lad was only 12, he had an interest and a talent for the work. When Noël could not accompany the boy, he sought the help of a young neighbor, Paul Vachon. Only 22, Paul had come to Canada as a young mason two years before and had sought training as a *notaire*. He would soon be in charge of making and keeping records of marriages, births, deaths, deeds and other legal documents for the colony. This skill made him ideal to assist young Jean-Pierre.

Having said their goodbyes to their families the evening before, Robert and Henri-Makya were unaware of their audience. As the sun reached tree level, they pushed off and headed for the river to the north while Noël took his tea and returned to the house.

"Did the boys get away?" Françoise asked as she began to prepare breakfast for her brood.

"Yes," he replied, "It looks as though the weather will be good." Taking a piece of meat from her frying pan, he said, "I had better get to the docks. I will eat there. This will, hopefully, be my last trip upriver this season."

Troyes, France: Congregation of Notre-Dame, the same day

Mother Louise de Sainte-Marie hurried through the halls to the chapel where she would meet with lay members of the Confraternity of Notre-Dame. Before reaching it, one of the nuns stopped her. "Sister, there is a gentleman here to see you."

"I am due to meet with the lay sisters," she responded, "What does he want?"

"I'm not certain, but he does look quite important."

Mother Louise hesitated, "I suppose I should go see. Where is he?"

"In the confraternity office, Sister," the nun replied, "I will take you to him."

With some reluctance, Mother Louise diverted to the office. Entering she saw a familiar face. "Goodness! It cannot be you. You are a world away."

"Not today," said Maisonneuve. "I can't come to France without visiting my favorite sibling."

"I was supposed to meet with the lay sisters of the confraternity," she reported, "however, that can wait. Let us go into the garden and visit."

As they strolled through the elaborate convent gardens, Maisonneuve explained, "I must confess, though I dearly love to visit you, I do have an ulterior motive."

The nun smiled, "No different than when you were a small boy. What do you need?"

The governor explained his position in *Ville-Marie* as well as the problems at hand. "I am here to recruit soldiers and settlers. We also desperately need nuns to teach the citizens and the natives."

"I expect we can find some of the good sisters who are up to the challenge."

"There is one issue, however," Maisonneuve admitted. "The nature of the mission would not be suitable for cloistered sisters."

His sibling frowned, "I see. Well, why don't I call a meeting where you can present your case?"

That evening Maisonneuve dined at the convent with his sister, who spread the word among the congregation. The following day he spoke, describing the needs and nature of the project. A large number of nuns came forward with interest, but none felt they could break with their cloistered vows. Finally one of the head nuns suggested, "We do have one young lady who is dedicated to working with and teaching the poor, but she is not ready for the cloister, she prefers to work outside the convent with the neediest. The Carmelite nuns turned her down due to her refusal to be cloistered. We should discuss this with her. Her name is

Bourgeoys—Marguerite Bourgeoys. She is from right here in Troyes."

The next day, Maisonneuve and his sister met with Marguerite Bourgeoys. A large, plain young woman, she was intelligent and well spoken. As Maisonneuve described the situation, her interest was obvious. Ultimately, she agreed to travel with him to the new world. At the end of his journey to France in late February of 1653, Maisonneuve set sail for the new world, bringing over 100 soldiers and settlers, but to his disappointment, only one lay sister—Maisonneuve, however, would not be disappointed with Marguerite Bourgeoys for long.

<u>*Québec*: August 15, 1653 (Ten months later)</u>

Finishing her day volunteering at the hospital of the *Hôtel-Dieu*, François met her neighbor, Anne-Ardouin, at *L'Auberge Oie Bleue* for tea. "Isn't that your husband?" Anne asked, pointing to a man hurrying across the square.

"It is—with Abraham Martin—and Jacques-Henri." Françoise stood and called, "Noël!" As the two men came to the table, she said, "I thought you were to be at the docks all day."

"We were," Abraham reported short of breath, "but we had an urgent message from Governor de Lauzon to meet at the fort—immediately."

"It seems," Noël added, "there was a very large Iroquois raid on *Trois-Rivières.*"

"Oh, dear God! What happened?"

"It may not be as bad as it sounds," her husband reassured. "We heard Pierre and his men held them off to the point the Iroquois are willing to surrender and sign a treaty."

"Praise the Lord!" Anne-Ardouin Badeau exclaimed.

"We have little time," Noël continued, "We are to meet at the fort immediately and after a short meeting be ready to sail upriver. We hear de Lauzon is fitting the two largest shallops with cannon for show. We may be gone some time—perhaps several weeks. He will send periodic reports to the city to keep you and others informed. The notaries, Paul Vachon and Madame Badeau's son, Jean, are coming. Jean-Pierre will have to manage the *concession* without Vachon or me. I know Robert has showed little interest since his return from his last trip north, but tell him he must aid Jean-Pierre until my return." He stood kissing his wife on the forehead. "We must run."

As the men disappeared around the road to the fort, Anne-Ardouin said, "This will be wonderful—to have some real peace at last."

"Yes," Françoise answered, "but do not hold your hopes too high. Nicole used to say, 'If something sounds too good to be true, it probably is.'"

Entering the fort office, Noël and Abraham joined a long table of officers and city officials just as the governor began. "It seems that more than a week ago, six-hundred Mohawk surrounded the fort at *Trois-Rivières.* I know this sounds impossible, but Captain Boucher and his men held them off patiently while systematically killing attackers. Eventually the chief surrendered and met with Captain Boucher who reports they are ready to sign a treaty—with all of French Canada!" Following a large hubbub, he continued, "I know this sounds unlikely; however, I believe we must go, put up our strongest front, and press for peace." He then announced who would go on which shallop, and the meeting adjourned for the docks where they set sail upstream.

Two days later, approaching the small harbor of *Trois-Rivières,* the men saw the fort sitting tranquil without much damage. In addition, a large band of Iroquois had set a camp outside the walls where they went peacefully about their business. More astonishing yet was the sight of a few French Canadians walking peacefully about the camp visiting with the natives. Noël and Abraham accompanied the officers to the fort while Jacques-Henri went to find the Iroquois chief.

In the fort, Pierre Boucher greeted them and took them to a meeting area where he reported. "They appeared *en masse* two weeks ago. We brought everyone into the fort while the Iroquois surrounded it. Fortunately, they could not break through our new fortifications. Our marksmen picked off as many as possible each time they charged. Our losses were relatively small, but as the days wore on, our men became fatigued and our supplies dwindled to almost nothing. At nine days, we had only 40 able men. Just when I thought we would have to surrender, they approached with a flag of truce. The chief has agreed to return all prisoners, be they French or Indian to us within forty days, and they will also come to *Québec* and *Ville-Marie* to seal the peace. He is leaving six children with us as a sign of trust. They are also declaring peace with the Algonquin— but not the Erie and others who will remain in jeopardy."

"It sounds as if you have solved almost everything," de Lauzon remarked.

"Not quite, sir—if you could stay a few days and we can arrange meetings with the chief and elders, I think it will help secure things." With the hint of a smile, he added,

"Also, if you can leave a ship's cannon with the fort, I think it will make an impression."

The following morning, Jacques-Henri appeared, having spent the night visiting with the Iroquois chief. "This man now sees war with French is too costly. They do, however, still want large part of fur trade. They believe they can live with Algonquin, but will continue to battle remaining Huron and their related tribes. I believe this may make Beaver Wars less bloody, but they will not go away." Pointing to his French audience, he concluded, "And do not forget, this peace is *only* with Mohawk tribe of the Iroquois Nation."

Governor de Lauzon did negotiate and sign a treaty with the Mohawk tribe to include peace with all of French Canada as well as the Algonquin tribes in the northeast. Following the celebration, the Mohawk headed west to take on the remaining Erie tribe, while the *Québécois* sailed downriver where they would soon hear more good news.

Québec: September 22, 1653

The sailing ship *Saint-Nicolas* was rather inconspicuous as French ships of the 17th century went—a simple three-mast craft, it did not cause any more excitement than any other ship as Abraham Martin brought it to the dock. However, when the gangplank lowered, Governor Maisonneuve disembarked with a broad smile. Rumors were spreading through the port even before de Lauzon appeared to welcome him.

When Noël arrived home from the docks, his wife was waiting inside for him. "I hear Maisonneuve returned today," she declared, demonstrating the speed which news flew through the colony.

"Yes," her husband confirmed, "He has over 100 top rate soldiers and a large number of new citizens. He also brought what appeared to be a solitary nun. I'm not certain what that means. What I do know is they are staying awhile in *Québec* to make plans. Along with peace with the Mohawk, this may bode very well for the French." Before his wife could reply, he added, "I have another piece of interesting news."

"What could be more interesting than this?" she questioned.

"On my way up to the house, I saw Paul Vachon who had been visiting our *concessions*."

"How could that be more interesting?"

Noël smiled, "He asked if he could call on our Marguerite."

Her smile broadened. "How wonderful! Anne-Ardouin next door told me he and her son are both getting *concessions* in Beauport and they are likely to become well-to-do. Just think, two of our girls married to *Sous-Sieurs*. Does Marguerite know?"

He replied with a laugh, "What do you think? By now half of *Québec* knows."

"We shall have to make preparations," she told him.

"You had better hurry," he told her. "He is coming Saturday night."

Two weeks later, Françoise was finishing her day at the *Hôtel-Dieu* hospital when one of the other volunteers approached her. "Françoise," she began, "we haven't visited for an age and I wonder if you have time to join me at *L'Auberge Oie Bleue* this afternoon."

Marie-Geneviève Juchereau was Noël's cousin from *Perche*. She and her husband had travelled to the new world with the Langlois in 1634. Marie-Geneviève and Françoise had shared a terrifying stormy night at sea when they were the only two women aboard who were not disabled by seasickness. The two women saw each other at the hospital and occasionally in town, but Françoise always felt separated by station.

Marie-Geneviève had been born into the same rank as Noël but married Jean Juchereau, a member of the old Company of 100 Associates and the current Council of *Québec*. Jean was a rich fur merchant and possibly the richest man in *Québec*. *Seigneur* of the entire concession of *Cap-Rouge* along the *Fleuve Saint-Laurent*, just upriver of the city, Jean and his wife lived on possibly the most elegant estate in Canada.

Françoise agreed to lunch and the two women left work on a fine autumn day, strolling to the *Auberge*, sharing thoughts of the old days that now seemed more exciting and romantic than they had been. When seated, Marie-Geneviève ordered wine in place of the usual tea. "I understand," she began, "your daughter is to marry young Paul Vachon."

"Yes," Françoise answered, wondering what this was about.

"Jean has worked with him on some financial and legal issues. He says he is a fine young man with a grand future."

"He has worked with Noël on the *concession*," Françoise replied. "We are very pleased."

"What I wanted to ask," Marie-Geneviève explained, "is would they let us hold the wedding at our home?" Françoise's mouth dropped open, "Well…"

Realizing the awkward position, Marie-Geneviève added, "I know this is unusual, but it was actually Jean's idea. He was looking out the other night and said, 'This would be a fine setting for a wedding.' All three of our children have married and gone. He has a great respect for *Monsieur* Vachon, Noël has been helpful to him—and Noël *is* my cousin." After a moment of silence, she added, "I know this is sudden and unusual, but ask your family and let me know. We can make any or all the arrangements."

"Thank you," Françoise answered with a smile, "I am certain Marguerite will approve." Standing, she added, "Now I must go do a lesson at the Ursuline Convent."

"Oh, what lesson?"

"There is a woman just arrived from France, Marguerite Bourgeoys. She is a lay sister who is to help with the native and French children in *Ville-Marie*. I am helping her learn Algonquin."

"Jean told me about her," Marie-Geneviève said with enthusiasm, "Could I go with you?"

Crossing the large square toward the Ursuline Convent, Marie-Geneviève asked about Marguerite Bourgeoys. "She is from Troyes, east of Paris," Françoise explained, "She went to join the sisters there but could not accept cloister and was not allowed to take vows. She stayed as a lay sister in what they call the confraternity, an organization that accepts laywomen who have not taken vows—I find it a little confusing. Anyway, when Governor Maisonneuve of *Montréal* went to see his sister, he met Marguerite. He wanted sisters to help with the children, native and French. They, however, must work outside of the organization and not be cloistered. Marguerite was perfect, and he hopes to find more like her. You will enjoy her. Her energy is boundless."

Warm for an October day, the trees still held much of their red and gold, but the light breeze off the land provided the occasional shower of color falling to decorate the lawn. Looking from the *Cap* high above the *Fleuve Saint-Laurent* to the southern bank beyond, Françoise told her husband, "I remembered it was beautiful here, but this is more than beautiful!" The guests gathered on the lawn as servants served drinks and refreshments. Jean Juchereau had offered a string orchestra, but Françoise and Marie-Geneviève had insisted on local music, so Jean Guyon and a number of other fiddle, drum and horn players performed traditional French country music. By midafternoon, the wind shifted in true *Québec* style to the north and the flurry of color soon became a flurry of white.

"Have no fear," Jean Juchereau announced to the guests, "We will adjourn to the ballroom."

The home was nearly as large as the governor's mansion, and the interior more ornate. Étienne Fortin continued to provide libation and dinner as the *Québécois* danced into the darkness before boarding their carts and heading home. Noël and Françoise took the newlyweds to their new home on Vachon's new *concession* conveniently located by her parents' place.

As they returned home, Françoise told her husband, "I can't believe *Monsieur* Juchereau would do all that for our children."

Her husband chuckled, "*Monsieur* Juchereau is a businessman, my dear, and he expects to get more than his return from your son-in-law as his career progresses."

Three weeks later, Governor Maisonneuve took his one-hundred new soldiers and nearly as many new citizens along with his solitary lay sister and headed back home to *Ville-Marie*. Three days later, Robert Langlois and Henri-Makya headed north just after Robert informed his father he may not come home that summer. As he watched them paddle off with a tear beginning in his eye, Noël realized he had not heard of the Beaver Wars since the peace at *Trois-Rivières*.

CHAPTER 27

Québec: Christmas day 1653 (Two months later)

To signal the end of Christmas mass, the bells of *Notre-Dame de la Paix* chimed joyfully as the faithful exited onto the square, squinting in the glorious sunlight reflecting off a new layer of snow that had coated the ground overnight. "What an absolutely glorious day!" Anne-Ardouin Badeau exclaimed, as she joined a few Beauport families in the square. "We never had winter days like this in *La Rochelle*. Winter was always gray and rainy."

"Some winters I would gladly endure rain," Perrine Boucher declared, "compared to the snow drifting over the roofs."

"Well," Anne replied, "this amount is perfect, only ankle deep."

"Jacques-Henri," Françoise related, "told me the holy man in the Algonquin village predicted this would be the worst winter in a generation."

"Oh, what does he know?" Perrine replied.

"Jacques-Henri claims he has never been wrong," Françoise told her, "and I put great stock in Jacques-Henri. At any rate, today is lovely and we are going to *L'Auberge Oie Bleue* to see Agnes-Anne and her husband, Jean-Claude." Putting her arm around Noël's, she led him in the direction of the inn. "It will only be us today," she whispered, "The children have an activity at the convent school and *Monsieur* Juchereau has invited Marguerite and Paul to his estate."

"Juchereau has Paul working on some land agreements," Noël related. "I knew he had plans for Paul, and I suspect they are going to advance his career."

When they reached the inn, they saw their daughter and son-in-law, Jean-Claude Pelletier, at a table. As soon as they sat, Françoise asked, "Did you see the midwife?"

"Yes, Mother," Agnes-Anne answered with some degree of irritation.

"And?"

Her daughter grinned, "She says I should be due about May!"

Françoise embraced her while Noël shook his son-in-law's hand. "Congratulations!"

Now 16, Agnes-Anne had decided it was time to stop chewing the Indian root. As predicted—and now confirmed, she conceived after her next monthly. The Langlois were at least as excited about becoming grandparents as Agnes-Anne and Jean-Claude were about becoming parents.

The day remained clear, while the *Québécois* sat around the tables discussing current issues. No one mentioned the Beaver Wars, which now seemed far away. Eventually they took their carts, now sleighs, and headed home. By the time they reached Beauport, the blizzard of a generation had begun to blow—as predicted by the Algonquin holy man.

Four weeks later, *Québec* lay buried in snow. Commerce in the city was at a standstill. All citizens remained in their homes where keeping fires burning and chimneys open was a daily ordeal, and the only available food was that stored before the great series of blizzards started. By the end of March, the slow melt began and ice and collapsing snow became primary concern of the citizens.

The Northern Wilderness: the same day

The difficult winter had been equally as brutal on Robert, Henri-Makya, and Mingan as they traveled snow-choked mountain passes. The failing health of the elderly Nixkamich had prevented him from accompanying the young men this season, but his tutelage had left them ready for the task. Along the way, they acquired another fellow traveler, a young man named Keme, from a nearby village. Together the four had weathered the most difficult season in memory, and as the weather began to break, they were quite proud of the feat. Now they were on their way back to the village, planning to arrive within a few days.

Normally, they hunted with their sled dogs, but today they were short of food and the presence of the dogs might frighten game away. Leaving the canines in camp, they walked silently on their *raquettes,* which allowed them to maneuver on top of the seemingly bottomless snow without frightening any prey desperate enough to leave its lair.

Approaching the summit of a mountain peak, Keme heard the sound of animals. Signaling his fellows to remain silent, he listened, but the sound of the creatures had disappeared, replaced by the growing sound of breaking snow. Keme held up his hand, alerting all to be still as he listened. It started as a ripple, and then began to groan. Soon it became thunder as they felt the awful sensation of snow moving under their feet.

Beauport: two weeks later

"I can scarcely believe we are all going to town," Françoise declared as Jean-Pierre brought the cart around. The worst winter in memory had caused most families to be homebound since Christmas, and only the occasional errand by dogsled allowed the Beauport residents any access to the city. The main outdoor activities were clearing snow from roofs and chimneys with the rare sled ride to hunt for nearby game.

Happily, winter was finally departing with the same rate it had arrived, as the sun returned, melting the snow with surprising speed. The significant slope from the Beauport homes to the river provided much-needed runoff, controlling the worst early flooding. Now the water over the heavy ice cover began to flow to the sea as the ice started to break.

The family climbed aboard, heading to the bridge over *Riviére Saint-Charles* and the road to the upper town. The church bell tolled as they approached for the first mass they had attended since Christmas. Françoise saw the person she was looking for and jumped off to join the crowd on the front steps. "My God, Agnes-Anne, you look ready to deliver right now," she declared as she patted her daughter's enlarging abdomen.

"The midwife says two more months," Agnes-Anne announced, "but Félicity-Angel came by with Jacques-Henri and she said the middle of May."

"She is always very accurate," Françoise agreed as she took her daughter's arm and entered the church.

Following mass, the families made their way to *L'Auberge Oie Bleue* to enjoy the brightest, warmest day so far this year. The Beauport families, as well as those from the upper town, had survived the brutal winter. Three of the new *engager* had succumbed, however, to the cold, all from not treating the *Québec* winter with the proper respect. When they rose to find their sleighs, Françoise said suddenly, "Dear God, I see a patch of grass."

The worst Canadian winter in memory was indeed approaching its end.

Québec: May 17, 1654

Spring appeared as always—snow melted, ice departed, songbirds returned to the meadows and, as predicted by Félicity-Angel, Agnes-Anne went into labor. Françoise had moved temporarily to the upper town to be close when the time came and brought her favorite midwife, Félicity-Angel. Following a prolonged labor, Noël-Guillaume Pelletier was born. "I named him after his two grandfathers," Agnes-Anne explained, but for brevity, he became Noël-Guy.

Three days later, Françoise deemed it safe to return home. Arriving at the Langlois house, she saw Noël and Jacques-Henri talking to an unknown native on the bank. When she saw her husband's face, she knew it meant bad news. Noël had Françoise and Félicity-Angel along with the two Indian men come sit on the porch where he began. "This is Ahmik, Jacques-Henri's brother. He has come down from the camp in the north with bad news."

Immediately sensing this was something bad about her son, Françoise held her breath, remaining silent while Ahmik began. "This winter our three boys, Henri-Makya, Robert, and my boy, Mingan, went to hunt in northern wild. Old chief, Nixkamich, who accompanied them in past, was gravely ill but gave permission for boys to go alone. He taught them well over past two years. They planned to stay out until late in season, so when they not return when great snow melted, we not concerned."

"Some sled dogs returned untethered and alone few weeks ago. We send three men to investigate—it easy to find as dogs led them. They had been hunting on great slope after big snow this year. They caught in avalanche."

Struggling from her shock, Françoise asked, "How did you know…?"

Anticipating the question, Ahmik explained, "My son and Henri-Makya, well preserved in snow, even find Algonquin Amulet on Henri-Makya."

"What of the third boy?" she questioned, trying to hold back her tears.

"He not as easy to identify," he replied.

"But why?" she asked.

Ahmik only shrugged, choosing not to tell the mother he was mauled after death—apparently by a wolf. Noël took his sobbing wife to the house. In the wilderness of Canada, joy and tragedy frequently crossed paths. The natives had buried the boys near the Algonquin village, but at Françoise's insistence on June 19, 1654, they placed a memorial stone for Robert Langlois in the church graveyard. A few days later, she returned alone to mourn. "I remember," she whispered, "when I was near death from the Iroquois arrow, you told me you knew God would not let me die." She began to sob, "I thought the same about you—but I was wrong." She fell to her knees and cried until she had no more tears.

CHAPTER 28

Fleuve Saint-Laurent: September 29, 1654

"Certainly a gorgeous day for a sail," Governor de Lauzon declared as the shallop approached the docks at _Trois-Rivières._ "Yes, sir," Noël replied, adding, "I would like to thank you again for allowing me to bring my friends. This ceremony means a great deal to them."

"Think nothing of it, Captain," de Lauzon replied, "It is special for me as well. I recall when you introduced me to him when he was very young. He has certainly turned into a great leader."

While Noël brought the craft to the dock, all his _Percheron_ friends gathered on the foredeck. "Look!" shouted Perrine Boucher, "there he is!" They all waved as Pierre signaled back, accompanied by a few soldiers, his father, Gaspard, and his wife, Jeanne, who held the hand of their two-year-old son. At 33, Pierre Boucher had risen to great heights.

"Hello, Governor," de Lauzon said, "how nice of you to greet us."

"It is my pleasure, Excellency." Pierre returned, "However, it will not be Governor until after the ceremony." His friends and relatives traded handshakes and hugs before he escorted them to the new, much improved, fort. Following a tour and dinner, he showed them to their quarters, and at noon the next day, they attended the ceremony. A cadre of soldiers marched while the band, consisting of a drum, two trumpets and Gaspard Boucher on his Jew's harp, played military music.

Several local residents spoke followed by de Lauzon himself. "It is always a pleasure to advance a soldier to the rank of governor of his region, and *Trois-Rivières* should be proud of their new leader..." He continued to list Pierre's many successful battles as well as his ability to govern his region, not missing the opportunity to laud him for such success at a young age. That evening there was dinner and a "ball" where the same band became orchestra. Sitting at their table, Françoise related, "The first time I met Pierre in *Mortagne*, he was eight years old, but even then it was apparent he was special—very special. I only wish his mother could..." she wiped a tear from her eye, then stood and took her husband's hand, "Dance with me, my dear, it has been a while."

The following morning, the ladies gathered around Pierre's new wife and son, while the men met in Pierre's office. De Lauzon began with the ever-present question, "How are you doing with the local Iroquois?"

"Rather well," Pierre answered. "There have been a few local skirmishes, but nothing serious, usually about women or liquor. I understand the real activity is well to the southwest by the Lake of the Erie. I fear that tribe will be extinct in a few years. My biggest fear, however, is what will happen then. The Iroquois have an instinctual need for battle and once the Erie are gone, they will turn elsewhere—I pray it is not here."

"What do you hear of *Ville-Marie?*" de Lauzon's chief officer inquired.

"I was there only three weeks ago. I met with Governor Maisonneuve. He is very encouraged. With his new citizens and soldiers from France, building is booming and they believe they finally have a viable defense."

"What about the lady from Troyes?" Noël asked.

"Marguerite Bourgeoys is real jewel for the territory. She is starting a school and building a confraternity of laywomen to help with it as well as the church. Her biggest issue is the lack of children. This stems from not only the relative paucity of women we see everywhere but also several outbreaks of measles, which have taken a toll on their newborn survival. She has been in contact with France and is hopeful to begin a program to bring more marriageable women to Canada."

Two days later, the shallop returned the group to *Québec*, and that evening, Françoise and Noël sat on their porch, enjoying one of the last warm evenings of autumn. "I saw Jean-Claude Pelletier in town today," Noël reported. "He told me if the baby continues to do well, they are going to move next spring to his *concession* near Montmorency. He has a man from France who knows sawmills and is putting one at the falls next year. Jean-Claude and Agnes-Anne will be half owners. Along with his *concession* he should do extremely well."

Looking off at the moon rising over the water, Françoise said. "That means both our married girls will be our neighbors in Beauport and with Paul Vachon's business, it looks as if both the children will be even more well-to-do than we." As she gazed back over the river, she added with a smile, "Why don't you get the Calvados? I feel like celebrating."

CHAPTER 29

Québec: Three years later, August 1657

"I guess I don't know the difference," Noël told his spouse. "Jesuits have been around for a long while and do a good deal of missionary work. That is why they are in Canada. The Sulpicians are a newer order, but they also do missionary..." Shrugging his shoulders, he said, "I guess I just don't know, other than Maisonneuve and d'Ailleboust seem to like these Sulpicians. They went to France, brought four back with them, and I am to take them to _Ville-Marie_—maybe I will know the difference when I get back, but now I need to go to the port and make arrangements for the voyage."

The past three years had been relatively uneventful. There continued to be occasional local skirmishes with the Iroquois who had all but annihilated the Erie Nation. The main issues for the colony remained slow fur trade due to native hostilities as well as the diminishing beaver population, but the more important issue was the slow French population growth due to the continued lack of women from France. When Noël returned for dinner, he announced, "We leave in the morning, but the governor asked that I bring you."

"Me?" she asked, "Why me?"

"He seems to value your judgement," he replied, collapsing into a porch rocker. "He also wants to bring Jacques-Henri and Félicity-Angel. To be honest, I think he fears these men are not clear about what they are getting into."

In the morning, they gathered at the docks with their fellow passengers. Along with the usual soldiers and citizens traveling to one of the outposts, they had Maisonneuve, d'Ailleboust, Father Gabriel de Queylus and his 3 young Sulpician assistants. Prior to boarding, d'Ailleboust warned Noël and Françoise some of the missionaries had spent the bulk of the crossing vomiting over the side of the ship. Today, however, the priests were pleased to meet their shipmates, admitting none of them had seen, least of all met, an Indian before. The first day was delightful and the four priests visited with Françoise and the Indians, which seemed to take their mind off *le mal de mer.*

By the end of the day, Françoise and her friends had been impressed by how anxious the Sulpicians were to learn about this new land. Unlike the Jesuits, they had no preconceived notions about *Québec* or the natives. Unfortunately, just before dinner, the wind shifted, sending the three young priests to the rail.

Late the following morning, they reached the harbor of *Trois-Rivières.* As usual, Governor Pierre Boucher was on hand to greet them. Although he had moved his family, now with three children, to Cap-de Madeline on the opposite bank of the *Rivière-Saint-Maurice*, he was still in town every day for business. The Sulpicians were anxious to hear the thoughts of someone from another outpost similar to *Ville-Marie*. Once the weary priests were off to bed, Françoise remained to visit with Pierre.

"You always know about these things, Pierre. How are these Sulpicians different from Jesuits? And why do d'Ailleboust and Maisonneuve seem to favor them?"

Pierre rose and brought a bottle of Calvados. Pouring two glasses, he began. "It seems the Sulpicians come from wealthy families more commonly than other sects. They also have a rather independent philosophy. They don't automatically embrace the message of the pope, for example. I think the two men feel the Sulpicians will fit better into the culture of Canada. Certainly, they feel that strongly enough to bring these four priests here at great expense. I guess we shall see, *Tante* Françoise."

She rose and kissed him on the forehead, "You haven't called me that for ages," and with a tear in her eye, she added, "I only wish your dear mother could be here to see what a great man you have become." She emptied her glass with the vengeance of a true Canadian and headed to bed.

Two days later, they approached the small harbor of *Ville-Marie* on the island of *Montréal*. The number of citizens waiting to greet them amazed Françoise. She had not realized there now this many souls in the settlement. Following the overwhelming greeting, they invited the Sulpicians as well as the fellow travelers to dinner in the great hall of the new fort. Maisonneuve gave a grand speech of welcome, including the fact the Jesuits had

216

recently vacated the city and most of the island, giving the Sulpicians full reign of the church and near missions.

Following dinner, when she had an opportunity, Françoise asked Maisonneuve where the Jesuits had gone and why they had left so precipitously. "It is no secret," his Excellency began as he filled his wine glass as well as Françoise's. "There is no love lost between these two religious sects. In addition, the Jesuits have always favored working in the wilderness with the native tribes." Walking her out on the small porch to enjoy the full-moon evening, he added, "The Jesuits also believe vehemently that one needs to die a martyr to go directly to heaven. That is why they seem to seek the opportunity to pursue a violent death at the hands of the heathen while attempting to save them." Again filling their glasses, he concluded with a smile, "Personally I'm not certain that is truly God's plan…In addition, I'm not certain it would be worth it." Françoise headed indoors, rescued from further discussion by the appearance of Marguerite Bourgeoys.

"I am so pleased I found you, my dear," the sister told her. "I have a great number of things to discuss—let us go outside and sit under the stars." Returning Françoise to the full-moon night, she began, "I have been given permission to build a church, and not just a small chapel, but a structure that will serve the needs of both the town of *Ville-Marie* and the whole island of *Montréal*." Filled with enthusiasm, she continued, "In addition, I am forming a congregation—The Congregation of Notre-Dame of *Montréal*."

Pausing to catch her breath, she continued, "We have started a school, we have but a few students, but attendance is growing. We can serve the natives and the French children, much as you do in *Québec*. Most exciting is that I am going to France next season to recruit a few sisters for the Congregation. I also hope to have an audience there for my plan to bring more eligible young girls to Canada."

"What is it called," Françoise queried.

"I call it *Les Filles du Roi*," she said proudly.

"The King's Daughters?" Françoise asked.

"Exactly," Bourgeoys explained, "Of course, they will not be his actual daughters. In fact I don't believe he has any—and if he did, they would be unlikely to come to Canada." Snorting a chuckle, she added, "and frankly not of much use."

"Well, what then?" Françoise queried.

"As it is," Marguerite began, "the only single girls who can come are the children of the wealthy. That is the only way they could afford the voyage, and it is doubtful they would be the hard-working peasant types we really need." Getting up to fetch two glasses of wine, she returned and continued, "In my plan, their way would be paid by His Majesty as well as a small dowry. This is the only way we will balance the genders of our colony."

"And does his majesty agree with this?" Françoise asked.

"Well, he doesn't know about it yet, I must explain it to him."

"Do you know the king?"

"Of course not," Bourgeoys chuckled. "I shall deal with that when I get there." As the hall was nearly vacant, it was apparent the evening was ending. Marguerite said, "I suppose we should be off to bed. I will tell you more and show you the new school tomorrow."

Françoise went to find her husband talking with a few soldiers, pondering what an exceptional woman Marguerite Bourgeoys had become in only one year.

218

CHAPTER 30

<u>Beauport: May 1658 (Nine months later)</u>

"I pray it doesn't rain," Françoise told her husband, as she loaded the baskets into the canoe. "I even said my mother's rosary for it."

"I'm not sure that would be high on the Almighty's list today," he replied as he pushed off shore.

"I know—it's just that this is Agnes-Anne's first picnic at her new home and I know how nervous she is." Agnes-Anne and Jean-Claude Pelletier had moved to his *concession* by Montmorency Falls and invited her parents and sisters, Marguerite and Jeanne along with their spouses. The downstream current along with a fresh westerly breeze brought them to the canoe dock at Montmorency in record time. Approaching the dock, she saw her son-in-law

219

waiting with a cart. "I was worried how we would haul all these baskets up the hill," she said, "but I see it will not be a problem."

Jean-Claude pulled the canoe onto shore with ease. Noël was pleased to see his son-in-law had now learned to do it without getting his feet wet. "I thought I would give you a ride," Jean-Claude told them. "It is a hike to our place." Once seated, Jean-Claude called to his two-ox team who began to haul them up the slope. Soon they came to the pleasant stone home of the young Pelletier family. As they pulled up to the porch, Agnes-Anne came to greet them with Noël-Guy, now four, well in the lead. He jumped into his grandmother's arms nearly bringing her to the ground. In spite of the fact, she had seen him only two weeks ago at mass, Françoise declared, "My goodness you've grown." Agnes-Anne took the baskets and ushered her mother to the house.

"The others won't be here for a while," Jean-Claude told Noël, "how would you like to go further up to see the mill?" Noël agreed, and the two men headed a short way up to the site of the new sawmill. "Part of the falls takes off from the main a ways up," Jean-Claude explained, "then forms this fast stream before beginning to fall again. This has been a perfect location for the mill. Just the right amount of current and we did not have to go all the way to the top. My partner, Levasseur, already has more work than we can handle. We may have to construct a second mill." He led Noël into the building where four men toiled and the sound of trees turning into boards was deafening.

When they returned to the house, they found the other two families had arrived, Marguerite and Paul Vachon with their one-year-old son and Jeanne who had recently married René Chevalier, a mason and stonecutter. René had arrived in 1654 from Anger in the Loire River Valley. Highly skilled, he had already obtained a *concession* in Beauport.

As the women cooked dinner, they gossiped about the latest news. Both Agnes-Anne and Marguerite announced they were pregnant. The three small children and the Pelletier's new puppy frolicked in the meadow. Watching the *Fleuve Saint-Laurent,* the men consumed Jean-Claude Pelletier's ale and talked. "Rumor has it," Pelletier told them, "that Governor de Lauzon is returning to Paris this season." Paul Vachon who was always up on important affairs told them, "I heard it confirmed in a meeting with him yesterday."

"Who will replace him?" Pelletier asked.

"They said," Vachon told him, "Pierre de Voyer d'Argenson—who is called de Voyer. He is from Tours. They say he believes we must stop worrying about the fur trade and concentrate on agriculture. He also thinks the Iroquois are not a problem." Adding with a grin, "In short, he knows little about Canada."

Stifling his laugh, Noël asked, "When is he expected?"

"I'm not certain."

"Abraham Martin left a few days ago to pilot in the first ship from France." Noël explained, "Perhaps he will be aboard."

Following dinner, Noël and Françoise headed back to the canoe for the slower upstream journey home, reveling in the success of their three oldest children. Although neither mentioned it, their joy was only dampened by their oldest son—languishing in an Algonquin grave in the northern wilderness.

Two days later, Françoise went to her volunteer work at the hospital of the *Hôtel-Dieu.* The ship from France had

221

arrived—however without the new governor. Around noon, Sister Marie-Forestier came to see her. "I received a note from the Ursuline Convent. Apparently there is someone there to see you, asking if you could come today."

She left promptly, hoping it was not a problem with one of her children. On arrival, she found somebody she had not expected. "Oh my dear, how good you could come," Marguerite Bourgeoys said as she embraced her. "I arrived from *Ville-Marie* two days ago and am leaving in three days on the ship for France. I wanted to discuss my voyage with you." She led her into the pleasant convent garden where they found a bench.

"I have had quite a winter," the lay sister related. "Governor Maisonneuve has been quite kind and is helping me build a chapel—the first permanent church in *Ville-Marie*! We shall call it *Notre-Dame de Bonsecours*. He has also provided me with a stone stable, which, as we speak, we are turning into a schoolhouse for the children. Most exciting is I am leaving for France to bring back teachers—and see his majesty about my *Filles du Roi* plan."

"Will the king see you?" Françoise queried.

"Well," she replied, "He will just have to—it is God's will."

Françoise chuckled all the way home, waiting to tell the story to her husband and envisioning Marguerite, marching up to the palace to see King Louis XIV.

CHAPTER 31

Québec: July 11, 1658

Noël carefully brought the French ship into the harbor. On it was the usual cadre of male *engager,* animals, machinery, soldiers and a very few women. It also carried the next governor of New France. Unlike de Lauzon, Pierre de Voyer d'Argenson was the very first person off the ship. He had all the trappings of a privileged Frenchman: his clothes were impeccable, his hair well groomed, and his attitude haughty. Unlike his predecessor, he did not address the crowd but immediately boarded his coach to the fort.

That evening, Jean Guyon visited Noël. In his position on the council, he had met that afternoon with the new governor. "How did you find him on your voyage in?" he asked Noël.

"Not much to say," Noël responded. "He was very aloof, unlike de Lauzon who was filled with interest and questions. I don't think we exchanged ten words."

"I'm afraid that is also the opinion of the council," Guyon reported. "He has little use for the Jesuits and believes we should make the fur trade a monopoly and put many of the voyageurs out to farm."

Noël refilled his neighbor's glass, replying, "I'd like to see how Benoît and Bernier respond to that."

"In addition," Guyon continued, "he seems to think we make too much of the Iroquois." Noël shook his head in disbelief before the conversation fell to lighter topics and the men finally said goodnight.

It came later that night—not on a grand scale, but many small attacks in multiple areas. It had been several years since any real assaults had been made on the capital. Most were fires, some with the theft of animals. Two buildings burned in the city itself and a few in the outlying regions, almost every area had at least one attack that night. Six *engager* were dead. In the morning, the raid was apparent as many fires continued smoldering. The new governor took a brief tour, stunned by the stealth and scope of the attacks, particularly the few that occurred near where he slept. His Excellency Pierre de Voyer had a new view of this land and its natives.

Three days later, former Governor Jean de Lauzon departed Canada forever.

Although the Iroquois continued a hostile posture with the occasional small raid, they had not struck again near *Québec* city during the ensuing month. The new governor was becoming familiar with the landscape but remained aloof. He had backed off his desire to make a monopoly of the fur trade, as it had no local support. The citizens did support increasing agriculture, but also tried to convince him it would require a larger population—particularly more women from France.

Beauport: August 1, 1658

Noël was just returning home from a two-week shallop voyage when he saw his wife pacing on the porch. Landing the canoe, he hurried to the house. "Thank goodness you're home," she said, "The most awful thing happened today. Did you hear about it in town?"

"No," he replied, "I had no report to make and went straight to the canoe dock. What is it?"

"Anne-Ardouin next door went out early to collect eggs in the hen house. When she returned, her husband was still in bed. She knew he had not been feeling well and started breakfast. When it was ready, she called him, but to no avail. When she went in—he did not respond! She ran over here and I went for Félicity-Angel." She paused to dry her eyes before continuing. "Félicity-Angel managed to wake him, but she says he is very ill with the fever and will likely not survive."

That Sunday after mass, a few Beauport neighbors met at *L'Auberge Oie Bleue*. The topic was their ailing neighbor. "I think Anne-Ardouin is worried about her farm," Mathurine Guyon reported. "She told me she wants to keep it, but her son François is busy—and doing well with his trade as *notaire*. Her oldest daughter is married, and her son Jean is seventeen but working fulltime as an apprentice rifle maker. That leaves only her seven-year-old daughter at home."

225

"But isn't she *sous-sieur* of the *concession*?" Françoise asked.

"Actually," Jean Guyon answered, "her oldest son inherits it. He is the *notaire* and will have no trouble managing it, but Anne-Ardouin wants to continue to farm her parcel herself."

"I see," Françoise said, standing to leave, "And now I see her solution. If you'll excuse me, I'll see if I can arrange it."

When she arrived home, Françoise went to the Jacques-Henri's camp, and in the morning, he arrived with a young native man and woman. "This is Henri," he told her. "He has just taken woman." Pointing to the young woman, "This Angélique, they want to help run farm. They help Miss Anne-Ardouin." Françoise went next door to discuss the prospect with Anne-Ardouin, who agreed gratefully. Soon the two neighbors each had an Indian camp behind the house, and Anne-Ardouin would be able to continue working her farm. As predicted by Félicity-Angel, Jacques Badeau died in his sleep two weeks later and was buried in the cemetery of *Notre-Dame de la Paix*.

Québec: Late October, 1658:

Heading home from giving the weekly shipping report at the fort, Noël walked, kicking the piles of late autumn color, dreaming of simpler times when he was a boy. The new Governor de Voyer was very different from de Lauzon. His opinions were ironclad, and he refused to consider a contrary point of view even when, in Noël's opinion, the contrary view was superior. However, as he gazed out on the deep blue *Fleuve Saint-Laurent* on this clear and possibly last warm day of the year, things did not seem so bad.

Passing *L'Auberge Oie Bleue*, he noticed his spouse at a table under a tree, having a heated discussion with a group of ladies. He stopped to say hello, and Françoise said, "If you are going home, I shall go with you. I came to the meeting with Mathurine but she is staying late."

While making their way to the lower town and canoe dock, he asked, "What were you meeting about?"

"It was a church meeting. It became rather heated."

"A church meeting? Heated?"

"Yes," she continued, "it seems odd. Of course, I don't have the experience of the others." Born to poor French parents around Paris, Françoise had no early religious upbringing other than a one-year stay at an orphanage. "In France," she continued, "there were lots of priests, then bishops, then cardinals and finally the pope, but because Canada has few people, we only have priests. When I first came in '28, the priests in *Québec* were Récollets and the Jesuits were out in the wilderness missions. When Champlain returned, there were only Jesuits who did it all. I never saw much difference. Now these Sulpicians are on *Montréal*, and as you told me, they don't see eye to eye with the Jesuits on many matters."

Reaching the canoe dock, Noël helped his wife board. As he paddled into the river, she continued, "Apparently we are now growing fast enough that there is talk of naming a bishop, but both sects, and the citizens of their respective areas, want it to be one of theirs. First, they will name a vicar. I never really knew what that meant, but Mathurine says it is someone who would have the duties of a bishop, but without the funny hat or something."

Noël had been smiling but now had to laugh. "So the question is who gets the hat?"

"No," she said with her *I am trying to be serious* voice. "But everyone is taking a side and taking it seriously, Maisonneuve and his people are for the Sulpicians and propose this Father de Queylus in *Ville-Marie* as Vicar of Canada, but our new Governor de Voyer supports the Jesuits and is totally opposed." Noël shrugged in his, *what is the difference,* fashion as she continued, "I don't really know, but people are all up in arms over this. It is like we are the Iroquois and the Algonquin."

Pulling the canoe up on their shore, Noël could not resist one more smart remark, "Are *we* the Iroquois *or* Algonquin?"

"Oh, you..." she began and pushed him playfully. Unfortunately, there was a rope behind him and he slipped into the cold *Saint-Laurent*. She began to laugh as he pulled himself to shore. He reached out and she gave him a hand with which he pulled her into the frigid river. Finally crawling ashore, they were both shivering but in gales of laughter.

Elisabeth came out on the bank to investigate the commotion. At 13, she was the oldest daughter living at home. "What in the world are you two doing?" she shouted with the air of an irate mother. Noël put his arm around his wife's shoulder leading her up to the house and casually replied, "Just discussing religion."

Winter did descend with its *Québécois* vengeance. Fortunately, the weather broke just in time for Christmas mass, and the faithful, filled with religion and cabin fever, headed to church. "What a glorious Christmas day," Anne-Ardouin told Françoise. "I have only been to town a few times since my husband passed." Pointing to a native couple on a bench nearby, she added, "I convinced Henri and Angélique to come. They usually go to the mission church, but I wanted them to see Christmas mass here."

After the service, the Beauport contingency retired to *L'Auberge Oie Bleue* where they retired to the newly enlarged interior to ward off the winter chill. "It seems the natives have settled down," Xainte Cloutier began, knocking her fist on the table for luck. "At least we haven't seen any this side of *Trois-Rivières* since summer."

"I only wish," added Mathurine Guyon, "we could say the same for the clergy. I heard that Maisonneuve and the people in Ville Marie have made their new priest, de Queylus, some level of vicar, and think that will make him a natural for bishop, once France can decide if the king or the pope will act."

"That will give the Sulpicians sway over the Jesuits," Xainte added, "and won't sit well with Québec."

"On the other hand," Jean Guyon added, "the Sulpicians are Normand and maybe some of them can make *real* Calvados." He stood signaling for more drinks.

Within the week, winter was back, and back to stay, as temperatures plummeted while the snow level rose. The *Québécois* did not know nor would they know until spring, that as early as December 8, the church of the Abby of Saint-Germain-des-Prés in Paris had consecrated an experienced Jesuit clergyman, the Normand, Father François de Laval, as Vicar Apostolic of *Québec* and Bishop of Petraea *in partibus infidelium* (in the land of the unbelievers). The Sulpicians had lost the battle.

CHAPTER 32

Québec: June 16, 1659

The docks and landing space of *Québec* filled with eager citizens as Abraham Martin carefully piloted the most recent ship from France to the mooring. The gangplank lowered and disembarkation began, first a few soldiers, then some citizens who appeared simple *engager*. "Look! That must be him!" Mathurine Guyon shouted, pointing to a thin but taller than average man in the simple black robe of a priest. As he stepped on the dock, Governor de Voyer and the Jesuit, Father Lalemant greeted him enthusiastically. The newly arrived priest shook their hands and began to greet other bystanders.

"Well, that cannot be him," Perrine Boucher declared, "He acts like a regular priest."

Making speeches under such circumstances was not de Voyer's style, but he saw he had little choice. Helping the prelate onto a small platform, the governor held out his hands and the crowd became quiet. "It gives me great pleasure to introduce Father François de Laval," he studied a paper he held before continuing, reading slowly, "Bishop in *Partibus* of Petraea, Vicar Apostolic in New France." Laval held up his hand, and the crowd cheered. The men stepped down and de Voyer headed to his awaiting coach, but Laval shook his head and pointed to the road to the upper town. De Voyer shrugged and the three men with their entourage began to trudge uphill toward the fort. When they reached the upper town, Laval pointed to the church and the entourage proceeded there for a short service before again heading to the fort. As they made their way with the prelate reaching out to touch hands and heads, de Voyer realized he was going to have a very long and, in his view, very bad day.

Three days later, the ladies of Beauport met for lunch at *L'Auberge Oie Bleue* where the topic of discussion was certain to be the new bishop. Council members, Jean Guyon and Zacharie Cloutier, had met with Laval, de Voyer, and several other officials. Their wives had then dutifully pumped them for information.

"Zacharie says he is a wonderful man," Xainte Cloutier began. "He stops to greet everyone and seems quite humble. He has already begun confirmations," she told them, explaining, "Because we have never had a bishop before, only those of us who came from France have been confirmed."

Françoise added, "He has already been over to the *Hôtel-Dieu* twice to visit the sick."

"What does this strange title of his mean?" asked Anne-Ardouin.

"I know that." Françoise told them. "They told Elisabeth in school that Bishop in *partibus* of Petraea means he is not yet a full bishop and Petraea is a place around Jerusalem. I don't know what that means, but Vicar Apostolic of New France means he can do anything a real bishop can do even before he becomes one."

"But I heard," Mathurine Guyon added, "that he is not yet a *real* bishop."

"He will be," Xainte reported, "but the Sulpicians wanted this Father Gabriel de Queylus in *Ville-Marie* to be bishop and are holding things up." Looking around and lowering her voice, she added, "but the governor received a letter last month from the Queen Mother—herself! She told him in no uncertain terms, that Laval can do *anything* a full bishop can."

François de Laval had been born to an aristocratic family in Chartres, and many *Québécois* took pride in the fact his mother was Normand. He went right to work, constantly in view, greeting and blessing people. When some of his shipmates fell ill to some epidemic, and were hospitalized in the *Hôtel-Dieu*, Laval visited and blessed them daily until they either they were cured or had died—sadly, mostly the latter.

The dispute for religious power between the Jesuits and Sulpicians continued, but de Voyer received a letter signed by young King Louis XIV stating *in no uncertain terms* that Laval was in charge of all areas of New France. De Voyer carried it on his person to show to his fellow citizens to the west in *Ville-Marie*. Laval visited a number of missions, preaching to and visiting with the natives. He was vehemently opposed to alcohol consumption among the tribes. Fortunately, he was less strict with his French-Canadian brethren.

Four weeks after the arrival of Laval, Abraham Martin piloted another French ship to the docks. This one had not been preceded by any word of who was aboard, so did not have much audience. Françoise had come to town to join her husband for lunch by the docks at *Taverne Terre Sauvage*. They watched the ship dock before Noël said, "I suppose I should go down and see if they need assistance." Françoise accompanied him, and when they reached the dock, disembarkation had begun. He told her, "I am going up to speak with Abraham. I may not see you until dinner tonight." She gave him a peck on the cheek and he disappeared.

Heading back toward the lower town, she heard her name called. Turning, she saw five women in black. The tallest was waving. Recognizing Marguerite Bourgeoys, she returned to the dock. "How wonderful to see you, my dear," the lay sister said, as she embraced Françoise with a bone-crushing hug. "I prayed I would find you before we depart for *Ville-Marie*. Please come with us, we are spending the next few days at the convent, and I have a great deal to report." Each religieuse had a small satchel of their worldly belongings, which they easily carried up the road to the upper town.

Once settled, the women retired to the convent garden. "Where to start?" Marguerite wondered. As they sat around a maple tree, she pointed to her companions, "These four sisters are coming to teach at the school—Indian as well as French students. They are all filled with zeal to teach as well as expand our services."

"What about your other plans...?" Françoise began, but before she could finish, Marguerite stood, "Oh yes, *the* most thrilling part. We have our plans laid out."

Françoise smiled. Not able to help herself, she asked, "Did you..."

"See the King?" Marguerite finished for her. "Of course, how else would we have managed?"

Amazed, Françoise questioned, "Did you actually speak...?"

"Yes, he was very gracious. However, of course, he was in a hurry. He sent me to two men, Messieurs Colbert and Talon. They and their assistants were very helpful. They have more eligible women than they can marry off, and we have not enough. It is as though it was a match—well, a match made in heaven. They are putting it together, girls from good homes where applicable, especially those whose fathers have passed on, but not forgetting the poor orphaned souls who have lost both parents. The King has agreed to pay a dowry and the cost of passage."

Françoise was speechless and would never again doubt Marguerite. Even if only part was true, it would be wonderful. Marguerite continued with unbridled enthusiasm. "Some will come to *Québec* and some to *Ville-Marie* depending on need and access. We hope to be running within a few years. We are going to begin recruiting and training sisters and lay sisters to house and care for them in both locations."

The visit continued with more details as well as pleasantries. Finally, Françoise said, "I should be going. Captain Langlois will want his dinner."

"I understand," said Marguerite, "I pray we can meet again before our departure. By the way, why were both Captain Martin and Captain Langlois on the ship?"

"My husband wasn't…"

"I was certain I saw him," the religieuse said. "In fact, I think I saw him during the voyage."

"Oh," Françoise began. "I think I might know why."

Arriving home, she saw her suspicions confirmed when she saw two men, both appearing to be Noël, on the porch. "If it isn't the twins," she said as she walked up on the porch. Seeing the near empty bottle of Calvados, she smiled, saying, "Not too much has changed."

Jean Langlois rose and embraced his sister-in-law. Looking at the bottle, he said, "We did save some for you."

She had not seen Jean Langlois for several years. Noël's younger, but almost identical, brother had run away to sea as a youth and worked his way up to ship's captain. About sixteen years earlier, he had left his ship and tried to settle down in *Québec* with his brother, but the call of sea caused him to sail away.

Françoise went inside. As usual, Félicity-Angel had prepared dinner with the help of Elisabeth and Mariette. Françoise rang the porch bell and the remaining brood assembled. The two older girls had finished school and were helping at the convent and at 13 and 14 years were eyeing marriage. Jean-Pierre at 18 was living at home and managing the *concession* with the help of Paul Vachon. Jean-Louis, 11, and young Noël, 8, were still in school. Jean-Pierre was the only child who vaguely remembered his Uncle Jean. The girls served dinner, and Uncle Jean regaled the family with tales from the high seas, not only France and Canada but other corners of the world as well. By dessert, both the younger boys had decided to become ship captains.

Following dinner, Noël announced, "Jean and I are going to visit Pelletier's sawmill tomorrow." Looking at the two younger boys, "Would you two like to come along?" Both cheered in the affirmative.

In the morning, Françoise and the two girls left to help at the Ursuline Convent and the *Hôtel-Dieu*. Jean-Pierre went to manage his father's *concession*, while the two men and the younger boys took the large canoe and headed to Montmorency. Upon arrival, the two boys scampered up to the Pelletier house with the men, gasping for breath, close behind. Following a brief coffee and biscuit with Agnes-Anne, Jean-Claude Pelletier took them to the mill, which was running at full speed. To Noël's surprise, his brother showed a more than casual interest in the project, asking each of the workers what they did and how everything worked. Eventually they made their way back down to Pelletier's house. Seated on the porch, Jean Langlois said, "This is impressive. What I think is with our knowledge of boats, Noël's of carpentry, Jean-Claude Pelletier's of the mill, and, given the nature of this community, we should begin to build boats."

Noël looked at his brother as if he had two heads, "What?" Jean Langlois began to describe in detail what he had in mind, and it soon became apparent he knew a good deal more about this than Noël had realized. Pelletier also reminded him of his family's coal business, which provided a secondary fuel source. By the time they arrived in Beauport, Noël was thinking this could work. In the morning, the brothers went to town and talked to a few other men before meeting with Abraham Martin, the colony's expert on boats.

"These boats you call large shallops," Jean told him, "are actually what is called a *barque* in Europe. I believe

236

we could produce them in higher quality—and in quantity. I think you have somewhat of a unique and untapped market here. If, as you say, the King and your new bishop are going to grow the population…" Standing, Jean said, "I think I will stay in town tonight, find a place to stay and talk to some people," adding with a smile, "perhaps some ladies as well." As Abraham Martin and Noël left the *Taverne Terre Sauvage,* Abraham told him, "You know, I think this could work, as crazy as it sounds."

Noël smiled, "I've been thinking of when we were boys. Jean always had good ideas—and they always got us into trouble."

CHAPTER 33

Ville-Marie: One year later, May 1660

Jacques Mirabeau was having a grand day. The sun was shining, the birds singing, and his dear wife had just informed him of her pregnancy. He had shut his shop early to attend to his side job, inspecting the town perimeter. Since the reconstruction of the palisade, the task had been simple—the new walls were virtually impregnable. Today was particularly easy as he was inspecting the interior. Picking up three stones, he began to juggle. Jacques had been quite skilled as a lad. He wondered if his first child would be a boy—the things he could teach him. Dropping one of the stones, he bent to retrieve it; when he stood, they were in front of him.

Where did they come from? How could he not have seen them? He brought his whistle alarm to his lips, but the knife in his throat stopped him short.

Québec: Two weeks later

Noël pulled his canoe into the dock. Going to the shipping office, he asked the dockhand if he had seen Abraham Martin. "Left in a hurry a couple hours ago," he was told, "heading west to *Ville-Marie*. Took a few soldiers."

"What was the hurry?" Noël asked with a puzzled look.

"Don't know, Captain," the dockhand reported with a shrug, adding, "Might ask those two voyageurs at *Taverne Terre Sauvage*. He talked to them first—they been suckin' 'em down for a few hours now."

Noël hurried over to find Benoît and Bernier at a table filled with bottles. "How's it goin', Captain?" Benoît asked. "You hear about the excitement?"

"No…what?"

"Have a seat," Benoît told him as he waved to the waiter for more refreshment while using his foot to push out a chair for Noël. "We just got back from way west." Pouring three glasses, he continued, "Once we made *Montréal* comin' back, we stopped at *Ville-Marie*. Anyhow, all hell was breakin' loose."

"What?" Noël asked anxiously.

"I'll tell ya if ya keeps still." Taking a long drink, he continued, "Like I said, we been out tradin' in the far west—where they still got beaver—did real good, too. We was comin' back loaded when we passed *Montréal* and decided to stop fer the night in *Ville-Marie*. Well, shit was flyin' everywhere. Seems their friends, the Iroquois, come back fer a visit. They got that new wall and all, but somehow the rascals got in, killed a guard and shot the place up. In the end, they took off with 17 citizens—I think maybe a couple women, too. Folks there say there was 160

239

of them Iroquois. I don't know how they could tell—I don't think any of 'em can count that high." Bernier snorted a chuckle and Benoît continued, "We hightailed it back here. They took us right up to see his majesty, the governor—man, is he a piece of work—he still don't get it. Anyhow, he got Abraham Martin who loaded on a few soldiers and took off west."

By this time, Jean Guyon had stopped by and joined the discussion. "Why are they back on the warpath after all this time?" he asked.

"Like I told you boys," Benoît replied. "They's always gotta be fightin' someone. They pretty much finished off the Erie. What they didn't kill signed on to join them. Then they turned back and went for the first place they saw."

"Have they been anywhere else?" Noël questioned.

"Don't know. We just hauled ass back here. But I suspects they'll be visitin' *Richelieu* and *Trois-Rivières* pretty soon—probably here, too."

Finishing his drink, Noël told the men, "I need to check with the shipping office before I go home. Thanks for the ale."

"No problem, Captain." Benoît said as he ordered another round.

Guyon stood as well, "I'll go with you. My ride has left and maybe you can take me home." Entering the shipping office, Noël asked the clerk about his status for the day.

"I think you are done for today, Captain."

"The governor didn't need me?" he asked.

The clerk looked around to see if they were alone and whispered, "I don't think you'll hear from him today, Captain."

"Why is that?"

Looking around again, "Well sir, when those two voyageurs came in, they took me and Captain Martin up to see his Excellency. He did not take the news well."

"In what way?"

The clerk again checked the empty room, "He looked real strange." Lowering his whisper, "I think he was scared."

"Scared?" Noël questioned.

"Well, sir. I know you won't tell anyone to get me in trouble, but I don't think he understands a lot in Canada. He certainly don't understand the natives. He looked like a little lost kid. He told Captain Martin to take care of it and locked himself in his office. I went up a few hours later and he had yet to come out. You men won't tell anyone I told you this, will you, Captain?"

"Your secret is safe with us," Noël assured him as he and Jean Guyon left, heading to the canoe dock.

On the way down, Guyon told him, "I'm not surprised about the governor. Frankly, I share the clerk's opinion. The thought of him in charge of a full-scale Indian war frightens me. And I agree with Benoît, I think the Iroquois *need* someone to fight."

Once they reached the canoe, he changed to a more pleasant topic. "So how goes the new boat-building enterprise?"

Pushing off shore, Noël replied, "Not bad for the first year. It is mostly my brother and Jean-Claude Pelletier. My brother, Jean Langlois, has moved down to Montmorency and has a workshop next to the lumber mill. He has a small cabin there and has moved in with an Algonquin girl half his age. I was down there a few days ago and things are moving along. He has hired two new *engager* who are carpenters—one with boat building experience. They just finished a small shallop. It looked good for the first try. We launched it, and it sails and rides well. Now he is going to move on to something larger. His plan is to make crafts more appropriate for our conditions and needs."

"Sounds impressive," Guyon noted. Then with a skeptical look, asked, "Does he have any experience with this?"

"I guess a little," Noël answered, "He has always been rather talented—in a weird way."

"What do you mean?"

"Well, when we were young," Noël began as he stopped paddling, "He always did odd things and even though he did them well, he always managed to get in trouble. When he was twelve, he ran off—I was fourteen at the time. He went to sea as a cabin boy—with little education, worked his way up to a captain of the line." Putting his paddle back to work, he concluded, "I have a feeling this venture may do well."

When he arrived home, he gave his wife the grave news about the raid on *Montréal*. She removed her apron and opening the door, she looked over the river to the *Citadelle* and asked, "Will they come here, do you think?"

"Hard to say," was his response.

"I guess, we must wait and see," was all she said before changing the topic abruptly. "Your daughter has a suitor."

"Oh? I didn't even know Elisabeth talked to boys."

"Not Elisabeth," she told him, "Mariette."

"Mariette is only fourteen!"

"Older than some of the girls, my dear," was her reply.

"Who is it?"

"François Miville," she told him, "son of Pierre Miville."

"LeSuisse?" he replied with a frown, referring to Pierre Miville's *dit* name, or nickname. "He isn't even French!"

"He *is* a successful and respected member of the community. He is a skilled furniture maker with a fine shop—which François will take over, and he has a *concession* in the upper town." She continued, "He is from *French-Switzerland,* but they lived in, and all the children were born in, Brouage, near Saintes." With a sly grin, she reminded him, "And you know who else was born in Brouage?"

"Yes, dear," he said, acknowledging he knew the port town of Brouage was the birthplace of none other than the Father of French Canada, Samuel Champlain. He stood and began to pace. "Then what about Elisabeth? Is she to be an old maid?"

She slapped him with her *torchon,* as the French called dishtowels. "She is only 15. She will be just fine."

Two weeks later, Abraham Martin returned and Governor de Voyer called a meeting of the council, military officers and some private citizens. To everyone's surprise, he had agreed to Abraham's suggestion to invite Jacques-Henri as well. To begin, they asked Abraham Martin for his report.

"It appears a large number of Iroquois managed to breach the walls of *Ville-Marie.* They killed a few men and took some citizens captive. On our way in, we heard no reports of attacks between here and *Montréal.* The opinion of those we spoke to, who live outside the palisade— mostly *engager* and voyageurs, is the Iroquois are at all-time strength. This is due in a large part to the number of Huron and Erie they have managed to take as slaves, or sometimes as willing warriors. In addition, a large number of the Iroquois are now armed with guns." Following few questions, mainly about the guns, he suggested, "I think it would be helpful to hear a native opinion. I see Jacques-Henri in the room, perhaps he will help us."

Jacques-Henri stood with some reluctance. Abraham Martin began with the obvious question, "What do the Iroquois want?"

Jacques-Henri replied, "Land, trade, tools, guns, liquor—mainly Iroquois want to fight."

De Voyer asked, "Will they kill the captured French?"

"If Iroquois wanted to kill them, they would be dead. They will want to trade them for these things they want."

De Voyer protested, "We cannot give them guns or liquor!"

Jacques-Henri pondered a while, "Tell that to families of two women they have taken."

One of the officers stood, "Should we give guns to Algonquin?"

Jacques-Henri replied, "Should Englishman and Dutch have given guns to Iroquois?"

Noël smiled at his friend's wisdom. Eventually the group decided to form a force of French soldiers, a few colonists, and some Algonquin warriors joined by the few remaining Huron to guard the city. In the ensuing weeks, there were further raids near *Montréal* as well as *Trois-Rivières*. Some captured Iroquois were exchanged for surviving *Montréal* citizens. However, it was news that arrived on a boat from France that would greatly affect the security and future of Canada.

CHAPTER 34

<u>Beauport: July 20, 1660, six weeks later</u>

Jean Guyon announced the news. A member of the council, he was among the first to be informed. "As some of you know, France has finally ended this interminable war of Spanish succession with the signing of what is called the Treaty of the Pyrenees. During this war, there were two regiments: the Salières and the Carignan Regiments. They have now merged to form the Carignan-Salières Regiment. Minister Colbert is considering sending us a number of these men to aid in our struggle with the Iroquois. A few of them are on the ship arriving today."

When the ship docked, the usual cargo of animals, equipment, *engager* and a few young women disembarked. Finally, a small but well-trained group of French soldiers appeared, and without a pause, marched directly to the fort. Although there were fewer than twenty soldiers, their appearance and professional demeanor gave hope to the colonists.

The following day, Governor de Voyer held a meeting for the council and select leaders. Seated next to de Voyer was a young officer in a brown uniform coat. "Gentlemen," de Voyer began, "I am certain you all know yesterday we received a group of soldiers from the newly formed Carignan-Salières Regiment. This is Lieutenant René Gauthier, their troop leader, who will tell you his mission and answer questions."

A good-looking man in his late twenties, Gauthier stood and gave a concise summary. Simply put, he and his men were to work with and train local militias. They would distribute a few of their number to each of the three posts, *Québec, Trois-Rivières,* and *Ville-Marie* on *Montréal.*

Following his short speech, questions were invited, and Jean Guyon rose to ask the most important. "Will France send more troops?"

"I certainly hope so, sir," Gauthier responded. "At the moment France is considering this question, but I suspect—and hope they will eventually send many more."

The regiment trained at the fort, marching and shooting by day and wandered through the town in the evening. One week after the military arrival, Noël and Abraham Martin were sitting outside the fort watching the soldiers practice a mock battle. At the end of the drill, Abraham said, "I can't watch this anymore, I need to say something." Walking over to Lieutenant Gauthier, he introduced himself.

Gauthier told him, "Yes, Captain, I remember meeting you on the voyage in. How did you like our drill?"

Abraham pulled on his ample beard, now entirely white. "Well, Lieutenant, I think if you were fighting the Spanish, you would do well. Unfortunately, you will be fighting our natives."

"A battle is a battle, sir," the soldier responded.

After more beard pulling, Abraham suggested, "Actually it is bit different here." Pointing over to his table, he added, "My friend, Captain Langlois, knows someone who may give you a few suggestions."

Realizing he should be careful with this much older respected citizen, Gauthier remained silent while Abraham continued, "My farm is just in back of the fort on the large plain—the locals call it *The Plains of Abraham*." He could not tell if Gauthier saw the humor, but continued. "Bring five of your men tomorrow morning, and I'll have our man come over. Maybe he can show you a few things." Gauthier was moderately aggravated at the intrusion, but knew enough to nod in agreement.

In the morning, he and four men appeared, properly armed, on the Plains of Abraham. The rest of his crew came to watch. Waiting was Jacques-Henri and four of his tribe, each armed with a bow. Abraham explained, "Lieutenant, these five men are going into the woods and will come out and attack, be ready to respond."

"But what if we shoot one?" Gauthier asked.

"Unlikely," Abraham answered, "however, don't aim too well."

The soldiers formed a line as the Algonquin disappeared into the woods. Soon they returned slowly, with bows ready. One of the soldiers took a single shot, and the natives turned, fleeing into the woods. Gauthier smiled, signaling his men to follow, and they ran in pursuit. Once in the woods, they could see no trace or trail of the Indians. Gauthier cautioned them to proceed slowly. Going ten feet further, the lieutenant felt a breeze by his right ear and an arrow landed in the tree directly ahead of him. He and his men turned to see the five braves with bows drawn and aimed—behind them.

Abraham Martin came between them. "Lieutenant, I suggest you and your boys stay and talk with Jacques-Henri. He can teach you a lot about fighting in Canada—like I said, it's not France." With a smile, he added, "Don't worry—his French is as good as yours."

Although upset that he had been bested, Gauthier remained calm, telling his men to stay. Soon he found Jacques-Henri disarmingly polite as well as helpful. By evening, he and his men were better prepared for wilderness combat, and to their amazement, had made a few new friends.

A few days later, they boarded a boat and Abraham Martin distributed five men each to *Trois-Rivières* and *Ville-Marie*. The rest remained in *Québec*.

<u>*Québec*: August 10, 1660</u>

At the very summit of the upper town, one can see what seems to be forever: downstream on *Fleuve Saint-Laurent* to the northeast, Beauport and *Riviére Saint-Charles* to the north and Fort Saint Louis and its palisades to the south. It was here one found the *concession* of Pierre Miville, known by his *dit* name, *LeSuisse*. Born in French-Switzerland and married in Brouage, France, Miville, his wife and 6 children immigrated to *Québec* in the early forties. A successful furniture maker, he had additional skills for making money and had amassed a certain wealth by various means.

When his oldest son, François, asked for the hand of Mariette Langlois, Miville insisted the marriage take place on his *concession* with its unprecedented views. Noël had no objections. He had provided a generous dowry for Mariette and was happy to forgo the expense of the wedding—particularly this wedding, where all the wealthy families were invited. The food was elegant, the music entertaining, and the grounds lit by fiery torches so the festivity could last well into the evening. Noël continued to marvel that even as he had acquired more wealth than he had ever expected, each of his children had married into even more.

The wedding was so delightful that no one mentioned the word *Iroquois.*

One month later, Jean Langlois launched his first large craft, an adaptation of the French barque, but better designed for the *Fleuve Saint-Laurent.* After a few short runs downstream, he took it into *Québec* harbor. It gathered several gawkers mostly from the shipping trade. Jean gave a tour explaining, "It is as large as the craft we call a large shallop and almost as large as a French barque, but it will maneuver better in our waterways." Once he had a good audience including the governor and a few soldiers, he took them out for a short ride to demonstrate its stability and maneuverability.

When they returned, Governor de Voyer asked, "What purpose do the two openings in the side serve?"

Jean smiled, "A little something to impress the Iroquois. They are for cannon." Noël smiled when he saw the governor's impressed reaction, realizing he and his brother were now involved in another possibly profitable venture.

CHAPTER 35

<u>*Québec*</u>: April 1661

Noël brought the new boat easily into the *Québec* harbor. His first long voyage of the season, and first long voyage for his brother's invention, had involved taking citizens and a few soldiers along with a few newly arrived *engager* to *Trois-Rivières* and *Montréal*. The dockhand took the lines, and as Noël first stepped onto the dock, he asked, "How's the maiden voyage, Captain?"

"Excellent," Noël replied, rubbing his hand gently on the railing, "I think my brother is on to something here." Looking at the dock, he added, "Where is everyone? I thought they would be anxious for a report."

"They's all up around the fort. Apparently the Iroquois are up to something in the south."

Noël's smile turned to a frown as he told the dockhand, "Finish up here. I'd better go up and see what's happening."

Making his way through the upper town, he saw very little activity. Arriving at the fort, he saw why. The parade grounds contained a number of citizens all in discussions. Seeing Abraham Martin and Jean Guyon, he asked, "What's happening?"

"Our old friends, the Iroquois," Abraham replied. "Seems the rascals have moved south and east to take on the Abenaki."

"That must explain why it is suddenly quiet in the west," Noël suggested. "Apparently, they had another raid in *Montréal* late this winter. They claim there were 250 braves, which I suspect is a bit of an exaggeration, but apparently 10 people were taken captive. However, they have not seen an Iroquois since then. Maybe the Iroquois are moving to the south."

"What we have heard," Abraham reported, "is de Voyer is sending a group of our soldiers including those brown-uniformed Carignan-Salières guys along with some Huron and Algonquin to break it up. The Abenaki have always been on our side of things."

When he arrived home later that night, he reported to his wife who asked, "Why would they do that? Did the Abenaki do something to them?"

"Not that I know of," he told her as he fetched two cups and the Calvados. "The Abenaki around here live on the south bank of *Fleuve Saint-Laurent* and downstream of *Québec*. They are a peaceful nomadic tribe, like the Algonquin. They even speak Algonquin. There are several around here, and most Canadians don't even know the difference." Opening the door and looking over the porch at the river, he added, "Maybe it's like Benoît says—the Iroquois just have a need to fight someone."

Three weeks later the troops returned, Lieutenant René Gauthier reported to the fort. "We were attacked before we reached the Abenaki village. The fighting was fierce—we lost five men. However, in the end, the Iroquois were also damaged, and their leader has asked to discuss terms of peace with the French." A short while later, a delegation of Iroquois arrived and discussions lasted three days. In the end, a temporary agreement to cease hostilities between French and Iroquois had been reached, and the Iroquois agreed to leave the Abenaki lands.

Québec: L'Auberge Oie Bleue, August 1661

"So tell me again," Noël asked, "how did this all come about?"

"You remember that big raid inside the walls of *Montréal* last May?" Abraham Martin asked.

"Yes, and you left right away with some soldiers."

"Right," Abraham replied. "What did you do when you found out?"

Noël thought for a moment, "I went up to the fort to see what happened."

Abraham asked, "Did you talk to Governor de Voyer?"

Noël thought for a moment, "No... I remember—he locked himself up in his office."

Abraham looked at Jean Guyon who was also at the table. "Tell him the rest, Jean."

Guyon drained his glass and pushed back, "Apparently, Bishop Laval heard about this episode. It is no secret he and de Voyer have never gotten along. Anyway, Laval wrote to the King and has finally received his answer."

Noël looked puzzled so Guyon went on, "The King is recalling de Voyer and has sent Pierre Dubois Davougour to replace him. He came in on the ship Abraham brought in today, and tomorrow, Laval is making the switch."

"I always thought de Voyer was a hog's behind," Abraham told them, "and I think it's about time to get rid of him."

Jean Guyon stood, "I have to go to the council meeting and see this play out."

As Guyon headed to the fort, Abraham Martin said, "Let's go down to the lower town, Noël, and see how the other half is doing." Approaching *Taverne Terre Sauvage*, he exclaimed, "I'll be damned, look who's here."

Walking over to the two voyageurs, Abraham said, "Look what the cat dragged in. Didn't you lads go to the far west again this year?"

Benoît stood and pulled over two chairs, "Take a load off, your honors and I'll tell ya all about it." They sat while he signaled for drinks and began. "We decided not to go this season, did so well last year we doesn't need to."

"Where have you been?" Noël asked.

"Down where the real actions gonna be, yer honor," Benoît answered, "down south in *Mary-land*."

"The English Colony?" Noël asked in surprise.

"That's right," Benoît assured him, "That's where the real action's gonna be. Besides, they's all Catholic down there so they don't care a shit about us." Bernier chortled. "See, down there," Benoît continued, "they also got them Susquehannock injuns. They's kind of Algonquin speakers and they gets along with them *Mary-landers*. Well, them Iroquois decides they's gonna take on the Susquehannock, so the English is givin' the Susquehannock guns."

Benoît pushed back and poured another glass, until Noël said, "I don't get it? Why is that good?"

Benoît pulled up to the table, looking at Noël, "Because the Susquehannock is pussies by comparison, and sooner or later the Iroquois gonna be fightin' the English." Pushing back and pointing at Noël, Benoît concluded, "And that's what I said all along needs to happen!"

Québec: October 1, 1661

Within days of his arrival in August, Pierre Dubois Davaugour had been installed as Governor of New France. Summarily discharged, de Voyer had departed for France on the same ship that brought Davaugour. The difference in the men was night and day. As astute as de Lauzon, Davaugour immediately had seen the poor condition of the colony and resolved to improve it. He met with Bishop Laval, the council, and local leaders within his first few days. Then he appointed the Jesuit, Father Paul Ragueneau, as head of the council. The priest had been in the Huron missions for many years and had been Superior of the missions for several of them. He was familiar with all three settlements and had recently been working in _Trois-Rivières._ In addition to Ragueneau, he appointed Noël and a few other community leaders to be non-voting members.

Davaugour then pressed Noël into taking him on a voyage to the three settlements along with Jacques-Henri with whom he discussed the multifaceted native culture and issues. Finally, he called a meeting of the council and local leaders. "Gentlemen, if we are going to grow this land to its full potential, we must have significant help from France. I propose we send an ambassador—a spokesman who is well versed in the colony and its issues. You, who have been here much longer than I, must help me decide who it shall be. Before we leave this room, I propose we choose our ambassador."

"Pierre? Are you all mad? He is only a boy!" Noël poured his second glass of Calvados while his wife continued, "Going to France—speaking to the King and all his ministers! They will eat him alive. Besides most of them are… are—perverts!"

Pushing the bottle toward her, he said calmly while stifling his laugh. "Sit down, my dear, pour yourself a drink. First of all, he will be forty years old next year, and this was a unanimous decision. It only took two hours of discussion. He knows the colony better than anyone does. He has led troops in battle successfully and has the most respected administration in Canada." Noël rose and walked to the door looking out at the cool autumn night. "Believe me, it is *he* who will devour *them*."

On October 22, 1661, young Pierre Boucher boarded a ship to France. His many friends, family members and others waved, bidding him farewell and good luck, as he sailed away with their fate in his hands.

Québec: Notre-Dame de la Paix, April 17, 1662

The cold spring drizzle set the tone of the gloomy day as her friends and family said their last farewells to Mathurine Guyon. Father Lalemant finished the prayers, and the gravedigger began to fill in the grave. "I just can't believe she's gone," Françoise told her husband. "I know it was expected, but I guess I never really believed it." Mathurine had fallen ill with a cough two months after Christmas. Sister Marie-Forestier visited her regularly but said she had an incurable croup. Following the service, the family returned to the church and her Beauport friends went to toast her memory at *L'Auberge Oie Bleue*.

"How will Jean get along all alone in the house?" Perrine Boucher wondered. "Now that all the children are married?"

"I heard Barbe and her family are going to move in," Françoise told her. The oldest Guyon child, Barbe, had already married when the group left Mortagne for Canada. She and her husband, Pierre Paradis, a master knife maker, had remained in France and had several children. They eventually immigrated to Canada a few years ago and lived in town.

"I guess we are all getting old," Françoise told her husband as they pushed the canoe toward home. "Even my bones are starting to creak."

"Don't be silly," he reassured her. "Mathurine was much older. You are only..."

While he struggled with the numbers, she replied, "51— that's ancient! And you are even... older."

The rain was diminishing and the sun tried to peak out as Noël pointed the canoe toward their dock, telling her, "And don't forget, every day has one of those." Looking up she saw the magnificent rainbow touching each bank of the great river.

One month later, Noël returned home from a particularly long trip to *Trois-Rivières* and *Ville-Marie*. Falling into a rocker, he poured himself a glass of ale. "These trips become more complicated each time," he told his wife.

"With the new troops and the increase in farming at the two western towns, I have more passengers and more cargo each trip." Pouring more ale, he added, "In addition Governor Davaugour is constantly sending envoys to the outposts—but I suppose that is a good thing."

Françoise came and sat beside him, stealing a sip of his ale. "I have another issue for you," she said. "This afternoon, Barbe Paradis, came over. Now that she has moved her family in with Jean Guyon, she seems to be in charge."

"I would expect nothing else," he said with a hint of sarcasm.

Ignoring his tone, she continued, "Barbe says her father is very depressed. He says he has nothing to do now."

"He's still on the council." Noël replied.

"Yes, but she says he needs something more—maybe something to do with his hands."

Noël rose and went to the window, as if searching for inspiration. "I know!" He said, turning to Françoise. "On my way home, Father Lalement stopped me. It seems Laval has decided to put a chapel in Beauport."

"It is about time, now we won't have to miss mass so often in winter."

"But the point is," Noël added, "this is a perfect job for Jean." Giving it more thought, he added, "But how do we get him to do it? He might just say he's too old."

"I know!" she exclaimed. Looking out the door, she reported, "I think he's home right now. Leave it to me."

Grabbing her shawl, she headed out the door, returning a short time later with a grin. "You have the leader of the chapel construction, my dear."

"How…?"

"I told him about the project and said they did not want to trouble him, and were going to ask *Monsieur* Beau. You know how he complains about Beau's arrogance and incompetence. Jean told me he would be delighted to lead the project—in fact, he insisted."

A few weeks later, Noël was coming up from the docks when he saw Jean Guyon. "I was just in town for supplies for the new chapel," he told Noël. "Why don't we stop for a drink?"

The two men found a table at *Taverne Terre Sauvage* where Noël asked about the chapel construction. "We are almost ready to begin," Guyon answered, "Robert Giffard has offered the land from his large Beauport *concession*, so it will be close to us and very convenient." Jean went on to describe the size, shape and other features of the project, which he had clearly taken under his wing. "I think we can even have a choir loft…"

Suddenly he was interrupted, "Well, good day, gents. How things going?" Benoît asked as he and Bernier joined them. "I hear you're buildin' a new church."

"Yes," Guyon responded, "Do you men want to help?"

Benoît pondered for a moment before responding, "Nah, Bernier is tough as nails, but we ain't so good drivin' 'em. Anyhow, we's movin' west again. Time to trade some pelts so's we can eat." Bernier grunted an agreement.

"How is the Indian war in Maryland going?" Noël inquired.

"Not so much fun this season, Captain. Them Dutchmen is gettin' friendlier with the Iroquois and them English is all in bed with the Susquehannock so they's kinda at one of them stalemates. I think them Iroquois might be ready to come make trouble again fer Canada."

Guyon stood, "I hope they do not, gentlemen, but if you will excuse me, I have a chapel to build. Good luck in the west." As the two men headed back to the docks, Guyon asked Noël's opinion. "I hope he is incorrect," Noël told him, "however, he is usually accurate. I guess we must hope Pierre Boucher will return this season with some help from France."

That evening Noël arrived home to more news from his spouse, "Elisabeth has a suitor—Louis Côté has asked to call."

"At least he's *Percheron*," Noël responded. "But it's going to be lonesome around here."

"More than you know. Jean-Louis told me he is moving to Jean-Pierre's cabin at the end of the summer. That leaves just young Noël and Tutu-*trois,*" referring to their third Indian dog by the same name, "and us."

"Where will the new couple live?"

"Just before his father died," she told him, "Louis Côté acquired a *concession* in Château-Richer."

"That far away?" he protested.

"It's only two villages downstream of here," she said. "Be happy she's getting married and again to someone of means. They are going to own the entire *concession* and he will manage it."

Beauport: Early July, 1662

Pulling his canoe onto the bank of Robert Giffard's large Beauport *concession*, Noël continued to be amazed at the progress. The fieldstone foundation had taken only one week, the floor and walls two more, now the roof was being added, and it was looking like a respectable church. "I'm pleased you could come today," Guyon told him.

"Our superstructure is up and we are ready for finish work." He continued with a sly grin, "I thought a skilled finish carpenter could give my men some assistance and advice."

"I hope I remember something," Noël told him. As they entered, he added, "I see you did put in a choir loft, just like the big churches. You even have a spiral staircase. Just like *Tourouvre.*" Guyon only nodded, Noël remembered that Jean had worked on the grand church of *Tourouvre* in *Perche*, and its crowning feature was its loft and long circular staircase built by a then young stonemason, Jean Guyon.

"We are getting our boards from Pelletier's mill," Guyon reported." Looking up, he added, "Here is someone I want you to meet." He brought Noël over to the largest man he had ever seen. "This is Pierre Tremblay."

Noël shook the giant paw that nearly crushed his hand. "I believe I have seen *Monsieur* Tremblay in *Québec.*"

As they continued the tour, Guyon told him, "He must be the strongest man in the world. Not terribly skilled, but strong! He came from Randonnay in *Perche* in the late forties. He worked around here at odd jobs for years, married and now has a small place in Château-Richer. We would not be half this far without him, but come here, I want you to show these boys how to do this trim."

By the end of the day, Noël realized how correct his wife had been. This project had brought his friend back to life.

Québec: July 15, 1662:

Piloting the ship *La Paix* into the harbor, Noël wondered how many people would turn out for today's arrival. He

260

hoped there would be a crowd, but at this point, only he knew this was the day French-Canada had been awaiting. Once secured to the dock, the usual *engager* and other travelers disembarked. Then came the soldiers, 100 strong. As the citizens on the dock realized what these men meant, they began to cheer and gather closer as two well-dressed gentlemen appeared—followed by young Pierre Boucher.

News of Pierre's visit to Paris had been sparse, but today, the citizens hoped the full report would be positive. The crowd on the dock maneuvered to bid him welcome. He greeted them patiently, shaking hands until a carriage arrived with two soldiers to whisk Pierre and the two men to the fort for an all-day meeting.

After the meeting, Noël and Jean Guyon met their Beauport neighbors at *L'Auberge Oie Bleue.* "Pierre and the two representatives from France met all day with the governor and his staff along with the council and city leaders." Guyon explained. "He gave an excellent presentation of what happened and what we may expect."

"What exactly did he say?" Zacharie Cloutier asked.

"We should wait for him to tell you himself," Guyon explained, "tomorrow evening he is coming to the Langlois home to explain it to us."

With the help of some of the other women, Françoise had her house ready to entertain by the time Pierre arrived with Noël and Jean Guyon. She had also laid out the rules for the evening, "Pierre will speak and we *will not* interrupt. Afterwards we can ask questions." Such advice would not work for long. When Pierre arrived, the mothers began to fuss over him, not fully ready to admit the twelve-year-old boy they had brought from France was becoming one of the most important men in Canada. Eventually they settled down and were seated.

"I left *Québec*, as you know, in October," he began. "I arrived in *La Rochelle* in early December. It took three long days by coach to reach Paris."

"Oh, Pierre!" Perrine Boucher interrupted, "What is Paris like? Is it as spectacular as they say?"

"Well, *Tante* Perrine, the Capital is enormous—it seems to go forever. Some parts are beautiful with wide gardens and splendid palaces, but much of it is poor—and it does not smell as nice as Canada." The ladies all giggled as he continued. "It was cool but not cold like here—it rarely snowed." Again, they all responded on how much colder Canada was.

Pierre spoke up, "I began at the Jesuit Seminary and spoke with the priests. Father LeJeune was there." This elicited each woman's need to comment on their memory of their favorite Jesuit before he could continue, "He spent a great deal of time with me, explaining how things would go and was with me or available almost the entire visit. This put me greatly at ease." His words resulted in a long discussion of Father LeJeune tales, including how *wonderful* he was to young Pierre.

"Then Father LeJeune took me to meet with Prince de Condé at his palace."

Xainte Cloutier's eyes popped, "Did you really meet the Prince? What is his palace like?"

"Yes, I did meet him," he answered calmly. "He is from the Bourbon family—the palace is luxurious. His family *was* Huguenot, but now he has the King's ear and is very influential. He was quite helpful to me and clearly has a great interest in Canada. He took me on a tour of Paris where we visited many palaces and public buildings. Most importantly, he introduced me to Jean-Baptiste Colbert and Count Jean Talon."

"I have heard those names," Françoise interrupted, "but who are they?"

"Colbert is to be the King's Minister. LeJeune said he will be the most powerful man in France. *Monsieur* Colbert told me if the King gets interested in Canada, Talon will be the Intendant for Justice in the colony—and may even come here."

Pierre continued describing places he went, what he saw, and what he learned. Eventually he came to the visit that everyone was anxious to hear. "Ultimately, we went to the Palace of the Louvre and saw His Majesty himself. He was extremely kind and welcoming. We spent most of a day discussing Canada. He had a number of questions, which told me he is very interested in it. Father LeJeune said since they have settled the European wars, the King is now ready to put a great effort and many resources into the colony—the King himself confirmed this."

At this point, Françoise could no longer contain herself, "Pierre, what is His Majesty like?" Smiling, Pierre answered with one word—"Young." before adding, "His Majesty is 23 years old. Here he is, master of a large part of the world and he is—*so young.*"

Françoise smiled inwardly that Pierre, who himself became a young leader in a hostile and little-known country, marveled that someone else was *so young.*

"But he is clearly interested in us," Pierre added, "and wants to help however he can. He told me he would send at least 100 soldiers and 100 settlers—which he did. Unfortunately, some of them were lost in our storms at sea. However, he seems to be committed to send a larger number of the Carignan-Salières regiment in the next two years. He is definitely dedicated to Marguerite Boucher's *Filles du Roi* program. I told him how the lack of women stymied our growth. He has promised to send as many young women as necessary."

The conversation continued well past midnight. It was apparent to everyone that young Pierre Boucher had indeed been the right man to send to the King.

News of Pierre's voyage and the renewed hope of assistance from France spread rapidly through the colony. The newly arrived *engager* easily found employment at various *concessions* to help build Canada into an agricultural power. The new soldiers began to train with Lieutenant René Gauthier, learning how to fight the Iroquois, and Pierre returned to his post as Governor of *Trois-Rivières* with a new level of respect.

Jean Guyon and his crew completed the new chapel, named *la Nativité de Notre-Dame de Beauport,* just in time for the November marriage of Louis Côté to Elisabeth Langlois. Sitting by their fire pit they had built to ward off the November chill, Noël and Françoise enjoyed the post wedding celebration. "Who would have thought we would ever run out of daughters?" she asked him.

Sipping his drink, he pointed to the constantly growing pack of children. "At least we shall never lack for granddaughters."

CHAPTER 36

L'Auberge Oie Bleue: late April 1663 (nine months later)

"Look! There they are," Françoise told the others, "Finally!" As Noël and Jean Guyon approached the table, she said, "We have been here since midday." Adding with a smirk, "We thought perhaps they had ordered your executions."

As her husband dropped into his chair, he replied, "No, something much more important." Suddenly the Beauport neighbors became serious. When Jean and Noël were called early in the morning for an *emergency meeting* of the council, they told the others they would meet them at the *Auberge* for lunch. When they had not appeared on time, the others had begun to worry. Seeing them, the waiter came promptly, and Noël ordered, "Something strong to drink and lots of it." Turning to his friends, he explained,

"Bishop Laval called the meeting, but he called for no executions, at least not yet."

When the waiter appeared with a bottle of the local apple brandy, Noël poured a generous cup, taking an ambitious dose before continuing. "Last night, Abraham Martin brought an early ship from France to the docks. On it was a courier with a special letter for Laval." Taking another drink, he turned to his friend, "You tell them, Jean, you understand this better than I do."

Jean Guyon, who was moving slower, showing his more than 70 years, remained sharp. "It seems His Majesty," he began, "delivered a decree taking personal control of New France. He has made Jean Talon the first Intendant of New France and his minister, Jean-Baptiste Colbert, Intendant of Justice, Public Order, and Finances of Canada."

"So what does this all mean?" Zacharie Cloutier questioned.

Guyon answered, "It means France suddenly cares about Canada, and Laval as well as the council view this as good—very good."

"What did Governor Davaugour think?" Perrine Boucher questioned.

"Not much," Noël told her. "The letter ordered Laval to find a new governor."

"Who will he choose?" asked Marin Boucher.

"Laval thinks this is a critical decision," Noël responded. "Even as we speak, Laval is at the dock telling the captain of the ship that brought the letter he must take Laval posthaste to France. He thinks that is where he can find a suitable man."

"So Davaugour will remain in charge?" Marin asked.

"No." Noël told him, "In fact, Laval is taking him back to France to leave him there. As we have seen, the bishop has rigid requirements for a governor."

"But who will be in charge in their absence?" Perrine asked.

Noël smiled, taking another sip, "Your young nephew, Pierre Boucher." Perrine looked at Françoise in amazement.

The conversation lasted well into the evening. When the Langlois and Jean Guyon reached the canoe dock, Françoise said, "I'll take the back seat and paddle, gentlemen, I think maybe you have had too much to drink."

Arriving in Beauport, they saw Jean to his house. Arriving at their own dark home, Françoise told her husband, "Young Noël said he was going to stay with his brothers at Jean-Pierre's cabin. When he finishes school this year I think he will move in with them. And we'll be all alone."

"We are all getting old," he replied. "Have you noticed how slow Jean Guyon is getting?"

"He is over seventy," she reminded him.

"He said his lungs hurt on the way to the meeting— probably indigestion."

Laval had to wait more than a week before the captain could ready the ship to whisk the impatient prelate to France. He left instructions with the head of the Jesuit house to watch the flock, adding, "I have no idea how long this will take. I must find someone capable, but also willing to take the job."

Three weeks later, Jean Guyon died in his sleep. His many friends and family put him to rest beside his late wife in the cemetery of *Notre-Dame de la Paix* in *Québec*.

<u>*Québec*: Early July 1663:</u>

Early in the season, Marguerite Bourgeoys had sailed to France on a special mission, and word had just arrived that she was returning soon with her cargo—the first *Filles du Roi*. Agents of Louis XIV had been hard at work screening and selecting young marriageable women for the program, and now Marguerite Bourgeoys would chaperone them from *La Rochelle* to the new world. Rumor had it that between 30 and 40 potential brides had been recruited.

Françoise Langlois, and Anne-Gasnier Bourdon, the wife of the long-standing engineer and consultant to the governors of New France, were to greet these women and house them temporarily until marriages could be arranged. The two women had a casual relationship, which had strengthened during the early months of summer when they met regularly at Anne-Gasnier's fine home at the top of the upper town.

"According to the communication we have just received from the ship," Françoise reported, "we are expecting more than 30 women. However, I have no information as to who they are or where they come from. Initially, we will house them in the Ursuline Convent. Once interviewed, we will keep most of them in *Québec*. However, a few will travel to *Trois-Rivières* or *Ville-Marie*."

"We will organize group visits from eligible men of good character," Madame Bourdon told her. "I only hope there will be enough interested men," adding, "Sister *Marie de l'Incarnation* has agreed to use the great room at the Ursuline Convent. Some of the more mature sisters will help chaperone. That way we can assure a high degree of decorum." Françoise wondered how long it had been since Madame Bourdon had been around young couples.

Two days later, Abraham Martin brought *Aigle d'or* to the docks. Anne-Gasnier Bourdon need not have worried about numbers of men. The word had spread quickly and the docks sagged with anxious bachelors. Once the ship was secure, the passengers began to leave. First came a few officials, then a troop of soldiers who received a rousing welcome, followed by the usual group of *engager*. Françoise and Perrine Boucher watched from the bank of the lower town as Marguerite Bourgeoys finally appeared, leading her flock.

Françoise was worried the bachelors might become rowdy, and she guessed from the nervous look on Marguerite Bourgeoys' face, she, too was concerned of a possible riot, but as the young women appeared, marching in pairs, the men maintained the silence and demeanor of Good Friday Mass. Their eyes wide, their mouths agape, but not a word uttered, as their fondest dreams and fantasies marched before them.

"Let us go meet Sister Marguerite," Françoise told Perrine. "I suspect she can use some help." As they made their way through the adoring crowd, Perrine reported, "I counted thirty-six in all. How wonderful!"

When Marguerite saw them, she waved enthusiastically. Once they reached her, she declared with relief, "Thank God, you were nearby. I did not know what to expect." Pointing up the road to the upper town, she told them, "I will lead the way to the convent and would be forever grateful if the two of you will follow from behind to make certain we lose no stragglers."

Marguerite motioned to the young women to follow and began the march up hill. Once they were on their way, the crowd also came to life, and the throng of men began to clap and cheer as the parade moved out.

Madame de la Peltrie, Anne-Gasnier Bourdon, and *Marie de l'Incarnation* met them at the door. "Welcome everyone!" de la Peltrie exclaimed. "Follow us, ladies, I know you are all weary, but we need to do a few preliminaries before you can eat and rest." Turning to Françoise and her friends, she said, "You ladies may rest as well. I suspect the next several days will be hectic." Pointing to a portly nun in the doorway, she said, "Sister Marie-Claude will take care of you."

Françoise had met the plump, and now elderly, nun many years ago in *Mortagne*. They had become good friends and some years later, the nun followed Françoise to the new world. As the *Filles du Roi* entered the great hall, Sister Marie-Claude led the three women into a pleasant library. "Have a seat, ladies," she said. "You look as if you might do well with a libation," she guessed, "particularly you, Sister Marguerite. Do you prefer red or white?"

Marguerite Bourgeoys looked perplexed, "Red or white…?"

"Wine, of course, my good sister."

"You serve wine here?" a stunned Marguerite inquired.

"But of course. The sisters are allowed a small glass with dinner and, naturally, most of the good fathers and many local men enjoy it." Lowering her voice, Sister Marie-Claude continued, "Bishop Laval prefers the reds of Bordeaux. He has each ship bring an adequate supply." As she poured four generous servings of red, she added, "You know if grapes are left to their own devices and merely fall from the vine to ferment on the ground, they become wine. In a way, it is the only nourishment manufactured entirely by God—*santé!*" They all took a sip. Marguerite Bourgeoys' eyes open wide, "Oh my!"

Once Marguerite had recovered, Françoise asked, "Tell us all about your adventure, Sister."

Taking a more adventuresome sip of wine, Marguerite began, "His Majesty's people have done a wonderful job. Young ladies apply through their parish, where they are screened before the parish priest recommends them. I was very pleased that there is a good deal of enthusiasm. It seems that in France there is a scarcity of men and abundance of women, I suppose due to war and disease." Looking up at Sister Marie-Claude, she asked, "Could I perhaps have another glass of wine?"

"The ladies on the committee," she continued with a renewed glass in hand, "should also screen them and decide to which town they should go. I believe you shall be surprised by the variation in the girls. A surprising number are from families with means—however, most have lost their fathers and do not have access to a significant dowry. Others are from working-class families, and another group is rather poor. It will be interesting to see how each group does."

Sister Marie-Claude looked at her own empty glass, suggesting, "Perhaps we should try a red from the region of *La Rochelle*." She began to open another bottle, while Perrine changed the topic asking Marguerite, "How was your crossing?"

"Overall, calm. Of course, we did have some storms but nothing compared to my last voyage." As she tasted a generous swallow of the *La Rochelle*, she smiled, "This is quite good, Sister—how do you come to know about wine?"

"I learned about wine in *Perche*," Sister Marie-Claude reported. "When I came to *Québec,* the convent was new and the sisters found they had to occasionally entertain the priests and city leaders. Since I had some knowledge, you could say I became the convent *sommelier.*"

Snorting a chuckle at her own joke, she poured more wine while Sister Marguerite returned to her story. "The young ladies had a private area in the *Sainte-Barbe* section of the hold. They each had their own small cot and place for their belongings. We ate and washed down there and each day had time to go on deck and take the air." Taking another sip she continued, "The problems came at night when they might sneak out and *fraternize* with the men! I would have to go search and sometimes found them in strange places—and positions!" she added with a smile. Taking more wine, her stories of nighttime passion grew. "One night I found a girl in a rope locker with a sailor. He was taking advantage of her." Lowering her voice, she added, "But not the usual way, she was on her knees and he was…well, behind her!"

Françoise decided they had better leave. She and Perrine excused themselves, saying, "We shall return tomorrow at midday to begin interviewing the young ladies." The two women laughed constantly during the canoe ride to Beauport.

The next day Françoise and Perrine arrived early. Marguerite Bourgeoys along with Madame de la Peltrie had made a short list of questions: name, age, place of birth and residence, schooling if any, and family history. They also charged the two women with getting a feeling for each girl. This would include their goals and what caused them to come to Canada. The women would soon learn each girl also came with a demeanor somewhere between adventuresome and curious to frightened to death.

Françoise's first interview was Marguerite Moitié from *La Rochelle*. She was 15 and came attached with a much more attractive young woman who clung desperately to Marguerite. "This is my sister, Catherine," she told Françoise. "She is a bit nervous."

Françoise took Catherine's hand, speaking gently, "Just sit in this chair, dear. You can listen and you shall be next." The youngster took the chair with caution.

Marguerite explained that their father was a master woolen maker, court officer and *sergent royal.* As a result, both girls came with a dowry. Unfortunately, their mother died some years before and their father had passed this year, leaving them orphans. When the opportunity to come to Canada presented itself, they took it. A married cousin had come to Canada with her husband in 1658 and now lived in *Ville-Marie*.

Catherine, who was one year her junior, shared this background, but was not certain she wanted to marry at her age.

Françoise's next *fille* was another girl from *La Rochelle*. Françoise Moisan was 18, also an orphan. Her late father had been a gardener, but she had no dowry. She had no schooling and no prospects, but she was very interested in marriage. Marguerite Bourgeoys had told Françoise that this was the young lady of the rope locker escapade. Françoise decided not to put that in her report.

The next young woman was Louise Gargottin, 26 years old from a small town near *La Rochelle*. Another orphan, she told Françoise that she had no money or prospects in France and was ready to accept any offer from *any* man.

Her last interview proved to be the most surprising. Jeanne Dodier was her oldest interviewee. At 27, she was from *Mamers*, a town near *Le Mans*. Her father had been a landowner of some means, but both parents were now gone. She did have a dowry. "My mother's sister came to Canada," she told Françoise. "She has died, however, and her son has given me the dowry."

"What was your mother's name?" Françoise enquired.

"Lemaire, Françoise Lemaire. Her late sister's name was Nicole."

Françoise's jaw dropped, as she asked, "And your benefactor's name?"

"Pierre," she replied, "but I can't remember what her married name was."

Françoise responded, "Could it be Boucher?"

"Yes!" Jeanne answered, "How did you know that?"

Françoise smiled and told her, "I believe you will find a number of people in Canada know your cousin."

At the end of the afternoon, the committee met, and each interviewer gave a short summary of each girl questioned. Some stories were funny, some sad, some confusing but all were interesting. Françoise and Perrine began to feel this was new territory for all concerned. Following reports, however, Madame de la Peltrie took the floor with confidence, "I believe we have what we need. Now we must organize the group meetings with prospective husbands. It should not be too difficult."

Again, Françoise worried that Madame did not totally understand men—or young women.

Four days later, the first such meeting took place. Over the previous days, the young ladies had been well-tutored in decorum and rules of behavior. Brought to the meeting

274

room early, *Les Filles du Roi* were stationed near a table in the far corner of the great room where Sister Marie-Claude would later serve a watery, non-alcoholic punch.

Chaperones included some of the more mature nuns as well as Françoise, Perrine and a few other wives who located themselves strategically around the room. Madame de la Peltrie had counselled them to ensure—or try to ensure, civil behavior. As the men entered, the three main chaperones would greet them. Madame de la Peltrie was born of great wealth and although she was kind, she exuded an air of superiority. *Sister Marie de l'Incarnation* was tall, thin and severe. Her mere glance put terror in men's hearts. Anne-Gasnier Bourdon had a kind and gentle air, but the men knew that her husband wielded great power.

The meeting was open to eligible men including those who had completed their *engager* contracts and were free to marry. Posted rules stated men must be clean, sober, and there would be no bad behavior such as fighting or swearing. The rules further explained men and women could visit freely, but that chaperones would be present. If at any time, a couple felt they had reached an agreement to proceed, they could visit one of the two *notaires*, Paul Vachon and François Badeau, who sat at a table, ready to provide advice and documents. Admission was on first come basis and stopped when Madame de la Peltrie determined there was no more room.

A full hour before entry, men began to gather at the door. A cross section of *Québec* males, some came well dressed and others wore soiled work clothes. Their ages ranged from 16 to 70. Occupations covered the waterfront of society, and although *engager* who had yet to fulfill their three-year contract were not allowed, some managed to gain entry.

At the appointed hour, Madame de la Peltrie opened the doors, announcing that the visitors should enter in an orderly fashion and give their name to one of the two nuns seated at the entry. This worked for the first ten men, after which pandemonium staked its first claim. However, as the first wave caught sight and scent of the women, inertia set in, and the two groups stood at some distance staring at each other, wondering how to proceed. Ultimately, one brave soul bridged the gap, crossing the imaginary Rubicon to say *bonsoir* to a *fille*. Eventually all girls were visiting, soon each girl had a few visitors—some had several.

Françoise, Perrine and the other wives began to circulate to prevent undisciplined behavior and violation of rules which proved a larger task than they had envisioned. As they maneuvered about, it was apparent several of the men were in violation of one or more of the posted rules. Françoise stopped one older gentleman from fondling a much younger girl's breasts. "Begging your pardon, Madame," he explained, "you wouldn't expect me to buy a milk cow without first examining the udder."

Later she saw a young man from Beauport passionately kissing Marguerite Moitié. When Françoise intervened, the girl pleaded, "I thought kissing was permitted," then whispering, "and he was so sweet!" From there Françoise was shocked to see Marguerite's shy sister, Catherine, allowing a young man to massage her backside. When Françoise approached, the young *fille* pleaded, "He was so lonesome—and I didn't know it would feel like that!"

In the course of the evening, many indiscrete acts were halted, although Françoise was convinced that even more went undetected. Overall, however, she felt the evening went as well as could be expected, and at the end of the event, a number of contracts had been signed. The bell rang at the appointed hour, and the men were escorted to the square and the *filles* to their bunks.

Noël and Marin Boucher had agreed to wait for their wives at the *L'Auberge Oie Bleue* across the square from the convent. When the women reached the table, they were tired and giggling. Françoise dropped into her chair, "Get us a drink, kind sirs," she said. "See if *Monsieur* Fortin has any good wine." Once served, they began to regale their spouses with tales of the evening.

"But tell, us," Noël said at a brief lull in the hilarity, "did they sign any marriage contracts?"

"Oh, yes," Perrine said, attempting to avoid laughing, "Forty-seven!"

Marin thought for a second, "How many girls do you have?"

Now laughing, she answered, "Thirty-five."

"But…"

Françoise explained, "I think Monday someone must go over things with *Les Filles.*"

Wednesday, Françoise, Perrine and a few other wives met with the three main chaperones. "Monday we met with the young women," Anne-Gasnier Bourdon explained. "It seems most of the girls come from circumstances where they have never been courted. When a man showed some enthusiasm, they immediately agreed to a contract, but as the night went on, they found more—should I say, *interesting* men, so they agreed to *another* contract."

"That explains the number of contracts," Perrine noted.

"Yes," Anne-Gasnier agreed, "but there is more to it. As you know, as with all French marriage contracts, either party may break it at any time before the marriage, even with no good reason." Pushing back her chair, she continued, "Another wrinkle occurred Saturday night after the group meeting. *Les filles* went to their bunks and gossiped into the night. Soon they found there were many more desirable men than they had met. In addition, they realized not every single man in the colony came to *this* group meeting. So, some canceled their contract—or contracts."

By now, the wives were laughing, and Françoise asked, "So how many contracts do you have now?"

Anne-Gasnier stood and looked out the second-story window with a beautiful view of the square. Turning, she answered, "One." As the audience laughed again, she added, "and that was Louise Gargottin, the oldest girl at 26, who has no dowry. She told Françoise at the interview she was ready to marry anyone who would have her."

"What do we do?" Perrine asked.

"Carry on," Anne-Gasnier told her. "Sister Bourgeoys is returning to *Ville-Marie* this week and will take six girls with her, two for *Trois-Rivières* and the other four for *Ville-Marie*. I for one," she added, "have not had this much fun since I was a girl. We shall continue our meetings until everyone is spoken for—and satisfied with their decision."

As the women rose to adjourn, Françoise asked, "Is the one contract going to be consummated?"

"Yes," Anne-Gasnier reported, "However, there is a wrinkle. Her man is a Daniel Perron, also from *La Rochelle*. He has a farm in *Château-Richer*. Like some from *La Rochelle*, he was a Huguenot and needs to officially abjure Calvinism, so they cannot marry until the first of the year. I have hired Louise Gargottin as a maid until that time. Our next group meeting for *les Filles du Roi* will be Saturday evening."

Over the course of the week, *les filles* traded stories, becoming considerably more perceptive in the art of courtship. Saturday they came to the great room with a different attitude. They were more subtle, demure, and aware that they were much more in demand than were the men. The men began to sense this and became very solicitous. *Les filles* sensed this as well and kept an arm's length, waiting for a man who fulfilled their needs. Contracts became less frequent and at the end of the evening, there were seven. Two days later, there were only five.

CHAPTER 37

<u>*Québec*</u>: September 18, 1663

A moderate crowd awaited the ship as Abraham Martin brought it to the dock. Noël had told his wife it was an important arrival as Bishop Laval was returning with the new governor. "That may be the case," Françoise told him with a grin, as the dockhands caught the mooring lines, "but even the bishop cannot draw a crowd to rival *Les Filles du Roi.*" Once the ship was secure, passengers began to march down the gangplank. "My goodness," Françoise exclaimed, "I believe this is the largest group of men we have seen on a single ship."

"Laval said he was going to bring back as many people as possible," Noël reported. "I suspect they are not all *engager* either—a few seem to be with women." Finally, the bishop disembarked, accompanied by a well-dressed man of a similar age. "I suppose I should go up to the fort

280

now. Bourdon said Laval would want to meet as soon as he arrived."

"I have a meeting at the convent concerning *Les Filles du Roi,*" Françoise said, "Anne-Gasnier Bourdon suggested we go to *L'Auberge Oie Bleue* afterward for dinner. Perhaps you can bring her husband and join us." Putting her hand on his shoulder, she added with a sly smile, "Now that young Noël has moved in with his brothers, we are free to do as we please."

Noël agreed, giving her a peck on the forehead, and headed to the fort.

A few hours later, Françoise, Anne-Gasnier, and Perrine Boucher took a table at the upper town eatery. Looking carefully at a paper she held, Anne-Gasnier reported, "Of our 30 *filles* we now have one-third who are married and one-third more who have signed contracts. I hope by the end of the year almost all of them will have wed." Setting her paper aside, she finished, "Unfortunately, Sister Bourgeoys sent word we may not have any *filles* next year."

"Why is that?" Perrine asked with a frown. "They seem to be doing well."

Taking a sip of wine, Anne-Gasnier told her, "Madame de la Peltrie told me France wants to wait a year to see what the outcomes are. However, she is confident it will start again the following year and hopefully with greater numbers."

"She told me," Françoise whispered, "that three of the young ladies have been caught having relations with men—two inside the convent walls."

Perrine laughed aloud, "I think that is pretty good for single French girls. I'm surprised there have not been more—at least they are not afraid to conceive."

Françoise choked on her wine, laughing at her friend's joke, adding, "I suspect there have been more."

"Looks like a good deal of fun for a church meeting." The women quickly looked up to see their husbands and the speaker, Pierre Boucher.

Perrine jumped up to embrace her nephew. "I thought you were back in *Trois-Rivières*."

"No, *Tante* Perrine," he replied. "I needed to remain and report to the bishop and new governor. But I am headed home in two days."

The women fawned over Pierre as usual. Eventually Françoise turned to Perrine's husband. "I didn't know you were going to the council meetings, Marin."

"They wanted another Beauport representative to replace Jean Guyon," he explained, "but I am just an advisor like Noël—we don't vote on important matters."

"Well, important or not," Anne-Gasnier Bourdon said, "tell us what happened, Noël."

"As you know," he began, "Bishop Laval went to France searching for a new governor. Apparently, his problem was not just finding someone capable, but more so was finding someone willing to come to Canada. However, *Monsieur* Bourdon can give us more information."

"Our new governor is Augustine de Saffray de Mézy," Bourdon reported. "He prefers de Mézy. He and Laval were at school together in Caen. De Mézy is a true Normand. Apparently, he is highly competent but was reluctant to come as he had some debts, but Laval paid those and de Mézy agreed. His Majesty has made the position a *vice-regal* post. This allows de Mézy to speak for the king himself. The bishop believes this will give Canada a new level of influence. Perhaps Governor Boucher can tell us more."

Pierre thought for a moment before beginning, "De Mézy believes we must put our efforts into agriculture rather than furs. Further, he feels we must continue to control the Indians. As of now, the Iroquois are hard pressed by the other tribes and have suffered in numbers from a recent smallpox epidemic. He thinks we need to go to whatever means necessary to defeat them permanently."

Jean Bourdon took a bottle of Calvados and poured a glass. Taking a swallow, he added his hope, "Along with Indians and agriculture, if the man is a true Normand, perhaps he can find a way for us to produce the real thing. This swill we call Calvados is apple brandy at its worst."

Once all the news had been reported, digested and revised, Noël told his wife, "We should be off, my dear, I must rise early tomorrow."

Françoise hugged and kissed Pierre, "Have a safe voyage if I don't see you before and say hello to your family. Tell your father I send him a kiss. I'm certain they, and all of *Trois-Rivières,* will be thrilled to have you home." When Noël and Françoise reached the canoe dock, she looked up, putting her arms around her husband's waist. "With that moon, anyone could find their way home."

Once away from the dock, she asked, "What do you have early tomorrow?"

"Our son-in-law, René Chevalier, asked Marin and me to help with the new seminary. Now that Laval is receiving regular funds from Paris," he added, "everyone is being paid—and paid well."

"Why do they need a seminary?" she asked. "The Jesuits already have the college across the square with plenty of room."

"Apparently Laval is going to start training new priests starting with all ages. The new building will house them and have class rooms, and I heard it will also have a retirement home for the older clerics." He added with a twinkle, "I think the bishop likes his comforts and is afraid he is at risk to retire with the common fathers. However, it all works for René. With Jean Guyon gone, he is now the master mason and stone cutter—so our daughter, Jeanne has little to worry about."

"I must go in early as well," she told him. "Perrine and I have a meeting at the convent about *les filles.* May we all go together?"

"Of course, we can take the large canoe—or the carriage."

"Dear God!" she exclaimed, looking up at the bright crescent moon, "Who would have ever believed we would be rich. Living alone—with a cart, a carriage and two canoes. The girls are all married to men with means, and the boys run our *concessions.* I heard Jean-Louis tell his older brother they should consider buying another." When they had secured the canoe, she took his hand and pulling him toward the beach, said, "Let's do something we have not done for a long while," and she began to disrobe.

"You aren't going into the river, are you?" he asked with a look of disbelief. "It's freezing!"

She pulled harder, "I shall keep you warm."

At sunrise, the two couples headed across the *Riviére Saint-Charles* to the lower town docks. "I have the agenda for today," Perrine informed her friend as they paddled to

284

keep ahead of the current. "Tell me if I have it correct. Of the thirty girls who stayed in *Québec*, ten are now married and ten have contracts. I think the nuns are going to move those with contracts to Madame de la Peltrie's home so they can plan for their marriages without being distracted by the others—not to mention the men at the meetings trying to give them another choice."

"Will her house be crowded?" Noël asked.

Both women laughed, as Perrine told him, "Apparently you have not been to Madame's home—it is almost as large as the convent. Do not forget, this was the woman who chartered her own ship to cross the ocean. At any rate," she continued, "the other young ladies will continue to attend meetings until they have decided their fate. Madame says they expect a few weddings will be in the winter and one or two girls may spend the winter with the nuns."

"That sounds like fun," Noël said sarcastically as they landed. The women merely frowned and Françoise said, "We will meet you at *L'Auberge Oie Bleue* for dinner. We will likely be late."

Walking to the upper town, the men stopped by the church, which sat nearby the seminary construction, while the women proceeded up to the convent. "My God!" Noël exclaimed, examining the structure, "the exterior is nearly finished!"

"While you have been sailing the river," Marin told him, "your son-in-law has been cracking the whip. Almost 300 men have arrived from France this season—a definite record, and many are building tradesmen. I believe the bishop has plans for this to be finished before next year."

They found René Chevalier giving orders to various teams. Greeting them, he said, "Marin, you know what to do. Captain Langlois, come with me."

"If you call Marin by his first name," Noël told the young man, "you can call me Noël."

"Well sir, it doesn't seem right," the lad replied. Noël only shrugged. Chevalier was pointing out a few jobs on which he wanted Noël's assistance when they saw a large man carrying a block that would normally take three men. "Have you met Pierre Tremblay?"

Pierre moved the mammoth stone to his left shoulder and offered his right hand to Noël. "We met," he said, "morning, Captain." As he walked on, Chevalier said, "If I had three like him, I would have this done before the snow."

Leaving the seminary later that afternoon, Marin suggested, "The women said they would be late, let's have a glass of ale at *Taverne Terre Sauvage*."

Approaching the venerable establishment, they heard, "Hey Captain!" There was no doubt who it was. When they turned the corner, they saw Benoît and Bernier. "Aren't you boys a little late getting in?" Marin asked.

"I guess we are, but we's getting ready to head west again. This year we did our tradin' in *Montréal,* and then took a little tour down the Champlain River and farther south to see them *Mary-landers*."

His interest sparked, Noël inquired, "What did you find out?"

"Well, Captain, we found the Iroquois beat the hell outta them Susquehannock. They had hooked up with the *Mary-landers* but that didn't do 'em no good. Iroquois had about 800 braves. The Susquehannock is still runnin' south. So the Iroquois up and got bored, and now they's taken on the English."

"Do you think we should ally with the English to beat the Iroquois?" Marin questioned.

"Hell, no!" Benoît answered, "Worst thing you could do." Marin looked confused, so Benoît continued, "As soon as you got the injun pressure off them Englishmens, they'd be up the Champlain and in the *Saint-Laurent* right quick. They's just waitin' to get their hands on Canada, and the only thing you can do ta stop 'em is make friends with them Iroquois and set 'em on them English."

Now totally confused, Marin said, "What?"

"Believe me, yer honor, these English want Canada, and the only group with enough balls to keep at them English, no matter what, is them Iroquois."

When the men left and headed to the upper town and dinner with their wives, Marin said, "I still don't get this."

"I didn't either," said Noël, "but now I think I see. Let us say the Iroquois are a mean dog. Now one thing a mean dog does is keep people away—like burglars. So let's say the English are our burglars and the Iroquois are the meanest dog we can get."

Marin began to laugh. Once he recovered he told his friend, "Noël, you certainly have a way of putting things." When they reached *L'Auberge Oie Bleue*, he added, "I hope there are no mean dogs in here."

CHAPTER 38

<u>Beauport: Spring 1664</u>

Always a fine but raucous affair, the first Sunday picnic of spring drew the largest crowd. Along the Beauport coast, the extended families gathered for fun, food, games or just to catch up with children, grandchildren and even some great-grandchildren. Noël and Françoise Langlois now had five married children, fourteen grandchildren, and no end in sight. These numbers paled, however, compared with many of their neighbors.

Looking over the scene, Xainte Cloutier remarked, "From here it is difficult to see why Canada isn't growing."

Perrine Boucher laughed, "Do not forget we came as five couples. Since then, most new Canadians are single men. *Engager* and even most of the non-indentured men come lacking a spouse. Marin told me we are expecting a few hundred new *engager* and a few hundred soldiers—all who come without women. This is why we need *Les Filles du Roi*, and why I am upset France has decided not to send any this year."

"At least they are sending men for the army," Françoise replied. Looking out with a smile at the pandemonium of games and socialization among the children, she ordered, "We had better get the food out. It seems we have our own army to feed."

One month later, Bishop Laval held a grand opening of his new facility, *Le Grand Séminaire de Québec.* The bishop was in grand form as he welcomed the families, officials and religious personnel. "I have modeled it after my own institution in France, *Le Séminaire des Missions Etrangères,* in Paris. We shall welcome men and boys with vocation for the priesthood as well as natives. We shall even...," he claimed with a sly grin, "welcome the Sulpicians."

"My word, this is huge," Françoise told her husband, as they walked through the cavernous space. "Oh, look there are some of the sisters, let's go see them." Strolling over to a table of treats and drinks, they saw Madame de la Peltrie, *Marie de l'Incarnation,* and a surprise—Marguerite Bourgeoys. "Oh, my dears!" Bourgeoys said as she gave hugs to Françoise and her husband. "Come have refreshment. I have wonderful news from France." Sister Marie-Claude stepped from behind the table and gave Françoise a bone-cracking embrace. Pouring two glasses of red wine, she handed them to the Langlois, whispering, "This is the bishop's favorite Bordeaux." Pouring herself a generous cup, she whispered, "It is very dear." Then she touched their glasses, adding, "*Santé!*"

Marguerite subtly set her empty glass on the table and looked away as Sister Marie-Claude filled it. Picking it up, Bourgeoys told Françoise, "Only yesterday, the bishop received word from his majesty. He has reconsidered and *is* sending some *Filles du Roi* this season, not many, I fear, but at least some." She looked about before draining her glass.

When Françoise returned to the head of the table, Madame de la Peltrie asked her, "Did the sister tell you the good news?" Françoise nodded and Madame told her, "We do not know as yet when to expect them, but I will call a meeting of the committee soon. All but two of our girls from last year are now married." Lowering her voice to a whisper, "And well more than half are *already* with child."

Québec: June 15, 1664

Coming back to the canoe dock after her day working at the hospital, Françoise could hardly miss the crowd at the dock. She knew the *Filles du Roi* were not anticipated for a few weeks, but her curiosity took the better of her, and she walked down to join the crowd. She strained to see the ship just appearing around the tip of *Île d'Orléans.* "Madame Langlois," turning toward the crowd she saw Lieutenant René Gauthier whom she had met through her husband. "Are you here to welcome the troops?" he asked.

She wanted to hide her ignorance, but decided on the truth, "Troops?"

"It has not been announced to the public but I thought, maybe your husband...?"

"Oh, he wouldn't tell me something confidential," she fibbed.

"Not really an important secret, Madame," he confided, "This is the arrival of the first company entirely of the new *Carignan-Salières Regiment.* We hope there will be well over 100 in all, and many more to come. There is a regimental captain onboard, Captain Dugué. He is Bretagne. I do not know him, but he will remove some pressure from me. We are hopeful Minister Colbert will send several hundred more troops by next year."

He began to walk toward the dock but stopped and turned, "Oh, by the way, your Indian man, Jacques-Henri, would he be willing to help train the men?"

"I would imagine so," she answered. "If you like, I will tell him you want to speak with him."

"That would be very helpful, Madame. He was very helpful to me." Gauthier walked toward the dock as Abraham Martin brought the ship in.

Having seen enough, Françoise turned toward the canoe dock when she heard, "I didn't know you were coming to see the troops." She looked over to see her husband.

"I was going to the canoe dock," she told him, "when I saw Lieutenant Gauthier."

"I'm meeting Abraham," he responded, "we are supposed to meet with the governor later today."

The ship was secured and suddenly the dock was alive with brown-coated soldiers and cheering citizens. "I'm going before the crowd gets too large," she told him, "You can tell me about it when you get home."

Once the military was away, the crowd dispersed and a weary Abraham Martin strolled slowly down the dock. "Moving a little slow today, Captain," Noël called out as he came to greet his friend and partner.

"These ships get harder to steer every year," he replied. "Hell, I'm…" he thought a moment while counting on his

291

fingers, "Shit! I'm 75 years old. We don't have any ships that old."

Noël put his arm around his friend's shoulder. "We still have to go up later and see the governor introduce the new men, but we have some time. Come with me to the *Taverne Terre Sauvage*, I'll buy you a drink."

"Better make it two," the old seaman replied.

Approaching the tavern, Abraham said, "There are our two friends. I don't know if I have enough energy for them."

"Cheer up, Captain," Noël told him. "Maybe they'll buy."

"Look who's here," Benoît said as the two captains approached, "Go get another chair, Bernier, let the Captains have a seat."

Bernier pulled a chair over and Abraham dropped into it. "What's the news this year, boys?"

"Big news, yer honor. So big this calls for shots and beers." Benoît ordered, and Noël asked, "What's up?"

"I see you just got some more soldier boys," Benoît said, "I think you're gonna need 'em. We went way south down Lake Champlain and down the Hudson all the way to New Amsterdam. The Iroquois was shootin' up the Dutchmen—serves 'em right for sellin' guns to them redskins in the first place." Drinks arrived and Bernier lit each shot. The men threw them back and chased them with the beer as Benoît continued. "Them Dutchmens was holdin' their own until the English shows up. Hell, they rode through that valley like the plague, shootin' everyone what's not an Englishman. When we left for the north, what Dutchmens was left was hightailin' it to the harbor and gettin' on boats back to Dutchmanland in Europe. Them Iroquois just limped away—but *they'll* be back."

"So, how does this affect us?" Noël asked.

"Like I been sayin' fer years, Captain, if we plays our cards right, this'll work to our advantage." Finishing his second round and ordering a third, Benoît continued, "Now you got these here soldiers—set them on the Iroquois. Right now, them Iroquois is hurtin' but they will come back like always. If you can kill enough of them, they's gonna make a truce with the French and go back after them English. Them English is just after farms and they want that whole valley up ta Lake Champlain and beyond fer farms. But if France helps them Iroquois, they can raid them farm towns and kick em outa here fer good."

Noël and Abraham finished their drinks and excused themselves to hike up to the fort and their meeting. "Do you think we should mention this to anyone?" Noël asked.

"Why not," Abraham replied, "couldn't hurt."

In the morning, Captain Abraham Martin, who had lived in Canada longer than any other Frenchman, was found dead in bed. The crowd of his mourners at *Notre-Dame de la Paix* rivaled that of Champlain.

<u>*Québec*: Two months later</u>

"Do you think this rain will ever stop?" Perrine questioned.

"It usually does," Françoise replied. "I'm just happy we can stand under the dock office canopy. Oh look! There it is." Laughing she noted, "The ship is only 100 feet away, I hope Noël can see the dock."

The ship came expertly into the mooring while the hapless drenched dockhands went to secure the lines. First came a group of *engager,* exhausted from a long, difficult voyage and blinded by the downpour. Eventually Françoise saw the young women. "I suppose we must go welcome them," Perrine said, pulling her hood over her head. The befuddled group on board the ship followed an equally confused nun down the dock where Perrine and Françoise waited.

"I'm Sister Geneviève from the Ursuline convent in *La Rochelle*," she told them. "Does it rain like this often?"

"No," Perrine replied, "sometimes it is quite heavy." The nun remained silent until she noticed Perrine's grin, causing her to emit a very un-nun-like giggle. "Unfortunately," Perrine told them, "We have a rather long uphill hike to the convent before you can get warm and dry." Perrine led the way while Françoise brought up the rear along the long muddy path to the upper town. Arriving at the convent, they quickly entered. Anticipating their condition, the nuns had a fire going and helped *les filles* out of their drenched garments while giving each a blanket.

As she removed her habit, Sister Geneviève unbuttoned her bodice, producing a wrinkled paper. "Here is a list of names," she explained while blushing. "It was the only place I could keep it dry."

Taking the list with authority, their hostess announced, "I am Madame de la Peltrie, I will be in charge of you for now. Sister Marie-Claude," pointing to the portly nun, "shall take you to your dormitory to get settled, warm and dry and have a short rest after which we will meet to discuss your visit."

As the group marched up the stairs, Madame de la Peltrie sat to look at the list while explaining to Françoise and Perrine, "Sister Marguerite Bourgeoys was hoping to be here by now, but she is doubtless caught in the weather." Reading aloud, "Fifteen young women, six private dowries—oh my, one of 800 *livres*! Ages fifteen to… oh my! To 46 years of age! Ah, the large dowry belongs to the older woman." Standing she declared, "At any rate, we shall follow the same protocol as last year. You ladies can interview *les filles* and we will begin group meetings for prospective spouses." Standing, she pointed to the office, "Let us began!"

Three days later, Jean-Pierre came to visit his parents, accompanied by his Uncle Jean Langlois. "Uncle Jean is going to move his boat building business down here, and I am going to join him."

"What do you mean by *down here?*" his father asked.

"Down on the bank of the *concession*. It will be closer to the market and to labor."

"But, what about the sawmill?" Noël enquired.

"Actually it began as Jean-Claude Pelletier's idea. He needs space and would like to have our workshop to expand the mill."

"But…" Noël did not have time for the next question before his son answered it. "He knows exactly how to make our boards. He can make them and move them here by barge. It will be much more efficient."

"And where will you get the barge?" Noël wondered.

His son answered with a grin, "We have already built it."

"Well, I guess…"

"Good," Jean-Pierre answered him. Turning to face his father, he added, "Also, I'm getting married."

Now totally overwhelmed, Noël sputtered, "What? Who?"

"Charlotte-Françoise Bélanger."

With this, Françoise's face brightened, coming to life, "How… how wonderful—keeping it in the neighborhood."

Charlotte-Françoise was a child from one of the early Guyon marriages in Beauport.

His mother hugged him, and his father reached out to shake his son's hand. Facing his son and his brother, Noël anticipated the next question as he asked, "How much will you need to borrow for this boat factory?"

Finally Uncle Jean spoke, "Well, brother, I've put enough away for the entire project just this summer." He waited for his brother's amazed reaction before adding, "When you live in a country where the way to get around is by water, building boats is a gold mine—you just don't need to dig in the dirt."

With a look of astonishment, Noël asked, "When will you start?"

Jean-Pierre smiled. "Not to waste time, we thought we would start moving tomorrow."

Later that evening Françoise told her husband, "I am very excited—I think this idea is wonderful!"

After spending the next day at the convent, Françoise arrived home holding a letter. "This was sent to me at the convent," she said, sadly.

"What is it?" Noël asked.

"A letter from Pierre—his father, Gaspard, died two weeks ago."

In the wilderness, nothing was certain, and joy did not last forever.

Ursuline Convent: two weeks later

When the women met to interview the new *filles,* they included a discussion on the wisdom of being patient and prudent before signing a contract. The women now felt more confident as the love-starved and lonesome single men of Québec attended the first group meeting with enthusiasm. This time each of the men signed in, and things seemed to go well in spite of a large discrepancy of numbers between eligible women and suitors. Once over their shyness, a swarm of desperate men surrounded each *fille*.

The parish ladies and nuns had made it clear that inappropriate behavior would not be tolerated. In spite of this warning, Perrine and Françoise pulled two couples apart, one in a small room off the kitchen and a second more daring couple locked in the throes of passion upstairs in a dormitory bed. At the end of the evening, the matrons had finally pushed the men out the door and sent the young *filles* upstairs, in theory, to sleep. However, everyone knew better.

As the house calmed down, Madame Bourdon came out with a handful of documents. "We have the contracts from this evening."

"How many?" Madame de la Peltrie asked.

Anne-Gasnier Bourdon tried to remain serious when she announced, "48 from 15 young ladies."

Madame de la Peltrie fell into a chair, holding her face in her hands, as the others tried to stifle their giggles. "How could this be?" the rich benefactress moaned.

Anne-Gasnier could not control her laughter, as she choked out, "The full moon?"

"There was no moon tonight!" de la Peltrie protested, bringing her head out of her hands.

Hiding her face with a kerchief, Anne-Gasnier replied simply, "Oh."

The next two meetings were more controlled. By October, there had been seven marriages, six additional reliable contracts and two yet unspoken-for *filles*. To celebrate their success, Laval invited the women in charge, along with their spouses, to dine at the seminary.

"Tonight," he told them once they had all arrived, "we shall dine in my private quarters." The fabled *private quarters* occupied much of the upper story of the seminary. All the wives had been dying to see it and were not disappointed when he gave them a full tour. Along the way, Perrine whispered to Françoise, "Do you suppose this is what the king's quarters are like in the Louvre?" The tour ended in the large dining room, constructed to facilitate a considerably larger group of diners. Dinner was exquisite, and entirely from *Québec* produce and animals—with the exception of Bordeaux wine. Following dinner, the Beauport contingency retired to *L'Auberge Oie Bleue* for a drink and gossip.

The *Filles du Roi* came under control, signing valid and lasting contracts. By late autumn, all but two *filles* were married or engaged. Marguerite Bourgeoys made a final trip of the season to *Québec* where she addressed the ladies at the home of Madame de la Peltrie. "We expect as many as 100 *Filles du Roi* next year. I shall go early to France and hope to chaperone as many as possible on the crossing. Following this, I am planning to build a residence for the newcomers in *Ville-Marie* and have discussed a similar facility in *Québec* with Madame de la Peltrie."

She then produced a bottle, "This," she announced, "is the first bottle of wine produced from French grapes on the island of *Montréal*. The vines came from northern France. Blessedly, they are able to survive our winters. The farmer who brought them has produced his first wine this season." She handed it to Madame de la Peltrie who poured a small glass for each. Marguerite stood. "*Mesdames et Bonne Sœurs,* as the men struggle to make this a safe and viable nation, we women shall make it a nation of families." Raising her glass, she shouted, "TO CANADA!"

They had never before heard her raise her voice.

At the same time, Noël was heading across his *concession* to the boat shop his sons and brother had built. When he reached the top of the rise overlooking the shop, he was shocked. He had not visited for some weeks, but instead of boats, they were building walls, greatly enlarging the facility. Walking down the rise, he came to his son Jean-Pierre. "What are you doing, lad? I thought you were going to build boats."

Jean-Pierre put down his saw. Wiping his hands on his apron, he replied, "We're expanding, Pa."

Noël's jaw dropped, "Expanding? You have only started—and you had more space than you needed in the beginning."

"I know, Pa," he admitted while repositioning the saw. "But we want more inside space that we can heat to work in through the winter, and we're going to hire more men—a lot more."

"Who is going to buy a boat in the winter?"

"Probably no one, Pa. We just want to be ready."

"Ready for what, son?"

"Well, you see, Pa," he replied, again laying the tool aside. "Uncle Jean and Jean-Louis took a new boat we made to *Trois-Rivières* to give it a good test—it tested great!" Putting his arm on his father's shoulder, much as Noël had done to him as a boy, he continued, "When they were down there, they saw Pierre Boucher who told them the government is bringing *hundreds—maybe a thousand* soldiers for a war with the Iroquois."

Noël remained unimpressed, "I don't think they're going to kill them with boats."

Jean-Pierre chuckled, "Probably not, Pa, but we figure they gotta get all these hundreds of men to the Indians."

"Son," he said trying to seem patient, "they have their own ships."

"Well, yes, Pa, but how far down the Richelieu River can they get in ships, and how about all the smaller rivers?" The boy shrugged before ending, "Pierre seemed to think it was a great idea. He even sent Lieutenant Gauthier over to show us what he thought would be a good design to move soldiers. Anyhow," he concluded, handing his apron and saw to his father, "as long as you're here, how about some help?"

Beauport: December 31, 1664

Françoise gave out a playful scream as Jacques-Henri brought the sleigh down the steep incline leading back to his camp. "Oh, *Mon Dieu!*" she exclaimed, as he stopped next to the steam hut. "I haven't had this much fun since... well, I suppose the last time!" Looking across the *Saint-Laurent* at the gorgeous winter day, she added, "It must have been ages ago, when we still had children at home."

Jacques-Henri unleashed the sled dogs while Félicity-Angel opened the flap on the steam hut. "All ready!" she announced. The foursome disrobed and entered the glorious enclosure of moist heat. Félicity-Angel passed a jug of native beverage while they relaxed and chatted about their long friendship and days gone by.

With the setting of the early winter sun, the Langlois returned to their home. They were greeted by Tutu-*trois*, their own Indian sled dog that was, as Françoise put it, "more lover than worker." After Noël stoked the coals, she stirred the porridge. Soon they sat alone and dined. "This empty house seems so huge!" she exclaimed, as the fire filled the walls with shadows.

"Enjoy it," he told her, "next weekend we have some of the children coming with God knows how many grandchildren."

"Let's just leave the plates," she said, "Get some Calvados and we will lie on the bear by the fire, like the old days." As she reclined on Robert's giant bearskin trophy, she said sadly, "For years I used to cry if I sat on this. I guess things like that do pass with time. Now I just dream of him and what he could be doing were he living."

He poured two glasses, whispering in her ear, "*Santé*."

Sipping hers, she smiled, "You know, this really *isn't* very good."

Laughing, he replied, "You are correct, but I don't know if I could get used to the real thing." She giggled nearly spilling her glass. "Tomorrow is a holy day. I think if the weather is good, we should skip the chapel and go to the *Cathéderal*," pronouncing the word with a snobbish air. "I still don't understand what had been *Notre-Dame de la Paix* last year, is suddenly *La Cathéderal de Notre-Dame de Québec* just because of Laval."

"You see," he began to explain, "now that he is Bishop..." She interrupted, "I know. It is just that I did not grow up with that, and it seems... well, silly. I think we have bigger issues in Canada. With all the soldiers fighting the Iroquois and all the new *Filles du Roi*, and..."

"Oh, I don't know," he said laying his head on the bear's as if it were a pillow, "I'll wager this year will be one of the calmest ever."

CHAPTER 39

<u>Northwestern wilderness: April 1665</u>

The tribe moved efficiently in nearly single file, as it threaded its way west though the hills and forests of their winter grounds. This was their annual migration to the Great Plains in the west where they could harvest the omnipresent buffalo, collecting enough meat to sustain the tribe through the next winter. More migratory than most bands of the Cree Nation, *Neigemain's* tribe was nearly always on the move, frequently expanding their region by entering unknown lands.

It was just such a venture that had caused them to find *Neigemain* eleven years before when a small band ventured far to the east during the year of the great snow. Crossing a snow-covered dome, they saw a human hand, protruding as if reaching from the snow. Digging, they uncovered *Neigemain* and three other braves. All appeared dead, but as the Cree prepared to leave, *Neigemain* moved. On careful inspection, he was breathing—but barely. Loading him onto the sleigh they used to carry game, they returned to their hunting camp, leaving the dome just as the wind advanced, again burying the remaining three corpses in snow.

His shallow breathing gained strength as they reached camp, where they lay him in a tent by the fire to warm. In the morning, he was almost conscious. As his color returned and his frost coating disappeared, they realized he was not Indian, only his dress and the Algonquin amulet around his neck were native. Deciding he must be a French backwoodsman who had abandoned his people, they began to spoon warm broth into his mouth bringing him back to life. During the retreat to their home camp, he improved daily and soon was walking, although his right side remained weak.

Since the Cree people speak an Algonquin dialect, communication, though strained, was possible. His thoughts and speech were jumbled, but it was apparent he had no memory of the past. In camp, a young squaw who had recently lost her mate began to tend him. She gave him a name in French, meaning *Hand-in-Snow*. Her name was *Oota-dabun*, meaning *Day Star*. Today, as they approached the plains and their buffalo hunting grounds, she followed her man in lockstep with their nine-year-old twin sons in tow.

CHAPTER 40

<u>Beauport: May 7, 1665</u>

Putting his tools back in place, Noël removed his apron and dunked his hands in the basin. "I'm taking off, boys," he announced. "I told your mother we would go to town tonight." Leaving the factory, he looked up at the sign, LANGLOIS BOAT WORKS. Smiling, he knew the sign had been designed to bring his money, labor and standing into the enterprise. Looking with pride at the several completed crafts standing in the yard, he realized his sons and brother had developed a boat similar to the common shallop, but made to move personnel rather than goods through the various small waterways of *Québec*. Moreover, they worked! Lieutenant René Gauthier had used one to move troops about and raved at its success.

Noël strolled the short distance to his home, enjoying the unusually warm spring day. The house was empty, as he knew it would be. Françoise was working at the hospital and would meet him in town. After bathing and changing clothes, he headed to the dock and pointed the small canoe to town. Struck by the lack of activity upon his arrival, he secured his canoe and headed to the upper town where he found a beehive of activity at *L'Auberge Oie Bleue.*

"Have you heard?" his spouse asked as he kissed her forehead.

"I haven't heard anything. There was no one at the docks."

"Well," Françoise began, as she pulled her chair closer to his as if to impart a secret nobody knew. "Last night, Governor de Mézy was troubled with a cough. He went to bed and never awoke—this morning he was dead!" Pouring her spouse a drink, she continued, "Sister Marie-Forestier said it was a rare type of croup—hopefully not contagious."

Noël was silent, obviously weighing the pros and cons of this news. Eventually he asked, "Who will be in charge?"

"Marin went to a meeting today," she said. "He thought it would be Pierre Boucher for now, but they are expecting troop ships from France in the next month or so. Whoever is ranking will be the temporary governor."

Noël did not comment, but after some thought, began to tell those at the table about the success of the Langlois Boat Works.

Québec: June 19, 1665

As hoped and predicted, the first ship from France, *Le Vieux Siméon,* had arrived. Aboard was a small group of

305

settlers who were shuttled off to the lower town square to make room for the main event—the first sizable group of soldiers from the Carignan-Salières Regiment. All in brown dress uniform, they marched proudly onto the dock to the cheers of grateful citizens. Captain Dugué was there to greet them along with their commander who would relieve Dugué of his yoke of responsibility as chief officer. From there Dugué led them to the fort, followed by a number of citizens.

A sizeable group of onlookers remained, however, in hopes of one other group. They remained in suspense for some time before Marguerite Bourgeoys appeared, followed by more than thirty *Filles du Roi*. The remainder of the group on the dock—mostly men, followed them happily to the Ursuline Convent. At the end of a long day, the men and women of the Beauport group, along with few others, met to discuss the day's events. A warm but moonless night, they sat outside of *L'Auberge Oie Bleue* illuminated by romantic torch lighting recently added by Étienne Fortin.

"Who goes first?" Françoise asked.

"Ladies first—as always," suggested Jean Bourdon, smiling. "They are generally more interesting in any case."

Anne-Gasnier Bourdon stood. Reading a paper under a torch lamp, she reported, "Sister Bourgeoys left for France on the first ship of the season. She has arranged for more than 100 *Filles du Roi* to come to Canada this season. This first group of 35 came from the area of *La Rochelle*. Tomorrow we will begin interviewing them and have the first group meeting in two weeks."

"Will the soldiers take part?" Marin Boucher asked.

"We inquired into this with Bishop Laval. He told us the soldiers are not to fraternize with single women until their tour is over."

"What about married women?" Perrine asked coyly, "I saw a few cute soldiers that I could fraternize with."

Once the laughter subsided, Anne-Gasnier continued. "There will be a group from Normandy next month and a final group from the French interior at the end of the season. Sister Bourgeoys reports they plan to bring close to 1000 *filles* before the end of the program." She sat, surrendering the floor to her husband and the other men.

Jean Bourdon had several papers but was not nearly as organized as his spouse. "Let's see…" he began, "Today the ship, *Le Vieux Siméon,* arrived with four troops of nearly 100 men from the port of *La Rochelle*. The ship is a…" dropping a few papers, he crawled under the table trying to retrieve them. Again standing he continued, trying to use the light from the torch, "It is a Dutch ship, chartered by a French merchant." Shuffling though his papers, he added, "one of…" searching the pages, "six—no, seven ships carrying troops are expected this season. These men are all seasoned soldiers and will start training tomorrow, including training with Jacques-Henri and some men on Indian warfare."

As he sat, still organizing his papers, Marin whispered, "How about the forts?"

"Oh yes," Bourdon stood, again trying to get the light when one of his pages caught fire. "Damn," he said, stamping it out while handing the others to Marin, "why don't you finish?"

Marin selected three of the papers and tore one into long strips. Then he set the two whole sheets at separated ends of the table and connected them with the strips. Then he took five bottles placing one on each sheet and lining up the other three bottles along the strips. "The top page," he began, "Is the *Saint-Laurent*, home of the French and Algonquin. The bottom page is Lake Champlain, home of Iroquois and English. The strips are the Richelieu River. This is the traditional route of the Iroquois to attack Canada. Each bottle is a proposed fort our troops will build, or in some cases, rebuild."

He poured a drink from the top fort-bottle before replacing it and continuing, "The fort at the *Saint-Laurent* is our post called Richelieu. The three on the river are Fort Chambly in the north, then Fort Sainte-Thérèse, then Fort Saint-Jean. Fort Sainte-Anne will be in the south, at the mouth of Lake Champlain. Once constructed, the forts will halt passage of the Iroquois and serve to resupply our troops. If we enlist local builders to help those from the military, we should have much of this done by next year." When Marin sat down, Bourdon added, "That is what I was going to say."

Less than two weeks later, a second ship, *Le Brèzé*, arrived with four companies and more men than the previous vessel. To the disappointment of the male onlookers, it carried no *Filles du Roi*. *Monsieur* Bourdon greeted the commander before they marched directly up to the fort. Neither Françoise nor Noël attended the day's landing. He was hard at work at the boat works and she at the hospital. That evening she reported what she had heard, "I believe one of the men is the commander of the troops. He and his ship were somewhere in the far south. They also hope there will be more *Filles du Roi* on the next vessel."

In the morning, Noël reported early to the boat works. Having become more involved in the project, he found it more enjoyable each day. He was just starting when Jean-Pierre came to him, "Pa, there's some soldiers to see you."

Still wearing his apron, with a hammer in hand, he went out to find a man in the uniform of regimental commander along with Lieutenant Gauthier, Captain Dugué and two soldiers he did not recognize. The leader stepped forward, "Captain Langlois? I am Alexandre de Prouville de Tracy. I arrived yesterday from the Caribbean where I have been dealing with the English and Dutch in the West Indies."

Noël had heard of de Tracy and knew he was to be the Commander-in-Chief of this new French force as well as Governor of New France until someone of higher rank appeared. Noël wiped his hand on his apron before extending it, "Forgive my appearance, Commander, I didn't know…"

"No problem, sir. I do some woodwork myself. The truth be told, when *Monsieur* Bourdon told me of your shop, I knew it was the first place I wanted to see." Removing his apron, Noël invited them inside. As they walked, de Tracy continued, "I understand you are a river pilot."

Surprised at the information de Tracy had already uncovered, Noël responded, "Yes, sir."

"I have always admired the skill of such men," the commander declared, inspecting the shop. "I knew Abraham Martin in Paris. I had hoped to see him here. Alas I have just heard of his passing." Noël nodded and de Tracy went on, "I understand he married your sister." Noël nodded as de Tracy added, "I visited her briefly last evening at her residence—what extraordinary views from her home."

"Noël, help me with this keel." Noël looked up to see his brother struggling with a keel, which blocked his view of de Tracy. Noël took one end and together they put it in place.

"Commander, this is my brother, Jean. He and my son own the shop."

De Tracy extended his hand, "Yes, I hear you are a captain of ocean boats." Jean did not wipe his hand before offering it to the soldier. "Yeah, but this suits me more. Would you like to have a seat?"

Noël was concerned this might seem forward to de Tracy. However, he sat immediately while telling them, "The purpose of this call, gentlemen, is I understand you are building crafts for army use." Now Noël was getting more worried until de Tracy added, "I would like to see one."

"Absolutely," Noël answered in relief.

"In addition, I understand you have an Indian man who has been helpful to our troops in introducing them to the… should I say unique, aspects of Indian warfare."

"Yes, sir. His name is Jacques-Henri."

"As I told you, Captain Langlois, we have just returned from the Caribbean. One thing I learned is even though our *business* was with the Dutch and English, knowledge of local customs and tactics frequently made the difference between victory and defeat."

Jean rose suddenly and removed his apron, "Well, hell, Commander. We have one of our boats moored outside. Get your men. We will take a ride! You can see how things work, and when we get back, we can go see Jacques-Henri."

De Tracy rose as if at attention and declared, "Excellent, sir—exactly what I had in mind. Get things done right away!" Putting on his hat, he added, "Gentlemen, I am impressed! This is definitely not what I expected in *Québec*!"

That evening an exhausted Noël Langlois was greeted by his wife, who was tired herself. "After the hospital, I went to the convent where we worked on *Filles du Roi*," she told him. "We expect more than three times the number we had the first year and anticipate ten times the work."

Dropping into a rocking chair, he described his visit with de Tracy. "This afternoon," he added, "Giffard stopped by. He offered us a new large *concession* on *Île d'Orléans*."

"Don't we have enough land?" she questioned.

"You never have enough," he answered, getting up to fetch the Calvados. "It is flat fertile ground with excellent water supply, perfect for farms or animals. I think I will work less at the shop and spend more time with the land."

Two days later, he received a note asking him to meet de Tracy at the fort. "Thank you for coming, Captain. I am about to take a tour of the territory and need your assistance." Going to a map of the area, he began. "I want three of your boats to begin. One for us to visit the outposts, one to leave with workers on the Richelieu River, and one for some men to stay a while in *Ville-Marie*." Putting plans for each fort on the desk, he added, "We will leave crews to begin early construction at the forts. As crews arrive this summer, they will be taken to the various posts to work. We will also need to recruit tradesmen from the towns. In *Ville-Marie*, I need to leave a few men to get the lay of the land. I am getting a sense that the people there are not entirely in agreement with those elsewhere."

311

Standing back, he concluded, "Can you leave in three days? And can you bring your Indian man?"

When he gave this information to his wife, she took it with surprising calm. "You go ahead; I will do your *concession* work. I will get young Noël to help. He has helped the older boys and he is almost 14."

Again, Noël was pleasantly surprised at how organized de Tracy and his men were. They had practiced with the three boats they had purchased, and each had at least two men who could sail the crafts. They had a group of soldiers as well as a similar group of new *engager* to begin work on the forts. Their first stop was *Trois-Rivières* to introduce de Tracy to Pierre Boucher.

"Our greatest difficulty," Pierre told him, "has been controlling the Richelieu River. As you will see, it is not as simple as it seems. No matter what we do, the Iroquois always seem to find a way around it."

At first, de Tracy thought this was naïve, but when they began their tour, he saw the many pitfalls. They left work crews at each of the four proposed forts to begin survey and foundation work, leaving one boat for the use of all. "As more help comes to *Québec*," he assured them, "they will be sent here and eventually we shall send more boats." As they left the Richelieu River heading to the Island of *Montréal*, de Tracy began to think the difficulties were behind him.

His worries were further relieved when *Marie de l'Incarnation* and Jeanne Mance met them on their arrival. They showed him around the town, which seemed well fortified and easily defended. He met with Maisonneuve who also seemed very helpful. When they left the convent, however, Mother *Marie de l'Incarnation* told them, "We shall help your men understand that this is a holy war, where the only things that matter are the glory of God and the salvation of souls."

Once they were alone, de Tracy told Noël, "Minister Jean-Baptiste Colbert has left no question that this is a secular, not sacred, war. He wants to develop the colony's economic potential—and these people in *Montréal* have already been given that information."

Next, they visited the Sulpician Monastery and Father Dollier de Casson who told them, "We do not need soldiers. Their vices are more than our people can bear."

By the end of the day, de Tracy told Noël, "Take your boat and whoever else needs to return. Leave the third boat and a few men with me. I need to visit longer with these strange people. I shall be along soon."

Noël and his few men worked their way back to *Québec*. A few days later, de Tracy returned and called Noël to his office. "As you were there and very helpful in my task, I thought it best you hear it from me. This is a *secular* war. If these people in *Montréal* do not understand this, they will be doomed. To that end, I have ordered Governor Maisonneuve to leave permanently for France—on the next ship."

CHAPTER 41

Summer of 1665 was the hottest in memory. Not only in temperature, but also in action at the port. Two more ships brought *Filles du Roi*, pushing the summer total over 100 potential brides, most of whom soon had contracts and eventually husbands. Françoise and her friends were constantly busy interviewing, chaperoning and organizing. In addition, Françoise's load was increased by managing some of the *concessions*. "I don't know how you do it," she told her husband in frustration one evening. "Most of the tenants and *engager* are delightful, but some are rude—almost hostile. They do not seem to understand everyone here has an obligation. When I am the least bit critical, they fly off. Maybe it is because I am a woman."

Sitting at the table, Noël laughed, "It *is* because you are a woman. These men have never taken orders from a member of the fair sex, unless it was their mother, spouse, or the baroness—and even then, they would never acknowledge it."

She came behind him and massaged his shoulders, "I guess I am just spoiled by having you."

"Do you want me to go talk to some of them?"

"No!" she said, regaining her determination. "I can deal with it."

Equally stressed, Noël was overrun with the onslaught of military men. As the number of boats going downriver continued to expand, he was home less often, even though he had shortened his hours at the boat shop. "We are expecting three more ships in addition to the four that have already landed. De Tracy estimates we will have over 800 soldiers by then, and many need to be transported somewhere—God, I wish Abraham was still here."

Sept-Îles, Canada: September 8, 1665

It had been years since Noël sailed this far downstream of Tadousac, but Laval had wanted a river pilot to meet this ship long before *Québec*. "With passengers this important," he explained to Noël, "I want no chance of running aground." As his boat met the ship in the miniscule fishing port, two Basque fishermen and a few members of the local Montagnais tribe greeted him. Shivering from the chill, Noël now remembered how soon winter arrived this far north of the capital. One of the younger pilots had sailed the small boat to deliver Noël along with the venerable first mate, André Bergeron. "If I need a copilot," Noël had explained to the bishop, "*Monsieur* Bergeron is more skilled than any captain." Since the rendezvous would be late in the afternoon, Noël had decided to anchor the ship

315

on the deep side of the small harbor, explaining, "We will depart at daybreak—it is safer."

The ship's ocean captain introduced his two most important passengers, "Captain Langlois, may I present Governor Daniel de Remy de Courcelles." Noël shook his hand with a slight bow, as the new Governor, who appeared unimpressed, said, "You may call me Courcelles."

The captain then took him, with an obvious increase in his deference, to the second man. "And *this* is his Excellency, Jean Talon, Intendant of New France."

In spite of his superior rank, Talon shook hands as if they were friends meeting in a bistro. "It is a pleasure, Captain. I hope we have time to talk on the voyage. I have a number of issues on which I would value your opinion. Indeed if your duties will allow, I should like to dine with you this evening in my cabin. My cook is just now preparing a *repas*."

Talon's cabin reminded Noël of a very small version of Laval's quarters in the seminary. Dinner was excellent, and the Intendant filled with questions of Canada. Once Noël had given him his opinions, Talon told him, "My hope is to turn this into a highly viable colony—going from fur trade to agriculture with introduction of many new crops. Clearly, to do this we will need a much larger population. Are you familiar with this new *Filles du Roi* program, Captain?"

Noël smiled, "Yes, my wife is quite involved."

"Excellent!" Talon replied, "I hope to increase the number of women as soon as possible. I also believe we can increase commerce and get into shipbuilding. In fact, I wondered where you obtained the interesting craft you brought to meet us?"

"Well, Excellency…"

316

"*Sir* will be sufficient, Captain."

"Yes, Sir. We have a small boat building enterprise in *Québec* and have been making these for the river traffic to aid in moving soldiers about."

"Excellent!" Talon responded, "Who is in charge?"

"Well, actually, Exc… Sir, my brother and my son."

"Wonderful," Talon replied, "It will be among the first things I want to see."

Looking up at Courcelles, Noël asked, "Governor, have you any questions?"

"Yes, tell me about the savages."

"Well, sir," beginning with caution, Noël said, "the native people are not necessarily savages. They are a diffuse group of tribes with variable characteristics, some are very warlike and some very peaceful."

"I doubt that these aboriginal creatures are *that* civilized," Courcelles challenged with distain.

Trying not to wander into a swamp, Noël simply replied, "You may be surprised."

"We shall see who is surprised," Courcelles said smugly.

During the following days, the difference in these two men became more obvious. Talon was interested in building a nation, Courcelles in hunting Indians.

Beauport: October 12, 1665

"You look upset," Noël told her as she fell into the rocker.

"I just had a run-in with one of the *engager*," Françoise told him. "Some of these people do not know how to behave—or accept criticism—especially from a woman!"

"Who is it?" he asked.

317

"You're too busy," she protested. "Anyway, young Noël is going to run the *concession* for the next two weeks while I work on Jean-Pierre's wedding." Standing to gaze out at the river, she changed the subject, "I'm so pleased they have decided to have it in the *Cathéderal*—I hope the weather will stay as mild as it has been."

La Cathéderal de Notre-Dame de Québec:
 October 19, 1665

When François Bélanger came from Normandie in 1636, he had become a tenant on Noël's *concession*. He married Marie Guyon, one of the older Guyon children who had come from France with the family. François Bélanger eventually obtained his own *concession* and became, among other things, a captain of the local militia. This marriage of Jean-Pierre Langlois and Charlotte-Françoise Bélanger represented a union between two of *Québec's* prominent early families and so drew the expected large crowd.

"I am so pleased we have good weather this far into autumn," Françoise told her husband as they exited the *Cathéderal* to the tolling of the new bells. "And *Monsieur* Fortin has done a wonderful job of adding tables into the square for our wedding meal." The family and friends dined, drank and danced into the late afternoon until a sudden wind shift and arrival of clouds caused them to begin heading home. Noël brought his carriage around and collected his spouse and the newlyweds for a ride across the *Riviére Saint-Charles* Bridge to Beauport. Jean-Pierre's brothers had moved into their own small cabin, vacating their larger residence for the new couple. Before taking his wife home, Noël deposited them in the new love nest.

The senior Langlois were just entering the house when the first snow of the season began to fall. Françoise poured two glasses of Calvados and they took them out to watch the weather. "I'll need to visit some of the *concession* this week," she told him.

"Do you anticipate any more trouble?" he asked with a worried look.

"No," she answered, absorbed in the snow becoming a blizzard, "I think I have everything under control."

Beauport: October 31, 1665

Returning from a five-day delivery of soldiers and equipment to the Richelieu River, Noël pulled his canoe onto the embankment, pleased to be home before nightfall, and pleased the weather had improved. Entering the house, he was surprised to see it empty. Pouring himself a glass of Calvados, he went back to the porch. As he looked out over the river, he heard a faint moan by the side of the home. He had expanded his porch around the side and as he turned the corner, he saw Françoise lying face up. Rushing to her side, he tried to arouse her but only elicited a weak groan. Putting his arm in back, he tried to sit her up, but he felt moisture. His hand was red with blood.

Setting her down carefully, he hastened around to the Indian camp returning with Jacques-Henri and Félicity-Angel. They turned her carefully and saw the source of the bleeding on her right flank. The porch held a sizeable puddle.

"Get her inside," Félicity-Angel ordered, and the threesome carefully moved her onto the bed. Félicity-Angel turned her and removed her dress, examining the wound, a linear, two-inch gash. "Knife wound!" she declared.

Examining the patient further, she said, "Lose much blood, I pack." Running to the back, she returned with a basket of items and carefully packed the wound. This seemed to stem the hemorrhage. Looking to her husband, she ordered, "Go quick for Sister Marie-Angelique!"

In spite of his age, Jacques-Henri remained one of the quickest runners and definitely fastest canoeist in the area. He was back with the nursing nun in less than three hours. Examining the patient and wound by torch light, she determined, "The wound is likely from a knife or other sharp object. It appears to have penetrated deeply and probably injured at least a kidney—maybe more. Obviously, she has lost a good deal of blood. At this point, there is nothing more to be done but wait and see—and pray."

By the following morning, Françoise had died without regaining consciousness. She was 54. Noël had her buried in the cemetery of the new Beauport Chapel where he could visit her grave regularly. A mass of humanity attended her funeral, including all her friends from Beauport as well as those in *Québec*. Pierre Boucher arrived two weeks later to pay his respects. Jean-Pierre and his new bride moved into Noël's house so he would not be alone.

The cause of her death appeared to be homicide, but there were no suspects. Some weeks later, Marin Boucher decided to ask Noël if he had any suspicions.

"She had been complaining of difficulties with some of the tenants and *engager*," he told him, "but, each person she had dealt with came to her funeral and appeared sincerely in mourning." He began to sob as he choked out, "I really don't know."

And he never would.

CHAPTER 42

Québec: December 3, 1665

Noël had spent the past month trying to recover from his grief. Jean-Pierre left for work every day asking his father if he would like to come with him, but Noël stayed home to mourn. Jean-Pierre's new bride, Charlotte-Françoise, tended him as if he were her own father. Marin Boucher had visited regularly, and finally on this day he suggested, "The sun is out, it's a gorgeous day. Let's take the sled to town and see what is up. You cannot spend the rest of your life like this."

Crossing the *Riviére Saint-Charles*, the dogs brought them to the upper town square where they encountered Jean Bourdon. "My wife is off working at the convent again," Bourdon told them. "I thought I would have something at *L'Auberge Oie Bleue*. Why don't you gentlemen join me?" Entering the interior, they found a table where Bourdon told Noël, "It's good to see you out and about, Langlois." Drinks arrived and he continued, "My first wife, Jacqueline, died in an accident—a terrible fall in 1654. Jacques, our youngest son, was only three years old. I was devastated—lost. Anne-Gasnier had been married in Paris, but after her husband's death, she came to Québec. My marriage to her saved me." He signaled the waiter to order as he concluded, "My advice to you, my friend, is look around. There are a number of widows in our segment of society—one may save you." Once the food arrived, Bourdon asked Marin, "I haven't spoken with you since our last council meeting, *Monsieur* Boucher, what do you think of our two new warriors?"

Marin considered the question. He knew his answer but remained a little insecure around Bourdon, a man who was born with more wealth and power than Marin had ever considered. However, he had brought Noël here and felt he must speak his mind. "Well, sir, I think we are dealing with reason versus passion."

Bourdon understood but smiled and responded, "How so, *Monsieur*?"

Marin paused to form a response. Noël had been out of the loop for a while and listened closely. "De Tracy sees the problem and realizes victory against the Iroquois will not be simple. I have taken him to Jacques-Henri's camp by Noël's a few times, and he listens and understands the Indian's advice. This is not a war in Europe. Battle in Québec requires a firm grasp of the natives, and if it is to be done soon, a firm grasp of the Canadian winter." He took a drink and decided to go further. "Governor Courcelles, on the other hand, believes it is simply a matter of force and the way is to do battle with the natives as aggressively and as soon as possible." Deciding to go even further, he added,

322

"I have taken Governor Courcelles to Jacques-Henri's camp on two occasions. I don't think he has thought any of the Indian's ideas are of merit."

Québec: Christmas day, 1665

Noël exited the *Cathédéral* on the arm of his daughter-in-law with Jean-Pierre following behind into the fresh December wind. "I don't think I have been here since your wedding," he told Charlotte-Françoise. "It is nice getting back with people."

"You need to get out more, Pa," she told him, squeezing his arm. "All your friends say they miss you." She added with a devilish grin, "Especially the widows."

"Don't start that, my dear."

"I'm serious, Pa, we can't live with you forever."

"I don't see why not," he challenged, getting into the game. "You are a better cook than your mother-in-law was."

"You're terrible, Pa," she said with a giggle, "but I'll let you go here. I see your friends are up there waiting to gossip about the governor or something."

Indeed, Marin Boucher, Jean Bourdon, and Zacharie Cloutier were waiting for him. "Look who finally came out of hiding," Marin said.

"What are you boys up to?" he inquired.

"Have you seen Governor Courcelles, lately?" Bourdon asked.

"Only once, a few days ago," Noël answered. "He asked me if we could take any more boats upstream. I told him we were done for the season—that the river is too bad to go that far in small boats. Why do you ask?"

"It seems," Cloutier said, "he is planning on taking the troops to defeat the Iroquois."

Noël's face lost its smile, "How will he get to Richelieu?"

"Marching," said Bourdon, with a greater frown.

Noël looked around and kicked a small drift of snow. "It has been a mild winter until now. It could be done—if it doesn't snow too much. Who will guide him?"

"We aren't certain." Marin replied, "We recommended Jacques-Henri, but Courcelles doesn't like him for some unknown reason. He said he was going to use someone from Matwau's tribe. Jacques-Henri told me he worries Matwau is not very reliable."

"I hope he has enough Indian raquettes, for all his men to walk in deep snow," Noël noted.

Marin answered, "Apparently not. Courcelles thinks the army snow boots are better."

"Doesn't seem to take advice very well," Noël said with more than a hint of sarcasm.

"Both Talon and de Tracy have tried to discourage him," Bourdon explained, "But like you say…"

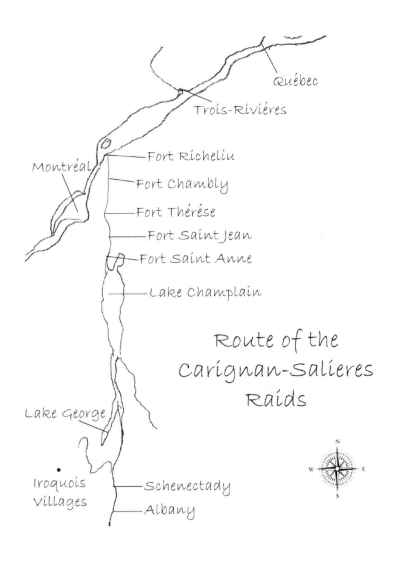

Québec

Trois-Riviéres

Montréal

Fort Richeliu

Fort Chambly

Fort Thérése

Fort Saint Jean

Fort Saint Anne

Lake Champlain

Route of the
Carignan-Saliéres
Raids

Lake George

Iroquois
Villages

Schenectady

Albany

CHAPTER 43

Governor Courcelles had assembled his troop of 600 men to battle the Iroquois. How to get to the Iroquois had proved a bit more complicated than he had envisioned. When he approached Noël for transportation by boat, he was informed conditions on the river now made this impossible. Marching, he learned, would be his only option. Being further warned this was difficult in the winter, he declared, "My men have accomplished missions more formidable than this!"

Courcelles now realized to march to the mouth of the Richelieu River he would need to get to the south bank of *Fleuve Saint-Laurent*. A relatively simple task in summer, the bitter cold, rapid current and numerous ice floes would now make it a bit more difficult. He called upon his guide,

Matwau who assured him it could be accomplished by canoe.

After three long, cold days of canoe shuttling, the troops assembled on *Pointe Lévy*, a small point of land across the *Saint-Laurent* from the *Citadelle*. Many were still cold and wet from the half-mile passage, accomplished by twenty Indian canoes fighting the ice floes back and forth.

Matwau explained the route downstream consisted of trails created by generations of Indians and Frenchmen hiking along the bank. "Sometimes goes into woods—just follow."

By morning, the soldiers had been able to dry and warm themselves by a large fire set on the bank. As they broke camp, Courcelles noticed only three Indians remained. "We guides," Matwau explained. Pointing upstream, he continued, "We go ahead and scout. You follow trail—no problem. If there trouble, we wait—no trouble, meet you at mouth of Richelieu River. Good weather three days, bad weather five."

Courcelles had calculated they would handle the nearly 100-mile hike in two days, but three was probably more realistic. He turned to give instructions to his second in command, Lieutenant Gauthier, who, to his dismay, had been drafted for the trip. Turning back, there was no sign of the native guides. "They do move quietly," Courcelles commented calmly, and then pointing ahead, ordered, "*Allons-Y!*"

By nightfall, they had gone no more than five miles. As they made camp, it began to snow.

"I appreciate the ride," Zacharie Cloutier told Noël as he climbed into the Langlois sleigh. "Otherwise, I would have had to go with my wife and the ladies hours ago." The women had a meeting concerning next year's *Filles du Roi*, and the men, a meeting of the council. In an act to increase the presence of early *Québec* families to the council, Laval had added Zacharie to join Noël and Marin Boucher. "I don't know if we have much to discuss," Zacharie declared. "Courcelles left to battle the Iroquois several days ago. No one has heard a thing."

Noël chuckled, "I suspect he would not call for help under any circumstances."

The meeting was rather dull, and there was no news of the warring governor and his men—which surprised no one. As they left, Cloutier said, "I am to meet Xainte at *L'Auberge Oie Bleue*. I can go home with her, but you are welcome to join us."

"Oh, I don't…"

Cloutier interrupted, "Come in—the weather is good and you know everyone."

Agreeing without enthusiasm, Noël tied the oxen. As they entered, he received a warm welcome. It was the usual group, with the exception of one lady whom he knew but could not immediately place. "Noël, you know, Marie-Crevet, of course," Xainte said calmly. Noël shook her hand gently, fibbing, "Of course."

Drinks were served as he recovered his memory. Marie was the wife of Robert Caron, who had been a tenant on his *concession* and later acquired his own. Robert Caron had died a few years ago so now she used her maiden name, which was common practice in *Québec*. After drinks,

Xainte said, "We need to go. I told our daughter, Anne, we would have dinner with them." Turning to Noël, Xainte asked, "Would you mind taking Marie-Crevet home?" Noël knew a trap when he saw one but actually did not mind and agreed.

While Noël and Marie-Crevet left for the sleigh, she said, "It is good to see you out. I haven't seen you since Madame Langlois' funeral." He only nodded as she continued, "I know when my husband died—my God, it is now ten years. I was devastated and rarely left the house."

"I know what you mean..." Noël suddenly realized he was actually talking about this. The conversation went on and changed to children and other small talk. As he reached his house he asked, "Would you like to come in and meet my son and his wife, or must you get home?"

"Actually, I'm in no hurry. My two children who still live at home are spending the night with my son and his family."

Entering the house, they found Jean-Pierre sitting by the fire and Charlotte-Françoise busy preparing dinner with Tutu-*trois* sitting at her feet, hoping for a dropped morsel. Jean-Pierre stood and his wife put down her spoon to welcome the guest. When Noël introduced them, Charlotte-Françoise told her, "I was at the convent school with your daughter, Catherine."

Taking her hand, Marie-Crevet told her, "She is married now."

"I know," Charlotte-Françoise replied, "I see her at mass." While Noël watched this pleasant conversation, he noted there seemed to be no surprise in the group.

Charlotte-Françoise invited Marie-Crevet to sit, asking, "Why don't you stay for dinner? We have lamb stew."

"Oh, I couldn't..."

"Oh please," Charlotte-Françoise continued, "We have too much and Father would not mind, would you, Pa?"

Left with no choice, Noël sat up, and said, "Of course not—I insist."

"Well, in that case…"

The meal was excellent and enjoyable. Charlotte-Françoise was a grand hostess and made everyone comfortable. Marie-Crevet told a little about herself. She was a bit younger than Françoise and came from Normandie. Following dinner, Charlotte-Françoise poured each a glass of Calvados. Marie-Crevet made a face. "Do you not like it?" Charlotte-Françoise asked.

Their guest blushed, "Oh not… well you see, I was born in Normandie, in the heart of the Calvados region—just outside of Caen. My father had an apple orchard and small distillery. It was said, his was among the finest. I make some now from time to time. If you like, I can bring you a bottle someday."

Charlotte-Françoise thanked her and asked, "Were you married in France?"

"No," she replied, "I was given the opportunity to come as a *fille à marier.* Shortly upon arrival, I met *Monsieur* Caron, but I fear I outlast my welcome. Perhaps I should get along."

Noël stood, retrieved her coat and walked her to the sleigh. It was beginning to snow and by the time they arrived at her home, it was a full-blown blizzard. As he helped her out, she said, "This is bad, even for *Québec.* I believe you should put your oxen in my barn and come in—it is no problem." With a smile that suddenly reminded him of Françoise, she added, "The children will not be home tonight."

Fort Richelieu: January 29, 1666:

What had begun as a hike in three inches of snow had deteriorated into a struggle through more than two feet. In addition, Courcelles' men had yet to find their three guides. Struggling though the rugged terrain, they had already lost a few men to cold and injury. Finally, they had encountered a river. "Get me Lieutenant Gauthier," he ordered his aide. At the beginning of the campaign, Gauthier tried to be as helpful as he could; after all, he had been this way by boat a few times. However, his commander had belittled all of his suggestions, so he decided to keep his opinions silent unless requested.

"You called, Excellency?"

Turning to see Gauthier, he said, "I believe we are back at the *Saint-Laurent*."

Gauthier looked out at the relatively narrow river and as calmly as possible said, "Excellency, I believe this is the Richelieu River."

"But how...?"

"The *Saint-Laurent* widens as one travels upriver, Excellency."

"Well then, where is this Fort Richelieu? We have a number of men who need attention."

"It would be to the north," Courcelles looked about in confusion, so Gauthier added, "That would be to our right as we face this river. As I recall, Excellency, at our meeting..." Gauthier did not think he needed to mention that Courcelles was at the meeting, "we heard most of the men would be moved to *Montréal* or *Trois-Rivières* for the brutal winter." He also decided not to mention that Courcelles had planned this journey—after that meeting.

"Then we head north." Courcelles announced, "Our men need attention and we need to meet our guides." Courcelles turned to continue north, when Gauthier said, "If you don't mind, sir, the Fort is on the opposite bank of the Richelieu River. The ice here is strong and we can cross. If we wait, it may be too thin further up."

Again, Courcelles regarded him with distain. "In this terrible cold, everything will be solid." Looking north again, he relented, "Well, if it will make you happy, Lieutenant." Their slightly smaller, but frozen corps crossed easily and headed north.

It took an entire day to reach the small outpost. "Looks vacant," Courcelles noted before he saw a rather obese soldier covered with Indian blankets approach.

"You men lost?" the soldier inquired.

"No!" Courcelles told him with his typical distain. "I am Governor Courcelles. My men and I are here to rid the country of the Iroquois. Some of my men are in need of medical assistance. Take us to your commander!"

"I guess that would be me, Governor. I'm Private Marcel Tremblay."

Approaching the end of his limited patience, Courcelles challenged, "How can you be leader?"

"Well, yer honor, ya see, there ain't but three of us here and I been in the longest—so I'm in charge, but follow me and we can git inside."

Tremblay led them through the gate. "We can put yer sick men and some officers inside—over there. The rest will have ta stay in the courtyard and build a fire. There ain't that much inside room."

Courcelles turned to Gauthier, "Lieutenant, you take care of this. Take me to your office, private." Entering the miniscule space, which was marginally warmer, three rats scurried off the desk. "Don't mind them, yer Honor. We let 'em run 'cause if we ain't got no meat, we can fry up a few."

"Where are my guides, private? I am supposed to meet my three Indian guides here."

"Ain't seen no Indians, yer honor."

"Damn savages," Courcelles said under his breath. Gauthier had decided it best not to point out to his Excellency that the Richelieu River was unfrozen, though filled with loose floes at this level.

Two days later, the sick and injured were in simple cots. Two of the local privates had gone hunting and provided meat for the rest of the throng. Courcelles took Gauthier to meet with Tremblay. "We are ready to continue our march, private. I am going to require you or one of your men to guide us."

Tremblay scratched all three of his chins, "We *could* go, yer honor, but we *was* ordered ta stay here. They said ain't no French troops due till summer."

"Well, perhaps you have a map."

Tremblay produced a tattered paper, "This is all I got of south of us, yer honor. They ordered us not to go south of here."

Courcelles threw it on the table, "I suppose we just follow the river south."

"I guess, yer worship—ain't never been, myself."

The next morning, while Courcelles assembled his troops, Private Tremblay appeared. "Ain't you got no sleds or them Indian *raquettes* fer the snow?"

"We don't need them, private."

"You boys must be strong. Hell, I couldn't get ten feet out there when the snow gets deep."

The phrase, "*when* the snow gets deep," frightened Courcelles but he kept it to himself as he ordered his men to march out. Later in the day, the snowfall returned.

Beauport: February 2, 1666

More holiday than holy day, the French Feast of *Chandeleur* was a bigger day in Canada than in France. Being Catholic, Bible skills in Canada were not what they were in New England. Not everyone understood why it was a holy day, but everyone knew today was the festival of the crêpe, a paper-thin pancake, usually wrapped around a sweet or salty filling. The French-Canadians preferred them sweet and had easy access to the perfect filling, maple syrup. Marie-Crevet called on Charlotte-Françoise two days earlier, inviting her and her two men to come celebrate with her and her children. "Even though her father was Normand," Charlotte-Françoise explained to Noël and Jean-Pierre, "she told me her mother was Breton—everyone knows they make the finest crepes."

In spite of significant snowfall the previous week, the sky was clear and the wind calm, making the sleigh ride to Marie-Crevet's home a pleasure. She and her children were waiting on the porch when they arrived. "This is my daughter, Catherine, and her husband Jacques Dodier," she explained. "They live over in Château-Richer, while Pierre and Aimee still live with me."

They all gathered in the kitchen where Marie-Crevet demonstrated the Breton manner of making the perfect crêpe before rolling them with syrup. No one would dispute they were the best ever. Following the sweet *repas*, the two younger children went off to do chores while the two young couples visited on the porch. Catherine and Charlotte-Françoise had been students together at the convent school and their men were both carpenters, so conversation was easy.

Noël and Marie-Crevet stayed by the fire sipping Calvados while enjoying more crepes. "I knew Madame Langlois," she told him, "both from church and working at the hospital. You must miss her greatly. I know as long as it has been since my Robert passed on, I still miss him."

Noël decided it was time to get personal. "Why did you come to Canada?"

Looking into her glass like a fortuneteller, she replied, "When I was young, there were few eligible men in our village in France, however one asked for my hand. It was only days from the wedding when he died in a farming accident. Because it was so close to the marriage, the few other eligible men worried we might have had... relations. It appeared I was destined for permanent maidenhood when a man came through the village, recruiting girls for the *fille à marier*. I enlisted and sailed that very year."

She stood to look out the solitary window, "It was not difficult finding a mate in *Québec*. *Monsieur* Carron saw me get off the ship and called the next day. We married almost immediately. He was a wonderful man—and hard worker. He received a *concession* and built from there. This house is on the final property." Sitting back she continued, "He was 44 when he fell suddenly ill. They took him to the hospital at *Hôtel-Dieu* where he died. They feared it was a pox, so he was buried that day." Taking her kerchief to dry a tear, "I was pregnant with Aimee at the time. She was born a few months later. Our oldest, Marie, was married a few weeks before Robert passed, but she died later in childbirth."

Pouring more Calvados, and drying a few tears, she said, "I went to work at the hospital, which is how I knew Madame Langlois. Now things are stable, one son and one daughter are married, the two older boys live down the coast and Pierre will join them when he finishes school this year—then it will be only Aimee and me."

Smiling, she pronounced, "Now you know everything there is."

Noël gave his short history, which she had already learned, from the women at church.

CHAPTER 44

Hudson River Valley: February 15, 1666

Courcelles and his troops had wandered along the river for over two weeks. Frequently challenged by forks in the river, they had managed to choose incorrect routes that bypassed the next four forts. When the waterway began to widen, Courcelles declared, "This must be Lake Champlain, this is real Iroquois country." This time he was correct, and the next day they happened upon a band of four natives camped at the lake. They began to flee south when they saw the French troops. "Sergeant," he told one of his most experienced men, "take a group of ten and pursue them. That way you can move more quickly. We will be right behind you."

Although the deep snow slowed travel, it facilitated tracking. By the next morning, Courcelles and his men came upon a battle scene. To his horror, the governor saw his ten infantrymen lying bloodied and lifeless. All stripped of their uniforms, four had been scalped. The sergeant hung by his neck from a tree. His hands and feet were missing. The loss of confidence was palpable as Courcelles ordered them buried. Unfortunately, the ground was solid ice forcing them to leave their comrades under the snow. Three days later, they came to a rise looking down on a small town—with houses. With enthusiasm, Courcelles took a small band of men and descended into the village. When he reached it, he had a communication problem. Courcelles knew English, but this was another language. One of his officers came down, "These people are Dutch," he explained. "The town is called Schenectady."

"Good, where are the Dutch officers?" Courcelles asked.

His man translated, "There are no Dutch officers, just civilians—they say the English have taken New Amsterdam."

Frustrated by this late-breaking news, Courcelles looked at the small map he had been given. "Ask him where this larger town with the trading post is, *Beverwijck*."

The man pointed south and his officer translated, "Five miles south."

When they reached that town, Courcelles found English spoken. This was, however, because the English had entirely taken this town and renamed it Albany. A group of English soldiers arrived demanding to know why the French were in English territory. Courcelles told the head officer his tale of woe, trying not to appear as incompetent as he had been. "This is now property of his Majesty the King of England," the officer declared. "We will house your men for a few days, but then you must leave."

Courcelles feared that if his men saw shelter, they would never leave. He politely refused and headed back to the remaining Dutch villagers in Schenectady. There he purchased provisions and finally learned the location of a Mohawk village. Two days later, they came in sight of the village. Courcelles sent two scouts who returned promptly. "There's no one here, Excellency—not much evidence anybody has been here for a while." His frustration reaching record levels, Courcelles started his men marching east, in hopes of finding another village, but the temperature rose, and rain fell in torrents.

Three days later, there was no letup, the mush of three feet of melting snow and the muck appearing beneath made the worst travel they had seen. Exhausted and demoralized, his men could scarcely progress. At this point Courcelles met with his officers who convinced him anything more would be futile. Broken and discouraged, he ordered his men to begin the nearly 600-mile march home.

At this point, natives began to make their presence known, not by appearing, but by occasionally removing a man from the ranks without being seen or killing one with an arrow in the back. All attacks were from the rear. When Courcelles reversed his course, the assaults continued from the rear. Five days from calling retreat, they were less than halfway home and had lost nearly 100 men—without ever having seen another Iroquois.

When the tattered troops arrived in Québec, the men still standing were severely affected by disease, malnutrition, and totally discouraged. Courcelles lashed out where he could, blaming the Jesuits, the lack of guides and anything else he could devise. Unfortunately, for Courcelles, the Marquis de Salières had come with the troops as a Colonel. He had argued with Courcelles before his departure, questioning the wisdom of the tour. Apart from rank, de Salières held a much higher social standing as well as the financial strings to the corps, and he lambasted Courcelles without mercy.

To add to the misery, the Iroquois, now rejuvenated by their success, began attacks with regularity as soon as spring arrived.

Beauport Chapel: July 27, 1666

When Noël had asked Marie-Crevet to marry him, the two had envisioned a small ceremony in a small church. However, the children from both sides, the Beauport neighbors and a few other close friends became a sizeable congregation. For witnesses, they chose young Noël Langlois and Aimee Caron. "We need to put some youth in this," Marie-Crevet told him with a youthful giggle. Three of Jean Guyon's offspring sang from his choir loft while Father Lalement, a relative of the many Lalements to preach in Canada and a cousin of the priest who had married Noël and Françoise many years before, performed the rights.

Following the ceremony, friends gathered outside on the lawn. The weather was perfect, the sort of day rarely seen in *Québec* outside of July. The women had prepared a picnic on the grounds. Someone brought a keg of ale and most of the ladies some food. Marin Boucher played his Jew's harp while one of the Guyon boys played his father's fiddle. After the meal—and no small amount of alcohol— the individual sexes gathered to discuss their favorite topics.

"I don't think Courcelles has been out of his office at the fort since he returned from his Iroquois debacle." Zacharie Cloutier said. "I heard nearly half the men who went will not be able to fight again this year—if ever."

"I heard Laval and Talon will scarcely speak to Courcelles," Marin added, "There is no question that the next attempt will be firmly in the hands of de Tracy—that is if there is another attempt."

Denis Guyon had taken over his father's role on the council. Living in town and controlling a number of *concessions*, he was definitely an *up and comer* of *Québec*. He told them, "There is little question there will be another campaign this year. At the last meeting, they claimed many more troops will arrive yet this season. They hope to have in the neighborhood of 2000 men by the end of summer."

François Badeau, the *notaire* who had escorted his widowed mother, Anne-Ardouin, added, "The Iroquois have definitely been emboldened by Courcelles. There are stories in town each day of small raids. Apparently, the threat is so severe, *Montréal* is keeping all citizens inside the walls. It is almost as bad in *Trois-Rivières*."

On the female side, the conversation was less bloody but no less intense. "Madame de la Peltrie told us," Perrine Boucher reported, "they expect only another 20 *Filles du Roi* this season, but they should arrive in the next few weeks. Marguerite Bourgeoys expects another 100 next year."

Anne-Ardouin added, "I don't care about that. My only unmarried son is François, the *notaire*." Lowering her voice, she whispered, "He doesn't seem to favor young ladies. What I need is a new *engager*. My old one left on the last boat to France, and I only have my Indian man, Henri, and his wife, Angelique, to run my place." With a smirk and another swallow of ale, she added, "And I'm too damn old to break in another man." Reconsidering her statement, she said to Marie-Crevet, "Don't get me wrong, dear, if I could land one like Noël, I'd grab him. But there ain't many like him around."

As the summer sun began to set, the revelers excused themselves. Noël and Marie-Crevet walked the short distance to their place. Aimee, her only remaining child at home, was spending the week with her sister. Jean-Pierre and Charlotte-Françoise had moved back to their old residence. Entering the empty house Noël lit a lamp. As they gazed into each other's eyes, she asked, "Do any of your children have your blue eyes?"

He stepped away, looking out the dark window to nowhere, "Only Robert, our oldest. He…"

She came back and embraced him, "I know, you told me—I'm sorry."

Kissing her forehead he told her, "You have nothing to be sorry about. It was years ago." He went to the cupboard and took a bottle of Calvados, brewed by his new spouse. Pouring two glasses, they toasted, "To our new life." He took a sip, then smiling, added, "I don't think I can ever go back to the old brew."

She snuggled up to him, "If you behave yourself, you won't have to."

When they finished their drinks, she stood, "I am ready for bed."

Entering the bedroom, Noël was a bit nervous, not knowing exactly what to expect with this woman who had been single ten years. Turning his back, he undressed. When he turned back, she was naked. Smiling, she said, "I have been waiting for this nearly ten years. How should we do it first?"

He realized he had been worrying needlessly.

<u>Québec</u>: August 11, 1666

As Noël sailed *Aigle d'or* around the tip of *Île d'Orléans,* bringing the harbor of *Québec* into view, he pondered, "How many times have I brought a ship around this point, and how many times have I done this with *Aigle d'or*? How many people has this venerable old ship brought to the new world?" He knew today's cargo would be particularly exciting to the people of *Québec*. He was bringing military might, new workers and future mothers of Canada. Only he, however, knew he was also bringing a prize coveted by the *Québécoise* for many years.

Approaching the dock, *Monsieur* Bergeron threw the lines to secure *Aigle d'or*. Once adequately docked, the parade began. First, future mothers of *Québec* as 20 *Filles du Roi* marched forward led by Marguerite Bourgeoys and greeted by Madame de la Peltrie. They soon trudged up to the convent as 200 military men paraded off and up to the fort. Last came a mass of *engager*—new workers for the New World.

Just as the onlookers thought the show was over, the ship's winch began to hoist cargo from the hold as six tired and confused horses were moved to the dock. Forgetting the soldiers and the women, the men of *Québec* were overwhelmed by something they had all yearned for since arriving in Canada but had come to believe they would never see.

A few days later, Noël and his new bride were rocking on the porch, enjoying the summer air. "Good evening, Langlois," a female voice called. Going to the porch rail, Noël looked down at his neighbor Anne-Ardouin accompanied by Charlotte, a young *metis* orphan she had taken in and a young man he did not recognize. "I brought my new man to meet you."

"Come on up," Marie-Crevet invited. As they reached the porch, Anne-Ardouin said, "Noël and Marie-Crevet, allow me to introduce François Allard. He came on the ship Captain Langlois brought in three days ago." They all shook hands and Marie-Crevet called to her daughter, Aimee, who was working inside. "Aimee," she told her daughter, "Anne-Ardouin has come calling, why don't you and Charlotte go for a walk? It is such a lovely day." The same age, the two girls had just recently met. A study in contrast, Charlotte was short, dark with straight black hair, but with softer features than a full-blooded Algonquin. Aimee, on the other hand, was tall with sandy hair, light complexion, and European facial features. The two girls headed to the bank as Marie-Crevet invited the adults to be seated.

"Aimee is rather shy," Marie-Crevet reported, "and Charlotte is the only girl her age nearby."

Once seated, Noël asked, "Where are you from, *Monsieur* Allard?"

Slightly taller and thinner than Noël, François Allard looked about mid-twenties, with dark wavy hair and striking eyes, one dark brown and the other bright green. "I come from a small town called *Blacqueville*, in the countryside near *Rouen*."

"What did you do in *Blacqueville*?" Marie-Crevet inquired.

"My father was a shoemaker. I didn't care for it, so I worked the farm near us that belonged to my friend's father."

"And what made you come to Canada?" Noël wondered.

"Well, sir, my friend and I went into Rouen one year ago to deliver produce. There was a man recruiting in the square. He told me *Québec* needed farmers—so here I am."

"Wasn't Jeanne d'Arc from *Rouen*?" Anne-Ardouin asked.

"No, ma'am, but she was burned there. There is a monument on that very square."

Noël disappeared into the house and returned with a bottle and glasses. "If you are Normand, sir, you may enjoy my wife's libation."

He poured four glasses. When they all had a sip, Allard said, "This is good, sir. I was told there is no good Calvados in Canada."

"This is as close as it gets." Noël lamented.

"Well, sir, my friend had an apple orchard, and we made our own. I think it was quite good. There are a number of secrets, but one is growing and choosing the correct apples."

Noël took another sip, "Perhaps you and my wife could start a business."

CHAPTER 45

Québec: September 1666

After a busy summer of preparation, de Tracy and Courcelles assembled their army of 1400 Frenchmen, overwhelmingly from the Carignan-Salières Regiment, with some French-Canadians and 100 Algonquin and Huron warriors. Talon and Marquis de Salières had made it clear that de Tracy, although outranked, was in charge. The men travelled both by Jean Langlois' small boats and by his brother's shallops to the mouth of the Richelieu River. Along the way, a company from Trois-Rivières under leadership of Pierre Boucher joined them.

The forces marched in multiple smaller groups, moving with much greater ease and sense of direction than Courcelles' men had when they travelled in winter. The soldiers from that first force who had recovered enough to repeat it kept their opinion of the relative wisdom of the two trips to themselves.

The plan was to break into three units, each arriving at Fort Richelieu one day apart. De Tracy led the first group to arrive. "I have sent Indian scouts ahead," he told his officers. "They will double back to warn us of problems.

Our course will be the one we discussed before leaving *Québec*. Once we make Fort Sainte-Anne at the mouth of Lake Champlain, to increase speed and have the element of surprise, we will prepare to travel light. This man," introducing Jacques-Henri, "will be our personal guide."

Pointing to his map, he continued. "We shall follow the Hudson River Valley. When we are still above the former Dutch post of Schenectady, we will head west to avoid detection by anyone there. Intervention by English or any remaining Dutch could be a disaster. Surprise in this venture is of paramount importance! We will travel fast and light. There are four significant Iroquois villages in the area that the English now call New York. We will attack each one in turn and move on. The forces behind us will do the same until the savages are totally defeated."

Three days later, de Tracy's force entered the first camp. It was deserted—recently deserted as some of the fire pits still felt warm. De Tracy called Jacques-Henri for advice. Examining the evidence, the Indian concluded, "They left quickly to set trap, but have made mistake. Iroquois expect slow attack as you described from winter—we moving fast." De Tracy set his men to burning fields and crops, and all tents and buildings in the village. They then began to pillage the remains, removing everything of value still standing.

He sent envoys to the units in the rear, instructing them to make haste. His men went to the furthest village and over the next two days, all the Iroquois camps were decimated beyond repair. The tribes did return, but as Jacques-Henri had predicted, too late. The French were waiting, and began to pick off as many braves as possible. The Iroquois finally retreated to the wilderness, destroyed economically, morally and physically. On October 17,

1666, de Tracy declared victory and claimed all the lands for the King of France, leaving nothing behind but ashes and corpses, along with the few frightened braves who remained hidden in the forest.

Québec: Late November 1666:

"I'm beginning to think it's colder every winter," Zacharie Cloutier told his friends while they worked their way down from the council meeting at the fort. "I think it's _older_ rather than _colder_," replied Marin, chuckling at his unintentional rhyme. "I'm afraid it is age," Noël chimed in, "I never worried about the last few runs up the river, now I dread them."

"How many more runs will you have?" Cloutier asked.

"Two or three—depends on the weather. They want to get most of the men out of Richelieu before it gets too cold." Gazing over at the upper town, he inquired, "You boys up for a drink?"

"Sure," said Zacharie, "but why don't we go down to _Taverne Terre Sauvage_. If we go to _L'Auberge Oie Bleue_, we're likely to see the same people we just left." Agreeing, they made the turn to the lower town.

"Well, look at who decided to come see the poor folks," they heard, as they approached the old tavern.

"I didn't think you boys would still be in town this late in the year," Marin said to Benoît and Bernier.

"We ain't goin' south this year," Benoît explained, "Not since them army boys got everyone's nuts in a knot to the south. No, sir, this year we goin' north—way north."

"Doesn't that mean you should leave earlier?" Zacharie questioned.

"No, yer honor, we's only takin' the canoe to *Trois-Rivières*, then up the Maurice River to a guy what lives with a couple of squaws. They raises sled dogs—the best. We gonna git us a great team and take off to the way north—up in Cree country. We hear they's had the best year ever and they's gonna be given away pelts fer *trois fois rien*," using the French term for *three times nothing*.

Benoît signaled for more drinks as he added, "Don't git me wrong. We's all happy about what happened in the south, it's just that the trade's gonna be in the shitter fer awhile. But, it was the right thing ta do. Like I always said, 'knock them Iroquois on their butts.' With the Dutch gone and them Iroquois makin' a truce with the French, only ones left fer them ta fight is them English. That'll keep 'em outta our hair for a while—just not forever."

Québec: July 1667:

Noël brought the ship, *Notre-Dame*, past the tip of *Île d'Orléans* where he could easily make out Jean-Pierre's new *concession* at the west end of the giant island. Much of the frontage was now clear of trees, and two new cabins were complete, ready for new settlers—and the settlers were coming. He had more than 100 on his ship today, along with forty *Filles du Roi*, and eight new horses.

Jean Bourdon had been compiling population statistics of Canada and reported to Noël and his friends. "After the first settlers from Perche arrived in 1634, there were far fewer than 100 souls—counting children and missionaries. In 1650 there were 1200; in 1663, 2500 and at the end of this year there will be 6300!" Noël smiled as he reflected proudly on how many of those new Canadians had entered this harbor on a ship he piloted.

When the ship approached the dock, André Bergeron threw out the lines with his classic surgical precision. The usual gaggle of citizens, eager to greet the newcomers, waited impatiently at the dock as Bergeron announced, "All secure, Captain."

Noël finished his duties and took his log. Marin Boucher was waiting at the end of the dock. "I'm glad you are back in time," he reported. "De Tracy and Talon have just returned from Fort Richelieu and negotiations with the Iroquois. A special meeting of the council has been called to begin in one hour." As a rule, council meeting attendance included most of the permanent voting members and rarely more than half of the associate members, like Noël and his neighbors. Today, however, everyone was present, including Laval, Talon, Courcelles, de Tracy and several ranking officers of the Carignan-Salières Regiment.

Talon took the floor. "We have just returned from upriver where we have completed and sealed a treaty with the Mohawk and Iroquois Confederacies." He took a sip from a glass that appeared more Calvados than water before continuing. "We agreed to consolidate the control of the fur trade in French hands at the expense of the Anglo-Dutch interests in Albany. This places us in a position to oversee *all* traffic of the fur trade in the region."

Taking another sip, he added, "We may place French-speaking traders and Jesuits in the Iroquois villages. To secure their safety, each Iroquois village will send two members of a leading Iroquois family to live among the French in the *Saint-Laurent* valley—a sort of friendly hostages."

As he stepped away from his podium, he told them, "One other subject, members of the Carignan-Salières Regiment may return to France or remain in Canada at their own choosing. Officers may acquire *concessions* and enlisted men may acquire land tenancy by the same means as any French citizen. We plan to offer land *concessions* to *any* military personnel in the Richelieu River valley and other areas where added defense may be desirable." Picking up a paper, he read, "Our prediction is that 450 men will choose to stay." Taking another sheet of paper, he added, "In conclusion, gentlemen, this is a great day for Canada. Three weeks from Saturday, we will have a ball for members of the council and officers. Bishop Laval has offered use of the new seminary including his private apartments. We have kept this news absolutely secret so you can all surprise your spouses."

After the usual questions, the men left for town. "I believe our spouses are anticipating us at *L'Auberge Oie Bleue*," Marin told Noël. "I hope you were not in a rush to get home."

As the men approached the now historic tavern of Étienne Fortin, they saw the wives deep in conversation and planning. "This *Filles du Roi* thing," Marin declared, "has given our women a new calling. Fortunately, most of us have few or no children at home these days. If we did, we would be hiring nannies like the rich people in the upper town."

Scarcely acknowledged, they joined the table as the women were listening intently to Anne-Gasnier Bourdon's report. "With the arrival of the latest ship, we have over 60 new *Filles du Roi* this year alone. About half have signed contracts at the two group meetings this year. Marguerite Bourgeoys claims we will have well over 100 by the end of the year and each year to come."

351

She stopped briefly to welcome the husbands, before sipping her drink and continuing. "The group of interested men has enlarged with the addition of many soldiers who have decided to stay and make their life in Canada." Turning the page of her report, she smiled, "Several of these men are officers and others who come with some means. In addition, Intendant Talon is plotting land parcels exclusively for farming to let to these men—if they marry a *Fille du Roi.*"

As Madame Bourdon finished her report, her husband jumped up to explain the Indian Treaty. When he had plodded as far as the second issue, his wife interrupted, "Jean, my dear, if the Iroquois are no longer on the warpath, we are happy and don't need every detail." Putting down his report, he grinned, "Well, I do have some more news that you will enjoy."

"Is it about the ball? We've known all about that for days." With a wide grin, she added, "I don't know when you boys will realize that men cannot keep secrets— particularly from their wives. We all even know what we will wear."

The couples headed home after dinner. Nearing the *Saint-Charles* Bridge, Noël asked, "What else did we miss at the ladies' meeting?"

"Perrine told us," Marie-Crevet began, "Pierre has some news. He is going to settle on some island near *Montréal.*"

"That makes no sense at all," Noël protested, "he wouldn't even be near *Trois-Rivières.*"

"That is all she knew," his spouse admitted, "but he will be at the ball, we can find out then."

Two days later, Noël arrived home at midday. "You're home early," Marie-Crevet noted.

"I have a surprise!" he announced with the enthusiasm of a young boy at Christmas. "Come see." He rushed her away from her chore, leading her to the porch.

She stopped and stared with her mouth agape, "A horse?"

"Yes, isn't she wonderful?"

"Where did you get it?" she asked, still in shock.

"From the eight I brought on the last ship. There were two extra, and Marin and I each bought one."

Walking down for a closer look, she asked, "Why do you need a horse? You have two oxen."

Pulling her over to see the fine points of the steed, he explained, "You can ride an ox but it's very slow. Also, we now have a carriage and a carriage *should* be pulled by a horse, and, of course, riding a horse is *much* faster!"

Putting her hand gently on the creature, she asked, "Where did you get the saddle and reins?"

"I bought them with the horse."

Walking around the animal, she asked skeptically, "Have you ridden a horse?"

"Yes." he answered with authority.

Walking around, again, now more skeptically, she inquired, "Where?"

He responded smugly, "In *St. Léonard-des-Parcs*. My father took me to the mayor's house and he let me ride his horse."

Now on her third tour, "When was that?"

He thought, then answered slowly, "1614."

"And you were how old?"

Thinking for a moment, he replied quietly, "10."

"And how many times?"

He responded more quietly, "Once." Nodding, she headed to the porch, explaining, "I have a pie in the oven."

Calling to her, he concluded, "I'm going to take it over to show Jean-Pierre."

"Be careful," she warned.

Returning to her baking, Marie-Crevet recalled her mother telling her that men reached a certain age where they returned to their childhood. She decided this must be it.

Two hours later, Marie-Crevet heard a commotion and went out on the porch only to see her groaning man being helped back by Jean-Pierre and Charlotte-Françoise with the horse walking slowly behind. Hurrying down to them, she asked the obvious, "What happened?"

"I fell off," he moaned.

For the remainder of her married life, Marie-Crevet would credit herself for not uttering the sarcastic statement that came to her mind. She merely helped the children get him into bed. "Should I call for Sister Marie-Forestier?" she questioned.

"No," he groaned, "I don't need her." As she touched his side, he winced and added, "Maybe you should get Félicity-Angel."

Marie-Crevet left, returning soon with the Indian nurse. Félicity-Angel removed his trousers revealing an emerging bruise from his waist, down the outside of his left leg to below his knee. She moved his leg and he groaned. She moved it more and his groan grew.

"Not broke," Félicity-Angel declared, and left, returning soon with her basket of wonders, and applied salve, binding the leg and waist. Finally, she gave him a potion to drink. "Stay in bed today. Tomorrow I come back." Leaving two walking sticks, Félicity-Angel departed and Noël fell asleep, a victim of her magic potion. Once outside she sighed, "Men," and walked back to the Indian camp.

Noël awoke some time later. It was still daylight but the house was empty. He sat up with difficulty and, taking the two sticks, lurched out to the porch. No one was in the yard, but as he looked downriver, he saw a cloud of dust. Soon he saw a horse, his horse, at full gallop in the cloud. As it approached the house, he could not mistake the rider—his wife. She came to a sudden stop, hopping off with ease. Tethering the reins to the porch, she saw her husband and asked, "How are you?"

"Sore," he answered leaving his mouth open.

"She's a good horse," she told him.

"How did you...?"

"Didn't I ever tell you?" his wife answered with a sly smile, "My father had a horse. I began to ride when I was four." She returned to her baking.

Séminaire de Québec: August 1667:

Noël proudly hitched his new horse to the carriage in which he would transport the Langlois and the Bouchers to the ball in honor of victory over the Iroquois Nation. As the new steed trotted across the *Riviére Saint-Charles* Bridge in the warm summer air, he began to feel he had truly arrived in society. Following the road winding to the upper town they arrived at a line of carriages and carts, a few pulled by the rare horse but many more by oxen. Once they came to a halt, a soldier took the reins of the horse and helped the ladies down. He tethered the horse while they strolled up to the entry of the grand seminary. Noël looked up at the ornate edifice, telling his friends, "When I was training in

France with Abraham Martin, we spent some time in Paris. I recall seeing lines such as this—people going to grand affairs." With a twinkle, he added, "Françoise would tell stories of picking pockets at events like this." As they entered the building, his twinkle turned to a tear, in memory of his first love.

The seminary's cavernous great-room was a jaw-dropping palace tonight, thanks to the efforts of Laval, Talon and the wealth of a few citizens. Removal of the Indian threat was an unprecedented victory, and *Québec's* citizens would rest easier and profit from it—at least for a while.

A small orchestra had been fashioned from a few talented local musicians with their simple instruments and a selected group from the military band. Food had been prepared by Laval's personal chef, and Étienne Forton stood at attention behind the bar, dispensing his libations with the assistance of Sister Marie-Claude.

The well-to-do from the upper town wore their finest clothes, some brought all the way from Paris. The military presented in dress uniforms while the rest of the *Québécois* had donned their best homemade threads. Looking about, Perrine Boucher noted, "When we first came to Canada, the entire population of the city would have been lost in a corner of this great room—but now look at us. *Québec* has become a real city."

There was music and dancing, drinking and dining, speeches and toasts—occasionally to excess. More importantly, there was exceptional fellowship, even for a close-knit community such as this. After dinner, Noël and Marin cornered Pierre Boucher, "We heard you were moving to an island, nephew," Marin declared. "Tell us about it."

"Yes," Pierre responded, "I have taken a *seigneury* of the entire îles Percées, across from *Montréal*, in the heart of Indian country. I will name it *Boucherville*. Things are becoming too—should I say, complicated, in *Trois-Rivières*. On the island I can live in peace and quiet—and finally write my book."

"Who will be governor of *Trois-Rivières?*" Marin questioned.

Pierre motioned to a man in uniform. When he joined them, Pierre said, "I believe you know Lieutenant—now Captain René Gauthier?" The men nodded and shook his hand. "Captain Gauthier," Pierre explained, "is to marry my daughter, Marie. I have named him Governor."

Marin's eyes had been continually widening during the conversation. "How will you live in the wilderness, boy?" he asked the 45 year-old governor.

"In peace, dear uncle," he replied, "in peace."

The celebration stretched into the early morning hours. When Noël noticed Bishop Laval sitting in his chair, snoring—the victim of excess Calvados, he told his wife and friends, "I suspect we should be getting back across the river. I hope the horse remembers the way. I'm not certain I do."

Arriving home, Noël lay on the bearskin, his head resting on the creature's head. "I just need to rest for a moment," he reported, and was soon snoring.

Québec, lower town: November 1667

Noël, Marin, and Zacharie Cloutier were returning to the canoe dock following a council meeting when they heard a call from *Taverne Terre Sauvage*. Looking over, Zacharie said, "Look who's back." As they walked over to the table occupied by Benoît and Bernier, Bernier rose to pull over three chairs. "How was the north country?" Marin asked. "It looks as you made it in one piece."

"Better than that, yer honor," Benoît declared, "Yer lookin' at two of the richest bums in Canada."

"It was that good?" Noël queried.

"Better, Captain, good thing we bought a few extra dogs so we could haul back as much as we did." Calling for more drinks, he continued, "We went way up by the big lake and was almost the only traders there. Them Cree— they had pelts like I ain't seen since I come in 1620. Traded 'em for less than half what we did down south last year. When we got back here, there was some big wigs from the Company at the market. They said good pelts is getting hard to find. They 'bout shit a brick when they saw ours. I jacked the price up almost double what I thought we'd get and they took 'em all—no questions asked."

"Did you hear anything about the Iroquois country?" Cloutier asked.

Benoît finished his beer and signaled for more. "Yeah, they said there wasn't squat on the market. Them Iroquois too busy botherin' them English to do business—I told ya that's what would happen."

"So are you going back north this year?" Noël wondered.

"You bet, yer honor. We gonna get two sleds and more dogs. The way I figures it, I might retire. I hear young Louis XIV's fixen' up that place at Versailles. If he moves, I'll go back to Paris, pay all my old debts and buy the Louvre from him."

Bernier giggled, "Louvre…"

"Well lads," Noël chuckled as he stood, "I have to go. If you can't make it to Paris, maybe I'll see you next season."

CHAPTER 46

<u>Northwestern Wilderness: March 1668</u>

Benoît and Bernier secured two large sleds with strong teams to pull them "way north." This year's snow was particularly vicious, causing them to arrive later than the previous year. They traveled well above the large lake, *Gitche Gumee,* someday to be called *Superior*, where they found a tribe whose pelts seemed even better than last year's. Visiting three trappers at the small village, Benoît settled into negotiations with a young brave traveling with two young boys. As Benoît began to barter, struggling with his Cree dialect, the native man in a hooded fur parka, pointed to himself, *"Parle Français."* As they began again, Benoît found the man's French much more understandable.

Benoît had learned that barter and negotiation were more complicated, and time-consuming, in this part of the wilderness, but for these pelts at this price, he could be patient. When they came to some understanding, the Indian stopped negotiating. Benoît knew this signaled an end of business today—time to relax. Their host lit a pipe and began to pass it. After two passes, Benoît asked, "How you know French?" Their host merely shrugged, "Just know." The man and his boys left, agreeing to meet again the next day.

In the morning, they bartered more and when everyone seemed in agreement, the Indian brought out the pipe.

When the pipe had been passed twice, Benoît pointed to the boys. "Names?"

The host pointed to each, "Mingan—Toguos."

"Gray Wolf and Twin," Benoît told his partner. "Seems simple enough."

Pointing to the man, he asked, "Your boys?" The man grunted while nodding. Benoît pointed again, "Mother?"

"Dead," was the answer. "Fall in big lake last year. Big lake never return dead."

Benoît nodded. He had heard that those drowned in *Gitche Gumee* never again resurfaced. The natives thought it was the work of the gods. Benoît thought it was the temperature.

Benoît thought he had time for one more question before becoming rude. Pointing to his host, he again queried, "Your name?"

"Neigemain," was the reply. *Snow hand?* Benoit thought to himself, *and in French?*

At this point, *Neigemain* and his sons packed up. On the morrow, it was tradition for them to meet a final time to change furs for items of trade before leaving.

The following day, they met again. *Neigemain* and his sons began to pack the two voyageurs' sleighs. As the sun ascended, they pulled back their fur hoods. Benoît was shocked. The boys were clearly *Métis* but *Neigemain* was definitely European. In spite of his dark hair, tanned skin and multiple scars, his eyes were steely blue. Benoît knew the boundaries when speaking with natives, so as packing finished, he took a chance.

"We," pointing to himself and Bernier, "come from *Québec*," pointing to the south. "Frenchmen," pointing to *Neigemain*, "look like you." Now he came to the delicate part. "If you like, come with us. Bring boys and sleigh with more furs. You sell your furs with us." Rubbing his thumb and forefinger together, "Big money." Then he looked into the blue eyes. "Maybe find someone you know—maybe not. You not like, come back here with us next year. If you like..." he just shrugged.

Neigemain went and talked to the boys. He returned shortly, "No, *merci*. We stay here." Benoît nodded, looking at the sky, he said, "We stay tonight, leave in morning."

In the morning, the two voyageurs rose before the sun and were packed and ready as it broke the horizon—just enough to reveal a man and two boys standing nearby with a large dog sled loaded with pelts.

Benoît looked over and merely nodded. Standing on the back of his sled he called out, "Let's go home!"

THE END

✦

AND
THE REST IS HISTORY

Although this is a work of historical fiction, most of the characters did exist, and most events did occur. As *Québec* grew and matured with immigration and the arrival of *Les Filles du Roi*, French-Canadians struggled to prosper in spite of weather, politics, and ongoing, sometimes devastating, inter-tribal warfare. This story ends, but history tells us more about some of the main characters we have grown to admire.

Noël Langlois died in 1684. Scholars believe he was the oldest man in *Québec* at the time. He and Françoise had 10 children and at least 74 grandchildren, but this is hardly a record for the early Percheron settlers in Canada. Statisticians tell us, considering the population of Perche at that time, those citizens who came from Perche contributed more people to North America than any other place of origin on earth. If you have the good fortune to visit Tourouvre and Mortagne in Perche (today officially named Orne, France), there are wonderful museums dedicated to the settlers of *Québec*. If you haven't already and are interested in following this storied path from Perche to Canada and even to the U.S., you are invited to begin with The Allards Series, Book One—The New World (1665-1676). The series is available through **Amazon.com**, and ends in Book Eight with WWII.

The remarkable life-story of Pierre Boucher is quite accurate, and he is certainly one of the fathers of Canada. He finally wrote his book, True and Genuine Description of New France, (1664), still read today.

The wonderful voyageurs, Benoît and Bernier, sadly are fiction, but the wisdom of Benoît was correct, as he predicted the day the Iroquois and other tribes would join the French to fight the English in what we now call the French and Indian War. You can experience the English side of this war with the story of the Deerfield Massacre of 1704 in my book, <u>Fearful Passage North,</u>

SELECTED BIBLIOGRAPHY

Charbonneau, Hubert, Bertrand Desjardins, and Jacques Légaré. *Le Programme de recherche en démographie historique (PRDH).* Montréal : Université de Montréal : n.d.

---. *The First French Canadians.* Cranbury, N.J.: Associated University Presses, 1993.

.

Denissen, The Rev Fr Christian. *Genealogy of the French Families of the Detroit River Region.* 2 Vols. Detroit: Burton Historical Collection, 1976, 1987.

Dictionary of Canadian Biography Online. Toronto: University of Toronto/Université Laval: 2003-2016.

Fischer, David Hackett. *Champlain's Dream.* New York: Simon and Schuster, 2008.

Gagné, Peter. *King's Daughters and Founding Mothers: The Filles du Roi, 1663-1673.* Pawtucket, R.I: Quintin Publications, 2001.

Jetté, René. *Dictionnaire Généalogique des Familles du Québec des origines à 1730.* Montréal: Les Presses de l'Université de Montréal, 1983.

Karkins, Karlis. *Trade Ornament Usage Among the Native Peoples of Canada.* Ottawa: Minister of the Environment, 1992.

Laforest, Thomas, J. *Our French Canadian Ancestors.* Palm Harbor, Fl.: The Lisi Press, 1984-1998.

Leitch, Barbara. *Indian Tribes of North America.* Algonac, Michigan: Reference Publications, Inc., 1979.

Michigan's Habitant Heritage: Journal of the French-Canadian Heritage Society of Michigan, Royal Oak, Mi., 2000-2016.

McNelley, Susan. *Hélène's World.* Middletown, De: Etta Heritage Press, 2014.

Nortier, Jacques. *L'Emigration Tourouvraine Au Canada.* Mortagne-au-Perche, France: Municipaité de Tourouvre, 1984.

Parkman, Francis. *Pioneers of France in the New World.* Boston: Little, Brown, 1885.

Simpson, Patricia. *Marguerite Bourgeoys and Montréal, 1640-1665.* Montréal: McGill-Queen's University Press, 1997.

Thwaites, Ruben Gold. *Jesuit Relations.* Cleveland: Quintin Publications, 2000.

Lifelong resident and student of the Detroit River Region, orthopedic surgeon Wilmont R. Kreis has authored ten historical novels along with three medical thrillers, The Corridor, The Pain Doc, and The Labyrinth. He and his wife, Susan, live in Port Huron, Michigan.

www.wilmontkreis.com

Cover Photo:

Lake Champlain

Made in the USA
Columbia, SC
09 March 2018